BEYOND COMMUNITARIANISM

Beyond Communitarianism
Citizenship, Politics and Education

Edited by

Jack Demaine
Faculty of Social Sciences and Humanities
Loughborough University
England

and

Harold Entwistle
Professor of Education
Concordia University
Canada

First published in Great Britain 1996 by
MACMILLAN PRESS LTD
Houndmills, Basingstoke, Hampshire RG21 6XS
and London
Companies and representatives
throughout the world

A catalogue record for this book is available
from the British Library.

ISBN 0–333–66020–X hardcover
ISBN 0–333–67744–7 paperback

First published in the United States of America 1996 by
ST. MARTIN'S PRESS, INC.,
Scholarly and Reference Division,
175 Fifth Avenue,
New York, N.Y. 10010

ISBN 0–312–16351–7

Library of Congress Cataloging-in-Publication Data
Beyond communitarianism : citizenship, politics, and education /
edited by Jack Demaine and Harold Entwistle.
p. cm.
Includes bibliographical references and index.
ISBN 0–312–16351–7 (cloth)
1. Citizenship—Study and teaching—Great Britain.
2. Communitarianism—Great Britain. 3. Educational sociology—Great
Britain. 4. Great Britain—Politics and government—1979–
I. Demaine, Jack. II. Entwistle, Harold.
LC1091.B48 1996
370.11'5—dc20 96–18827
CIP

---

10 9 8 7 6 5 4 3 2 1
05 04 03 02 01 00 99 98 97 96

Printed and bound in Great Britain by
Antony Rowe Ltd, Chippenham, Wiltshire

Contents

vi   *Contents*

List of Tables

List of Contributors

Len Barton is Professor of Education at the University of Sheffield. His publications include *Making Difficulties: Research and the Construction of SEN* (with Peter Clough) (1995) and *Disability and Society: Emerging Issues and Insights* (1996). He is editor of a number of journals including, *Disability and Society*, the *British Journal of Sociology of Education*, and *International Studies in Sociology of Education*.

Wilfred Carr is Professor of Education at the University of Sheffield. His publications include *Becoming Critical* (with Stephen Kemmis) (1985), *Quality in Teaching* (1989), *For Education* (1995) and *Education and the Struggle for Democracy* (with Anthony Hartnett) (1996). He is an editor of the journal *Curriculum Studies*.

Jack Demaine is Senior Lecturer in the Faculty of Social Sciences and Humanities at Loughborough University. His publications include *Contemporary Theories in the Sociology of Education* (1981). He is a member of the editorial board of *International Studies in Sociology of Education*.

Harold Entwistle is Professor of Education at Concordia University in Montreal. His publications include *Antonio Gramsci: Conservative Schooling for Radical Politics* (1979), *Class, Culture and Education* (1978), *Political Education in a Democracy* (1971), *Education, Work and Leisure* (1970) and *Child-Centred Education* (1970).

Ken Fogelman is Professor of Education and Director of the Centre for Citizenship Studies in Education at the University of Leicester. He contributed to the Speaker's Commission on Citizenship and his publications include, *Citizenship in Schools* (1991) and *Developing Citizenship in the Curriculum* (with Janet Edwards) (1993).

Rob Gilbert is Associate Professor in the School of Education at James Cook University, Townsville, Australia. His publications include *Studying Society and Environment: A handbook for teachers* (1996). He is a contributor to the *British Journal of Sociology of Education*.

Anthony Hartnett is Senior Lecturer in Education at the University of Liverpool. His publications include *The Social Sciences in Education* (1984), *Education and Society Today* (with Michael Naish) (1986), and *Education and the Struggle for Democracy* (with Wilfred Carr) (1996). He is an editor of the journal *Curriculum Studies*.

Geoff Hoon is Labour Member of Parliament for Ashfield in England. He was a Member of the European Parliament from 1984 to 1994. He is a graduate of the University of Cambridge and has lectured in law at the University of Leeds and the University of Louisville. He is Vice-Chair of the Westminster Foundation for Democracy.

Bryn Jones is Senior Lecturer in Sociology in the School of Social Sciences at the University of Bath. His publications include *Work and Employment in Europe* (1995).

Elizabeth Kingdom is Senior Lecturer in the Department of Sociology, Social Policy and Social Work Studies at the University of Liverpool. Her publications include *Women's Rights and the Rights of Man* (with André-Jean Arnaud) (1990) and *What's Wrong with Rights? Problems for Feminist Politics of Law* (1991). She a member of the editorial board of *Social and Legal Studies* and *Res Publica*.

Kenneth Levine is Lecturer in Sociology in the School of Social Studies at the University of Nottingham. His publications include *The Social Context of Literacy* (1986).

Ruth Lister is Professor of Social Policy in the Faculty of Social Sciences and Humanities at Loughborough University. Her publications include *The Exclusive Society: Citizenship and the Poor* (1990) and *Women's Economic Dependency and Social Security* (1992). She is a member of a number of editorial boards including the *Journal of Social Welfare Law* and the journal *Benefits*.

Sally Tomlinson is Professor of Educational Policy and Management at Goldsmiths College, University of London. Her publications include *The School Effect: A Study of Multiracial Comprehensives* (with David Smith) (1989), *Multicultural Education in White Schools* (1990), and *Ethnic Relations and Schooling: Policy and Practice in the 1990s* (with Maurice Craft) (1995).

Introduction

Communitarians, conservatives, socialists, social democrats, liberals, and communards all put different emphases on the notions of citizenship and community, but most want to turn what are seen as attractive-sounding terms to political advantage. This book investigates different notions of communitarianism and citizenship and considers their application within a number of fields – in particular politics, social welfare and education.

Politicians and social theorists are increasingly concerned with questions of environmental, social and political conditions and rights. Many writers focus on issues involved in the institutionalization of rights, with questions of social justice and with the principle of equality. For some observers, ideas about citizenship and community run counter to the market, or are seen as alternatives to it, but for others they fit comfortably within market ideology. Questions of citizenship, of consumer rights and other legal rights are seen in terms of empowering citizens but also in terms of encouraging citizens to behave responsibly within their communities and families. Whilst there can be no doubt that most observers regard the responsible conduct of citizens as a goal worth pursuing, difficult problems lie with questions of how (and indeed whether) responsible citizenship can be achieved. The chapters of this book look beyond communitarian ideology to investigate more detailed discussions of citizenship and the problems it poses.

In Chapter 1, Jack Demaine argues that whilst communitarianismis not new, it has become fashionable as a result of the efforts of the American sociologist Amitai Etzioni and the publication of the book *The Spirit of Community* (Etzioni, 1993). Demaine provides a detailed account of Etzioni's argument on the 'communitarian family' and its relation to the 'communitarian school'. He examines some of the criticisms of Etzioni's notion of the communitarian citizen and adds some critical observations of his own before turning to a discussion of questions of the politics of education and the family which, he argues, lie beyond Etzioni's communitarian ideology.

Elizabeth Kingdom situates communitarianism and its legal expression, new republicanism, within the broad debate about the adequacy of rights discourse to radical democratic politics. In Chapter 2,

1

'Gender and Citizenship Rights', she shows how communitarianism and new republicanism offer critiques of rights-based forms of citizenship which are attractive to feminists. But, Kingdom argues, some visions of 'community' are inimical to feminist politics and new republicanism adopts values which have excluded women from the citizen body. One remedy is to ally new republicanism to politics of difference. To take that position, Kingdom recognizes, is to invite the criticism that difference politics cannot engage with practical policy issues; such as the devising of a national curriculum. Kingdom maintains, however, that this position loosens the hold of problematic political discourses and encourages the more strategic type of appeal to social rights found in the 1994 Commission on Social Justice.

Rob Gilbert examines the implications for citizenship of cultural and economic change in the post-industrial global environment in Chapter 3, 'Identity, Culture and Environment: Education for Citizenship for the 21st Century'. He reviews aspects of the renewed interest in education for citizenship, arguing that it must address the problems of political participation in ways that acknowledge the characteristics of contemporary global change. He suggests that conventional approaches pay insufficient attention to the issue of identity, and that education for citizenship often fails to relate to the chief concerns or experiences of young people. To motivate students, education for citizenship must connect with their developing identity and their sense of what is important. The political economy of culture and the environment are potentially powerful means to this end.

In Chapter 4, 'Civic Education, Democracy and the English Political Tradition', Wilfred Carr and Anthony Hartnett argue for a 'civic education' that prepares citizens for life in a fully democratic society. Such an education must acknowledge that citizenship is a contested notion, and that it is through the process of contestation that the relationship between the citizen and the state is being continuously redefined. In Chapter 5, Ken Fogelman continues the argument that citizenship education has to deal with issues that are politically and morally contestable. He argues that this places particular demands on teachers, who must be able to handle open debate and conflicting views sensitively. This is partly a matter of their specific skills but is also dependent on the context within which they are working. Citizenship education can only be effective, he argues, if those attempting it have the confidence and support of politicians and the wider community.

Kenneth Levine examines the issue of citizenship and literacy in Chapter 6, 'Literacy, Citizenship and Education'. He argues that the National Curriculum for English pays lip-service to the linguistic dimension of democracy delineated in the Kingman Report but makes no systematic attempt to deal with significant aspects of political life or to promote seriously the often invoked ideal of active citizenship. In their treatment of Standard English, the Kingman Report and the subsequent proposals for English in the National Curriculum fail to appreciate that a multi-ethnic society will tend to be a multilingual society, and that this imposes a political obligation not simply to tolerate but actively to encourage and support linguistic diversity. Levine argues that the citizenship rights of linguistic minorities have been endangered and the seeds sown of future social resentments and antagonisms.

In Chapter 7, 'Ethnic Minorities, Citizenship and Education', Sally Tomlinson examines the politics of exclusion of ethnic minorities from a 'citizenship' which has itself been changing over the past forty years. In Britain, where, she argues, the school curriculum is still permeated by residual Victorian beliefs in white superiority, there remains a resistance to the idea that ethnic minority groups can be included within the national identity and can exercise full citizenship rights. Tomlinson questions whether education can influence non-rational ethnocentric beliefs in white superiority, and she discusses the implications of minority exclusion from recognition as both British and European citizens.

Geoff Hoon, a British Member of Parliament who until recently was a Member of the European Parliament, provides a detailed account of developments towards European citizenship in Chapter 8. Hoon argues that whilst particular difficulties *are* to be found within Member States, at the European level there has been a determined effort to make equality of treatment of citizens a practical reality. The difficulty has been to persuade national governments that they should abandon some national traditions and prejudices. Whilst the idea of granting a common European citizenship is seen by some as a step on the road towards a United States of Europe, and some politicians and citizens are enthusiastic about that, others are concerned that legal rights extended to European citizens amount to more than those extended to citizens by the individual constitutions and lawmakers of the Member States. However, as Hoon points out, in a strict legal sense European citizens already enjoy particular rights by virtue of a European Constitution which is enshrined in the Treaty on European Union.

In Chapter 9, 'Political Citizenship, Activism and Socialist Beliefs', Bryn Jones argues that it has become fashionable to associate the rise of new forms of political activism with a renaissance of active citizenship. However, this focus on grass-roots activism tends to neglect a corresponding decline of lay political activism with respect to mainstream political parties; a decline which might, if widespread, have serious implications for broader democratic systems. His chapter examines the evidence that this latter form of political citizenship is in decline.

In Chapter 10, 'Citizenship, Rights and Local Government', Ruth Lister examines the prospect of local government promoting active political citizenship beyond the limits of participation in local elections. Lister argues that because it is closer to the people, local government is better placed to promote citizenship than central government. Local community development initiatives, in partnership with community groups and the voluntary sector, can help people find confidence and help them enhance the skills they need to be active citizens. Despite the difficulties they face, local authorities can still make an important contribution to the quality of social citizenship enjoyed by local residents. Lister argues that in recent years a growing number of authorities have been committed to anti-poverty strategies of various kinds, despite the ever-tighter constraints within which they operate. The integration of economic and social development, service and benefit delivery policies which are sensitive to the needs of disadvantaged groups, and the promotion of advice and advocacy services, are all valuable strands in the web of social citizenship at local level.

In Chapter 11, 'Citizenship and Disabled People: A Cause for Concern', Len Barton argues for the development of forms of political discourse that will enable all citizens to participate in democratic debate and dialogue, and he insists that this must include disabled people. In the final chapter, 'Knowledge of Most Worth to Citizens', Harold Entwistle addresses perceptions, nurtured by the media, that modern youth displays widespread cultural illiteracy which must have deleterious implications for democratic citizenship. Arguing that citizenship has wider cultural ramifications than the merely political, he proposes what has always been the educational recipe for free citizens: a liberal education, constantly renewed to accommodate new forms of knowledge and developing human interests, and appropriately concretised in order to speak to a variety of student needs, talents, aspirations, strengths and limitations.

In a book of this kind there are bound to be differences of emphasis and argument. Each of the authors takes responsibility for their own contribution. And we want to add a cautionary note at this point. Whilst argument over citizenship, rights, community and changing familial structures involves discussion of the role of education, we argue that it is wrong to regard education as some kind of panacea. There *is* an emphasis on education in this book, and education for citizenship is important, but readers will recognize that the editors and contributors are well aware of the vital importance of factors which lie outside the sphere of influence of education and education systems.

Jack Demaine, Loughborough University
Harold Entwistle, Concordia University

1 Beyond Communitarianism: Citizenship, Politics and Education

Jack Demaine

Communitarianism is not new, but it became fashionable in the early 1990s largely as a result of the efforts of the American sociologist Amitai Etzioni and his associates. In his book *The Spirit of Community* (1993) Etzioni tells readers that in 1990 a group of fifteen 'ethicists, social philosophers, and social scientists met in Washington, D.C., at the invitation of the author and his colleague, William Galston' (pp. 14–15). As they explored matters that 'afflict our society', the members of the group agreed that the simplistic political dichotomies that have dogged debate over social issues, and the discussion of issues in oppositional terms, involves unnecessarily divisive argument which is 'antagonistic to the spirit of community'. The group found that they shared a 'distaste for the polarization of debate and the "sound bite" public life, the effects of teledemocracy'. Moreover, the group was troubled by what they saw as an evident reluctance on the part of citizens 'to accept responsibilities'. Etzioni goes on to say that 'We adopted the name *Communitarian* to emphasize that the time had come to attend to our responsibilities to the conditions and elements we all share, to the community' (p. 15).

Notwithstanding the attention that Etzioni's *The Spirit of Community* has attracted, other notions of communitarianism and of communitarian citizenship are available. Different communitarianisms seek to foster particular citizenship values, with many writers focusing on issues surrounding the institutionalization of citizenship rights, questions of social justice and the principle of equality. Whilst most writers share a concern for individual responsibility and activity, some notions of citizenship emphasize consumerist values. Differences in focus also involve differences in terminology so that, for example, socialistic versions of communitarianism often use the term 'new republicanism' (see Walzer, 1983; Mouffe, 1988; and Hirst, 1990 for critical evaluation). Of course, Etzioni's group could not deploy such a term for fear of association with the American Republican Party, and in any case the group's arguments could hardly be regarded as socialist. On the other hand, when the socialist members of the European Parliament (who are in the majority there) use the term 'communitarian policies' they do not have Etzioni and his associates in mind. Rather, they use the term simply to refer to the policies pursued within the European Community.

Communitarian debate and experience precedes and goes well beyond Etzioni's recent version. Indeed, Rosenblum (1994) registers the 'waves of communitarianism' which swept America during the first half of the nineteenth century and again during the 1960s and 1970s. Like the Paris Commune, discussed by Karl Marx in *The Civil War in France* (1871), they rarely lasted and, as John Humphrey Noyes notes in his *History of American Socialism,* 'all died young, and most of them before they were two years old'. But the communitarianism Etzioni and his friends seek to foster is not commune bound or 'place-based'. They envisage a wider movement, transforming and maintaining the 'supracommunity, a community of communities – the American society' (Etzioni, 1993, p. 160), and they consider their ideas relevant to Britain and to much of the modern West. Modern communitarianism is not concerned to establish short-lived enclaves but to transform whole societies through a 'change of heart' amongst their citizens.

The notion of 'the active society' and the question of the responsible conduct of citizens in their social and political context is a theme that has dominated Amitai Etzioni's life's work (see especially Etzioni, 1968). He is a distinguished sociologist with an international reputation. Whilst *The Spirit of Community* continues themes established in a series of important and well respected books and academic articles published over the last forty years, this latest offering does not compare well with his earlier work. There is a real sense in which *The Spirit of Community* is not an academic book at all; this is evident in its general style and particularly in its presentation of evidence and argument. The book is tendentious, and relies heavily on personal anecdote, differentiating it dramatically from, say, *The Active Society* (Etzioni, 1968) or *Modern Organizations* (Etzioni, 1964), and his *A Comparative Analysis of Complex Organizations* (Etzioni, 1961).

Delaney (1994) provides a useful introduction to the 'liberalism–communitarianism debate' which became an established theme of political philosophy well before Etzioni's meeting with Galston and their friends. Philosophical debate has been developed in and around the work of writers such as John Rawls, Robert Nozick, Ronald Dworkin broadly on the liberal side, and by writers such as Alasdair MacIntyre, Charles Taylor, and Michael Sandel on the communitarian side – although, as Delaney cautions, labels can mask important differences. Despite the new populist spin given to it by Etzioni and his associates, they add nothing to communitarian philosophical theory. But Etzioni is much more concerned with the need to establish a new communitarian *movement* for social change than with philosophical theory. After all, the philosophers have only interpreted the world; the point is to change it. Etzioni appears passionately concerned to change America, and much of the West, if not the whole world. Indeed, he notes that communitarianism might not suit everyone and suggests that 'the people of China, Eastern Europe, and Japan might well need to move in the opposite direction: to make more room for self-expression, to slash excessive government control, and to roll back severely enforced moral codes that suppress creativity and impinge on individual rights' (p. 25). A telling remark, which lumps together very different, diverse societies with differing histories, politics and ideologies; a remark that should alert readers to a need for caution when assessing Etzioni's views.

In Etzioni's version of communitarianism, the central need is thought to be that of establishing a 'set of social virtues, some basic settled values, that we as a community endorse and actively affirm' (p. 25). Communitarians say that they do not want to return to 'the traditional values of the fifties' but they do want to 'push back the pendulum' from the eighties; 'a decade in which "I" was writ large, in which the celebration of the self became a virtue'. The nineties 'call for an age of reconstruction, in which we put a new emphasis on "we", on values we share, on the spirit of community' (p. 25). Citizens need 'a change of heart. True, some of the matters at hand can be addressed through changes in public policy, but first and foremost we need a change in philosophy, a new way of thinking, a reaffirmation of a set of moral values that we may all share' (p. 18).

THE COMMUNITARIAN FAMILY AND EDUCATION

For Etzioni, the decline of the two-parent family lies at the heart of the problem of modern Western society. His kind of communitarianism strongly favours the two-parent family; he bemoans its decline and suggests ways in which its dominance might be reclaimed. In practical terms, the 'millions of latchkey children, who are left alone for long stretches of time, are but the most visible result of the parenting deficit' (Etzioni, 1993, p. 56). But as we shall see, Etzioni offers little more than a register of allegedly visible aspects, and ignores decades of research by fellow sociologists and educationists.

Etzioni tells readers that communitarians accept a certain amount of change in the family as inevitable and they are even willing to recognize that 'in some contemporary families children are cuddled by their fathers and disciplined by their mothers (but) what matters most is the two-parent mode' (p. 61). He asserts that 'another essential feature for a family effectively to carry out its parenting mission is *a mutually supportive educational condition*. The parents, as educational agents, must be mutually supportive because their specific educational goals are in part contradictory' (p. 61, emphasis in the original). Etzioni argues that whilst 'goading children to achieve generates stress', at the same time 'reassuring them generates a relaxation response'. Consequently, 'only if the parents are basically in agreement can they make education work and avoid being unwittingly played off one against the other by their children, to the detriment of education.' (p. 61).

According to Etzioni, the mutually supportive educational condition is threatened, and in many cases destroyed, not only by divorce but by the exigencies of the dual-income couple. But he has lived long enough in the USA to understand that he risks being attacked as a sexist and anticipates his critics: 'Hey, you're dumping on women!' and, 'You believe that women must stay at home and attend to the family's children! Women have the same right as men to work outside the home!' he hears them cry. But Etzioni attempts to slip out of the firing line by avoiding the questions he has anticipated and by simply asserting that, 'As I see it this is *not* the issue; the issue is the dearth of parental involvement of both varieties: mothers and fathers' (p. 55).

In place of argument with his critics, Etzioni goes on to endorse a University of Denver project 'to train couples to handle conflict', adding that it has been found that 'couples who learn how to argue well were unhappy at first but became more satisfied later. The divorce rate after six years for couples who had undergone the training was half that of couples who had not' (p. 79). But the image he paints of rowing couples does not fit too comfortably with his earlier stress on the need for couples to display a united front in dealing with their children's education. Slipping away from the argument here, he merely asserts that despite such experiments, legal change may still be required to slow down marriage in order to slow down divorce: 'to avoid the rush to divorce, we need to further slow the rush to marriage' (p. 78).

Etzioni's assertion of the need for stricter marital law can hardly be claimed as novel thinking; but it is also narrow and misleading thinking. In Britain, for example, there were fewer marriages in 1995 than in any year since the Second World War. Whilst the decline in marriage may contribute to a subsequent decline in divorce, it is obvious that Etzioni's focus on formal marriage and on divorce will tell us very little about the modern family as such, or about the powerful social changes that influence family structures. The availability of effective contraception and the legal and ideological empowerment of women which has gathered pace over the last two and a half decades are important and need to be supported and sustained. Such change, together with the more recent decline in job security and the decline of unskilled male occupations during the last decade or so, has had important consequences for young men and women. These changes go a long way to explain the changes in family structures. Etzioni wants to wish away and ignore powerful and continuing social trends which have real conditions, but no amount of argument about 'what ought to be' will alter them.

In a critique of Etzioni's views, Ray Pahl (1995) is dismissive of communitarian argument about 'what ought to be. If the desire is to celebrate and support those who engage in communal and collective endeavours then we should see who actually does this, rather than those who ought to do it. In practice those who are most in need of supportive and communal activity are lone parents. Those in the very category pilloried by communitarians are setting up support groups for themselves, and various other cooperative activities for others' (p. 21). Pahl turns the argument against the two-parent family, 'most praised by communitarians – the doting, caring parent taking their childcare very responsibly, and devoting considerable time to their children, have little time for much else'. They are exhausted by dual income-producing work, by their travel to work, having to collect children from their minders, taking them on visits to relatives, to swimming and to ice-skating. 'The harassed, time-challenged middle mass (*sic*) are obliged to be highly selective in how they choose their friends and associates. Those who do have the time, energy and inclination to engage in public-spirited work are more likely to be single' (Pahl, 1995, p. 22).

One problem here is that in his attempt to counter the communitarian view of the two-parent family Pahl throws one stereotype at another. The point surely is that all childrearing is hard work; sometimes harder for lone parents than for those in circumstances where more than one adult can share the labour, and often hell on earth for those in poverty. And activism, be it political or 'community-spirited', is not determined necessarily by marital status or by family circumstances. There are legions of lone parents, child-free couples and singles who are not 'active citizens' to contrast to those who are. No doubt the harassed middle mass, as Pahl calls them, *are* selective in their community activity (isn't everyone?) but their contribution should not be underestimated, neither need it be despised. Part of their contribution is sometimes in support of lone-parent families.

The idea that there is a necessary division between two supposedly distinct family life-styles is inaccurate, unhelpful and in many instances would be regarded as insulting. As the British director of the National Council for One Parent Families pointed out recently, research carried out by the Policy Studies Institute (1995) and published in *Changes in Lone Parenthood, 1989–1993* shows that 'lone parents are the friends and family we all know – women in their twenties and thirties, who were married or in a stable relationship when they had their children' (quoted in *The Guardian*, 28 September, 1995). The research 'totally undermines the arguments of those calling for cuts to lone parent benefits (and) it shatters the myth of lone parents as feckless, irresponsible women' (ibid.).

THE COMMUNITARIAN SCHOOL

As the argument in *The Spirit of Community* unfolds, we find that Etzioni has more or less given up on the family, arguing that in order to restore the 'moral infrastructure' of communities, 'schools will have to step in where the family, neighborhoods, and religious institutions have been failing'. In what he refers to as the 'Communitarian's ideal world, children would come to school, with their basic characters well formed and their values sufficiently internalized'. Once children were enrolled in school 'their character traits' would be 'further reinforced at home', allowing teachers to concentrate on passing on information and skill (p. 89). But this is Etzioni's *ideal state of affairs* which, he tells us, does not exist in much of America today. In fact, he argues, children's characters are 'underdeveloped' and there is a lack of 'commitment to values' because 'families have been dismembered or the parents are overworked, or consumed by other concerns and ambitions'. Moreover, if schools do not attend to this basic 'lack of character and moral values' they will turn out people who are 'deficient workers, citizens, and fellow community members' (p. 90).

Helpfully, Etzioni defines what communitarians mean by 'character' and 'core values'. Character refers to 'the psychological muscles that allow a person to control impulses and defer gratification, which is essential for achievement, performance, and moral conduct' (p. 91). And the 'core values, which need to be transmitted from generation to generation, contain moral substances that those with the proper basic personality can learn to appreciate, adapt, and integrate into their lives: hard work pays, even in an unfair world; treat others with the same basic dignity with which you wish to be treated' (p. 91). 'Self-discipline' is the 'master key' to 'education for character', and moral education is the essential component of teaching. 'Unfortunately', says Etzioni, American schools 'have been reluctant to engage openly in moral education', in part because of an overcrowded curriculum but also because moral education is 'very controversial' (p. 101). Despite these supposed obstacles, he argues that schools need to play a leading role in the task of constructing the communitarian citizen by inculcating 'a shared set of moral values'.

The sociology of education has long been concerned with the question of the role of values in the process of socialization, seen as the shared responsibility of the family, the school and other social institutions (see Demaine, 1981). An important difference between Etzioni's account of the internalization of values, and that available in traditional sociology, is that whereas the latter can be read as postulating a more or less normative condition of success, Etzioni postulates failure but *hopes* for success. Etzioni's account amounts to little more than a simple plea for 'what ought to be' and, as such, it compares unfavourably with other long established accounts of the process of internalization of values. Indeed, Etzioni's *The Spirit of Community* ignores decades of academic research in education and sociology. It is now more than 60 years since the American sociologist Talcott Parsons and his associates embarked on a series of academic papers and books which elaborate a sophisticated account of the place of values in sociological theory[1]. Their work on the role of the family and the school in the inculcation of values involves an account of mechanisms of differentiation. Parsons deploys Freudian psychoanalytical theory in his structural-functionalist account and, although it has been criticized (see for example, Savage, 1980; Demaine, 1981), it offers very much more than Etzioni's crude characterization of 'the psychological muscles' and their supposed effects.

Despite the emphasis Etzioni places on moral values, and on the need for a 'change of heart amongst citizens', he is forced to concede that institutional change is necessary if the 'communitarian spirit' is to supplant the rampant individualism said to grip American society. However, when it comes to spelling out specific detail of public policy for social institutions such as the family and education, Etzioni's argument lacks credibility and there is certainly no originality in his thought. The fervour for 'spiritual change' soon gives way to a rather dour appeal for the introduction of 'national service' as the 'capstone of a student's educational experience' (p. 113). He suggests that the latter need not be military service, although it could be in the 'armed forces, the Peace Corps, VISTA, or the Conservation Corps' (p. 113). National service would be 'character building' and, as well as providing the 'capstone' experience, a beneficial effect would be to 'remove many unemployed youths from the streets; it would provide them, often for the first time, with legitimate and meaningful work; and it would help protect them from being enticed into crime' (p. 113). Skill acquisition would be a bonus but, 'above all, such service would provide a way to develop the character... much of the potential impact of national service lies in psychic development, in enhancing the individual's self-respect, sense of worth, and outlook on the future. More importantly, national service would also provide a strong antidote to the ego-centered mentality as youth serve shared needs (*sic*)' (p. 113). But Etzioni's suggestion of national service completely ignores a range of well-rehearsed objections and it completely evades the question of the reform of education systems as such.

As we noted earlier, when we moved from examination of his argument over the family to argument over the school, in Etzioni's discussion there is a shifting emphasis on different social institutions. On earlier pages of *The Spirit of Community* hopeful sites for moral revival turn out to be sites of failure and difficulty on later pages. Indeed, we must move on again now to look beyond the family *and* beyond the school for the source of the problems of youth today.

THE McDONALDIZATION OF YOUTH CULTURE

Etzioni doesn't like McDonald's, nor for that matter, Kentucky Fried Chicken, Roy Rogers, Dunkin' Donuts, Hardee's, Burger King or Baskin-Robbins. It's not the fast food, the hamburgers, chicken pieces and ice-cream they sell that he finds so distasteful, but the experience they provide for youth. He insists that we have to 'look beyond the school itself to examine those factors that hinder or provide opportunities for generating educational experiences' (p. 109). Etzioni has looked beyond the school and he doesn't like what he sees. He estimates that in America about 'two-thirds of high school juniors and seniors these days have part-time paying jobs, many in fast-food chains, of which McDonald's is the pioneer, trendsetter, and symbol'. He argues that the 'McDonald's kind of job is rather uneducational in several ways' (p. 109). Unlike the lemonade stands and newspaper rounds of his own youth, which *did* provide an education in self-reliance, self-discipline, self-supervision, self-scheduling and an introduction to the work ethic, the McDonald's kind of job is 'highly structured and routinized' (p. 109). 'There is little room for initiative, creativity, or even elementary rearrangements. Thus, the fast-food franchises are breeding grounds for robots working for yesterday's assembly lines and not practice fields for committed workers in tomorrow's high-tech posts' (p. 110). We will leave aside the question of whether the national service that Etzioni favours is any more or less likely to produce the human robots he thinks he sees being turned out as youths take on 'the McDonald's kind of job'.

Etzioni suggests not only that the experience of American youth today compares unfavourably with the experience of his own youth (more than half a century ago), but that it also compares unfavourably with the experience of *European* youth today. Somewhat panegyrically, he asserts that 'Many Europeans have a rather different view of the work ethic: their teenage children are expected to spend their time skiing, improving their tennis or ballet, even honing their manners – not pumping gas' or staffing fast-food joints. Whilst there can be little doubt that youth is highly differentiated on *both* sides of the Atlantic, it seems highly unlikely that a significantly larger proportion of European than American youth has the opportunity and experience Etzioni imagines; and of course the McDonaldization of Europe has been gathering pace in recent years. The lack of adequate funding for post-16 education and the rapidly declining financial support for British university students may well lead to the Americanization of further and higher education unless new policy is introduced to halt it (see Bines, Perry and Demaine, 1992).

Back in the USA, according to Etzioni, robotic cash-laden youth is not only learning bad habits but also squandering its ill-begotten gains on 'trite elements of American consumerism: trendy clothes, trinkets, and whatever else is the fast-moving teen craze'. He is concerned that many teenage Americans 'find the instant reward of money, and the youth status symbols it buys, much more alluring than credits earned in algebra, American history, or French. No wonder quite a few would rather skip school, and certainly homework, to work longer hours at a Burger King' (p. 112). The communitarian answer to the problem of 'moral decline' said to accompany the McDonaldization of youth culture is more regulatory supervision of the youth labour market, together with the reasserting of parental authority and the introduction of a year of national service. Etzioni sees no need to investigate the effects of national service in countries that already have it, and there is no room for any doubt that its effects would be quite as communitarians imagine.

The Spirit of Community can be read as the thoughts of an embittered man sinking in a sea of crazy American teenagers; his life flashing before him, reflected in the rose-tinted glasses of his own youth. His contempt for 'the youth of today' is graphically illustrated in a cartoon he has selected for inclusion amongst the pages of his chapter titled 'The Communitarian School'. A grotesquely attired, hapless male is depicted pointing a TV remote control at a pile of books and complaining 'I keep forgetting... How do you turn these things on?'. It was never like that in Amitai's day. Leaving aside questions of his caricature for European youth and American 'teens' as he calls them, the significant point here is that his communitarian discourse does not provide the basis for a credible 'youth policy' or education policy for Western societies today. Again, notice how Etzioni began by arguing that schools need to take over responsibility from 'the failing family' and other social institutions, but rather than setting out policy for schools, turns *back* responsibilities to the family and other social institutions. In lieu of detailed policy argument readers are presented with appeals to 'changes of heart' and a circular (and inconclusive) account of the supposed roles of various social institutions in inculcating 'appropriate moral values'.

IDENTITY AND INDIVIDUALITY IN THE FRIENDLY SOCIETY

In his critique of communitarianism, Ray Pahl identifies forms of communal activity very different from those favoured by Etzioni. As we have seen already, Pahl cites the self-help activities of lone parents, contrasting them with the two-parent families heavily favoured in Etzioni's version of communitarianism. Moreover, Pahl argues that the desire for individuality and for new identities that has developed out of new life styles cannot be wished away or ignored; neither should it be simply equated with individualism. Pahl argues that beyond communitarianism lies the possibility of encouraging the development of a 'diverse, tolerant and friendly society based on creative individuality' (Pahl, 1995).

Pahl accepts that contemporary communitarians seek to foster the development of 'an environmental movement dedicated to the betterment of our moral, social and political environment', but he challenges Etzioni's ideas on, amongst other things, the loci of such a development. For example, work-based and professional communities have become sites of intense competition, stress and anxiety. 'Employers' strategies to control and discipline workers have been very effective: downsizing, delayering, contracting out, hiring on short-term contracts and similar measures create an uneasy and anxious workforce. The feel-good factor remains elusive' (p. 21). On the other hand, the idea of place-based community is limited, in part, because 'the local community is very rarely the locus of important social decisions'. Pahl cites James Coleman's 'brilliant pamphlet' *Community Conflict* (1957) which, nearly forty years ago, predicted that 'the prospect for the future is towards an increase in the proportion of externally caused community controversies'. Pahl argues that community spirit based on *conflict* is more and more related to national affairs and national decisions, and illustrates the point by referring to the likely effect of planning to put a high-speed rail link through 'comfortable Tory-voting England'. The activation of community spirit will 'frequently reveal a can of worms, it can also set community against community' (Pahl, 1995).

Etzioni has little to say about the diversity of community life, despite the wealth of anthropological and sociological evidence produced over the last fifty years, and a seemingly endless debate over 'the family, individual and society' (for a critical discussion, see for example Sennett, 1977). Pahl argues that if sociologists have exposed the myths and fallacies of the idea of community, the questions remain, 'Why does the idea refuse to lie down? Why are political leaders in America and Europe so keen to adopt communitarian rhetoric?'. He suggests that at least part of the reason is to be found in the desperate need to find a 'middle way between the public and the private', and in the fact that some of the communitarians' suggestions sound good for some sections of the population: 'it is easy for people to take on board those they would like to believe in and overlook those aspects that might make them feel uneasy if they subjected them to close scrutiny' (p. 21).

In Pahl's response to communitarian argument, the exigencies of the 'friendly society' demand that politicians and others recognize 'the deep-seated urge for individuality among people in our society' (p. 22). Citing Anthony Giddens' *The Transformation of Intimacy* (1993), Pahl argues that friendship is a 'pure relationship' in which 'we do not immediately calculate what we have to pay back for being comforted'. Politicians have 'probably neglected to consider friendship seriously because they cannot see clearly how to fit friends into an institutional context. Family-supportive policies are one thing... but friend-friendly policies – what on earth would they entail?' Unfortunately, Pahl doesn't tell us either. Instead, readers are to consider the 'new potentials for identity' and are warned, rather cryptically, that by being 'wary of the selfish self of the 1980s, we are in danger of ignoring the self-conscious self of the 1990s'. A fair warning but not an adequate basis for social policy; no wonder the politicians are left confused.

Pahl derides the politicians' alleged neglect of 'friend-friendly policy' but provides little more than bland description himself: 'Friends help each other, support each other and maintain links over long periods of a person's life'. So what? One could just as accurately say that friends might move away, keep in touch perhaps via an occasional Christmas card (if at all) and never be available to help or provide support. No doubt some friends who live close by do function as Pahl suggests, but friendships can be much more varied and fluid than he implies. There is nothing in his discussion of communitarianism, or of friendship, to indicate how policy might be drawn up to provide the 'support' that he regards as so necessary. He is at pains to insist on the importance of recognizing the individuality of persons and, of course, right to reassert that politics is personal as well as institutional. But if real alternatives are to be constructed in the arenas Pahl regards as problematical and important then much more detailed policy work is needed.

Like Pahl, Nancy Rosenblum (1994) is concerned with individual identities, but whilst Pahl provides very little detail on the 'friendship associations' that constitute his response to communitarianism, 'friendship groups' are central to what she refers to as 'romantic' communitarianism. Rosenblum is particularly interested in 'elective' communities which she characterizes as 'groups voluntarily formed by individuals oriented by subjective values, personality, and affective desires' (p. 58). In similar vein to Pahl, Rosenblum suggests that 'contemporary communitarian theory may be conceptually unequipped to take elective community into account' because the concept 'unsettles familiar categories and distinctions' (p. 58). Nevertheless, she argues that self-made identity unencumbered by hereditary conditions together with voluntary association constitute an 'exemplary expression of the public life of American society, a distillation of the distinctive relation between democratic society and personal identity' (p. 59).

Whilst contemporary communitarianism is also concerned with identity politics, Rosenblum argues that 'the romantic heart of identity – its resistance to closure and its susceptibility to the workings of imagination – is rejected; instead, personal and political identity are said to be socially constituted' (p. 85). For Rosenblum, romanticism is key to the dynamic relation between American democracy and communitarianism. The self, self-consciousness, individual identity, friendship and friendship groups lie at the heart of communitarianism and are not an alternative to it. But she concludes that much of this is beyond contemporary communitarianism. In *The Spirit of Community* Etzioni seems to be more concerned with the issue of national identity cards (he would like to see them introduced) than with questions of individual identity[2].

CONTESTED CITIZENSHIP

Whilst different communitarianisms seek to foster particular forms of citizenship, as we have seen, most share a concern for individual responsibility. Citizenship theorists, whilst not neglecting the question of individual responsibility, have focused more on citizenship rights and on issues surrounding the institutionalization of rights. Just as there are contested versions of communitarianism, there are contested notions of citizenship. But broadly, the main concerns of citizenship theorists are with civil, political and social rights; with social justice, the obligations of citizens, and the principle of equality.

There is a burgeoning literature on the concept of citizenship and on the means of encouraging its development (for example, see Barbalet, 1988; Heater, 1990; Lister, 1990, 1991, 1995; Ranson, 1990; Carr, 1991; Fogelman, 1991; Turner, 1990, 1993). Discussions of citizenship usually take the work of T. H. Marshall (1950, 1964, 1981) as their starting point. Marshall was concerned with the growth of citizenship in terms of a process of equalization of civil rights, political rights and social rights within the adult population. He addresses these three components of citizenship in *Citizenship and Social Class* (1950), arguing that citizenship is a status involving a broad equality in capacities with respect to rights and duties, whilst social class is a system of inequality. He argues that it is 'reasonable to expect that the impact of citizenship on social class should take the form of a conflict between opposing principles' (p. 29).

This notion of conflict between opposing principles has fuelled debate over social policy, with certain writers (see for example, Titmuss, 1958, 1970) arguing for the primacy of one set of principles over the other. However, Marshall maintains that a compromise can be found in what he refers to as the 'hyphenated society' (Marshall, 1981). He argues that post-war Britain is characterized by democratic-welfare-capitalism, where the hyphens indicate that the political, welfare and economic sectors can be considered both as interdependent and as partially autonomous. As Hindess (1987) points out, Marshall prefers this to the dominance of any one principle and suggests that 'the hyphenated society can survive only if it is recognized that both the welfare sector and the mixed economy are contributing to the creation of welfare' (Marshall, 1950, p. 131). As far as education systems are concerned, there is no shortage of examples of attempts (largely unsuccessful) to postulate the dominance of one sector over another, one set of principles over another. Writers such as Bowles and Gintis (1976, 1986), for example, have provided theoretical argument which has been deployed by commentators on contemporary education to allege the dominance of class and capitalism over the principles of welfare embodied in education (for critical discussion see Demaine, 1981; also see Ranson, 1990).

In a paper in a recent collection titled *Citizenship and Social Theory* (Turner, 1993), Barry Hindess argues that the notion of citizenship involves doubtful sets of claims. In particular, he argues that the Marshallian account of citizenship as 'a principle of equality that has been more or less adequately institutionalized in the societies of the modern West presents a misleading account of the character of these societies' (Hindess, 1993, p. 30). Moreover, he argues that what is at stake in modern notions of citizenship is the thesis that certain basic values or principles are realized in social life; that they 'control activities of the relevant kind within the constraints given by external conditions' (p. 30). Hindess notes that Talcott Parsons provides an elaborate version of the realization thesis in his account of the institutionalization of central values in the social system and their internalization in personality systems. The problem for Marshall's concept and indeed for the more elaborated version presented by Parsons is that, despite the theoretical sophistication of the latter, the thesis depends on an over-simple view of ideas and their effects. For Hindess, similar objections can be raised to what he refers to as the 'mystification thesis'.

The latter involves the suggestion that, rather than describing society, ideas about citizenship constitute a form of mystification. Distancing himself from this thesis, Hindess illustrates the point by reference to Marxists' claims about democratic politics and to Weber's account of 'democratic ideas serving to legitimate a distinctly modern form of rule'. Lenin's account of the political character of Western democracy as a 'shell for capitalism', a form of class dictatorship masquerading as a system of popular rule, and Weber's legitimation thesis both involve (in different ways) ideas about citizenship as a mystification or masking of the 'true' character of society. Like the realization thesis, the mystification thesis depends 'on an over-simple model of ideas and their consequences' (Hindess, 1993, p. 31). It is not that ideas about citizenship don't play a significant part in social and political life; they do, but their consequences cannot simply be read off from the ideas themselves or from their appearance in various forms of political discourse[3].

EDUCATION FOR CITIZENSHIP

Ideas about citizenship have certainly played a significant part in recent discussion about the role of education in democratic societies. The contested character of the concept of citizenship has not in itself constituted too serious an obstacle to the growth of the idea of 'education for citizenship', although there are concerns about the appropriate character of citizenship education, and doubts about the extent of its effective implementation as a component of the school curriculum (see Fogelman, 1991; Carr, 1991, and their contributions to this collection).

In Britain, the Right Honourable Bernard Weatherill MP, Speaker of the House of Commons, set up a Commission on Citizenship in 1988 to consider, amongst other things, the teaching of citizenship in schools. Its report, titled *Encouraging Citizenship*, appeared two years later but, writes Speaker Weatherill in his foreword to the report, 'From the start the Commission publicly advocated that a place should be found for citizenship studies in the curriculum' (Commission on Citizenship, 1990, p. vi). In the same year that the Speaker's Commission published its report, the National Curriculum Council (NCC) published a booklet titled *Education For Citizenship* (National Curriculum Council, 1990) as part of its Curriculum Guidance Series. In addition to official discourse emanating from central government and its agencies (and to some extent as a response to it), there are now serious arguments amongst educationists about the need explicitly to promote citizenship in schools, rather than leaving it to some ill-defined process often referred to as the 'hidden curriculum'. Teachers are urged, and indeed are required, to take a greater interest in the capacity for the development of citizenship in schools.

According to official discourse, the development of citizenship within schools is to be promoted in terms of 'the values by which a civilised society is identified – justice, democracy, respect for the rule of law' (National Curriculum Council, 1990), and it is said that 'education for citizenship is essential for every pupil. It helps each of them to understand the duties, responsibilities and rights of every citizen'. Moreover, the National Curriculum Council document states rather starkly that 'all citizens can and must be equal'. Although it does concern itself with wider issues of political participation, *Encouraging Citizenship* places an emphasis on an 'active' citizenship in terms of voluntary and community work. *Education For Citizenship*, on the other hand, performs a largely technical function, setting out a 'framework' for school activity elaborated around 'objectives' and 'content'. Objectives are said to be concerned with 'knowledge, cross-curricular skills, attitudes, moral codes and values' (National Curriculum Council, 1990, p. 3). 'Content' refers broadly to 'the nature of community; roles and relationships in a pluralist society; (and) the duties, responsibilities and rights of being a citizen', and more specifically with 'the family; democracy in action; the citizen and the law; work, employment and leisure; public services' (p. 5). Citizenship is to be considered within a range of 'activities, opportunities and experiences' which are related to the National Curriculum Key Stages 1, 2, 3 and 4. These activities, opportunities and experiences might appear and occur as cross-curricular issues which are integral parts of specific subject areas of the National Curriculum and more generally as aspects of whole-school policy (p. 15).

Beyond its largely technical function, *Education For Citizenship* is lacking in specifics. One of the few points of detail is its recommendation of a book titled *The Tiger Who Came to Tea* (Kerr, 1968) for use with children in the early-reading age-range. Of all the books that could be recommended for such children, *The Tiger Who Came to Tea*, first published by Collins in 1968, is an astonishingly outrageous choice. In this words-and-pictures story-book, the tiger who comes to tea behaves in a friendly but thoroughly anti-social manner in that it eats all the food and drinks the taps (faucets) dry – unbelievable, but then it is intended for four- and five-year-olds. This anti-social behaviour results in Mum's inability to have Dad's evening meal ready on the table when he arrives home from work. On his arrival, heroic Dad is able to rescue the hapless mother and child by taking them out to eat in a cafe. And of course it's Mum and daughter who we see in the supermarket next morning buying in food to replenish the larder. Even a minimally informed review of the literature available for early readers would throw up much more appropriate material. Quite why the National Curriculum Council needed to look back to the 1960s remains as mysterious as the choice of the book itself.

Another Collins publication from that era, *He Bear She Bear* (Berenstain and Berenstain, 1974) paints a picture of a quite different social world. In this book, both the female and male characters are depicted as potential parents but also as truck drivers, crane, train and bulldozer drivers, painters, builders, firefighters, police officers, doctors, teachers, musicians, airline pilots and much else. They are also depicted working in a circus where one of their joint tasks is to tame twelve tigers; a pity the National Curriculum Council was unable to tame even one tiger. None of this should be taken to imply that there is nothing of worth in *Education For Citizenship*, but the case of *The Tiger Who Came to Tea* does demonstrate an obvious need for vigilance in the selection of suitable educational material. The disappointing official discourse on citizenship produced by the National Curriculum Council compares unfavourably with the excellent material produced by The Citizenship Foundation[4].

CITIZENSHIP, CONSUMERISM AND EDUCATION

The recent focus on the idea of education for citizenship coincides with moves towards the promotion of consumerism in education, and the question arises as to the compatibility of the two developments. In a nutshell, the question is whether self-managed, market-oriented schools of the kind promoted by 'new right' policy (see Demaine, 1993) might be more or less appropriate institutions for the promotion of citizenship values and 'community spirit' than schools that are controlled by local authorities.

The promotion of consumerism in education is evident in many western countries where there has been sustained political pressure for reform from the 'new right'. Briefly, the new right argues for the 'privatization' of all schools: they should become independent, self-governing charitable trusts with control over their own budgets and their own pupil enrolment policy (see for example, Sexton, 1987; and see Demaine 1988, 1990, 1993 for critical evaluation). Such schools would operate under quasi-market conditions in that their income would come from education vouchers and from cash paid by parents as 'top-up' fees. The new right regards the removal of teachers' national pay scales, the re-writing of individual teacher contracts and the break-up of teachers' capacity for trade union activity as necessary to the future development of the market in education. According to the new right, the governing bodies of schools should be 'free to hire and fire' teachers, whilst parents should be 'free to choose' the school at which to spend their education credit vouchers, and free to top them up with cash. The new right justifies its argument for privatization (in part) in terms of the advantages of the 'empowerment of citizens' in the control of their schools, suggesting that citizens are more likely to feel closely involved with their children's education when their school is self-managed; and more especially when parents form part of the management group (see for example, the No Turning Back Group, 1986).

Of course, a school of almost any formal status can have a 'citizenship policy' as part of its curriculum, and indeed those British schools subject to the National Curriculum are legally obliged to have such a policy. It is debatable whether a privatized, self-managed, market-oriented school of the kind envisaged by the new right could provide a more or less appropriate focus for community activity than a school under local authority political control. Opponents of the idea of a market in education argue that in so far as it encourages a scramble for places in secondary schools, and pits parent against parent, it has the potential to *undermine* community spirit. Of course, much depends on the character of the local market and the relative status of the schools themselves. Specific local conditions will determine the extent of any scramble that might provide potential for bitterness in the local community and for opening up what Pahl calls 'a can of worms'. Opponents of the market argue that a community school under local authority political control can provide a focus for community activity and 'spirit', and that such a school is well placed to provide good access and accountability to its community.

The Conservative Government in Britain has not yet travelled all the way down the path proposed by the new right, but it does appear to be following the new right line on education policy (Demaine, 1993). Voucher schemes have been piloted in further education and nursery education and, although they have not been introduced into the primary or secondary sectors, there are those who argue that Britain now has many of the features of a voucher economy in education without the need to issue them formally (Thomas, 1990). On the other hand, the fragmentation of local authority-controlled education systems has not proceeded at anything like the pace proposed by the new right. By October 1995 only 1,072 out of around 25,000 schools had opted out of local authority political control to become what are known as Grant Maintained Schools (GMS), a status legislated for in the 1988 Education Reform Act. The British Conservative Government has been so concerned at the slow pace of reform towards its goal of a wholly self-managed national school system that it has made repeated attempts to hurry the process along; often without much success[5].

During the same period in which Grant Maintained Schools have been promoted, a policy known as local management of schools (LMS), also introduced by the 1988 Education Reform Act, has led almost all schools to the point where they are effectively self-managed, whilst still remaining formally under the umbrella of local authority control. An effect of Conservative education policy has been that by 1996 most British schools had a much greater degree of 'self-management' than was the case in 1979 when the Conservatives began their long period in office. However, this 'self-management' has to be assessed in the context of the centralization of the curriculum, and measures taken by the Treasury to exercise controls over the funding of the education system as a whole.

The differences between LMS and the GMS are real enough, but they are not so different as to make a blurring of the distinction between them impossible in most cases. Indeed, such a blurring became the policy of the British Labour Party during the early part of 1995, when the party published its policy document *Diversity and*

Excellence: A New Choice for Schools (Labour Party, 1995). New Labour under new leadership would not significantly erode the capacity for self-management that many schools have developed and now enjoy (see Demaine, 1993). The British Labour Party wants all schools to benefit from local community involvement, and wants to combine elements of a market (particularly with respect to parental preference or 'choice') with the benefits of community accountability. The extent to which it is possible to make such a combination work depends on particular local circumstances, and the issue cannot be settled in the abstract. These questions are pertinent in Britain and in many other western countries where, as Etzioni and Pahl both register, the political left and the right see potential for education to provide the vehicle for the 'Big Idea' of community involvement and the promotion of active citizenship.

In Britain, the Conservative Party has been concerned to promote community and citizenship as its 'Big Idea' in education and in other areas of social provision. When Margaret Thatcher lost the leadership of the Conservative Party, and with it the office of Prime Minister, she was replaced by John Major who surprised many commentators by referring to his commitment to a 'classless society'. Subsequently, when John Major introduced the notion of a 'citizen's charter' and the theme of citizenship as *his* Big Idea for the 1990s, some commentators saw this, together with the reference to a classless society, as an attempt to establish a 'new image' for the Conservatives and as a distancing of Major from his predecessor. Others saw Major's citizenship in terms similar to the consumerism of his predecessor, and the reference to 'classlessness' as political rhetoric. Nevertheless, Major was quick to establish the Citizen's Charter Unit within the Cabinet Office and to present proposals for a Citizen's Charter to Parliament. The Conservatives produced a series of policy documents and legislation referring to different aspects of the public services under the general heading of the promotion of the Citizen's Charter. As far as education is concerned, it is clear from *The Parent's Charter* that the consumer-customer is deemed to be the parent rather than the child. Thus, citizenship was to be developed within the schools as part of a programme of educating the citizens of the future, whilst at the same time schools themselves were to be regarded as entities to be marketed for the citizen-consumer-parent.

CONCLUSION

Communitarian ideology has been highlighted in Britain by Etzioni's 1994 lecture tour, by his television appearances and by the promotion of the book *The Spirit of Community*, so much for his despising the tele-democracy! Communitarian ideology has been afforded particular significance by political commentators in Britain who see it as a ready-made theme for the new leadership of the Labour Party. The British Labour Party is thought, by some, to need a new 'Big Idea' as a counter to the right-wing Tory idea of the market and the individualism it is said to entail. The notions of citizenship and community[6] might form the focus of a new ideology for New Labour but, as we have seen, others have pointed to the dangers.

Consumerism, citizenship and communitarian ideologies are not necessarily incompatible and education policy provides an illustration of the way the mish-mash of ideas has been taken up and used by different political interest groups and parties. Indeed, communitarians, conservatives, liberals, social democrats, socialists and communards put different emphases on the notions of citizenship and community and want to turn attractive-sounding terms to their advantage. Whilst Hirst (1990) suggests that there is no evidence that western electorates 'can be made to behave like "citizens"', many observers consider the responsible conduct of citizens a goal at least worth pursuing.

Almost three decades ago Etzioni wrote that the prerequisites of the 'active society' include, 'political education and consensus-formation to assure a more effective commitment than persuasion can provide' (Etzioni, 1968). In his more recent work Etzioni has moved towards the view that persuasion, and much more, is necessary. Although there are different kinds of communitarian, and some who recognize and want to celebrate difference, Etzioni and his communitarian allies would wage war on a range of social actors whose conduct appears to deviate from 'normative' behaviour alleged to have prevailed in an era before the Vietnam war. Indeed, ideological parallels can be drawn between Etzioni's recent communitarianist venture and the strategic thinking of American war planners during that conflict. The similarities are striking. In both cases, we have a 'hearts and minds' campaign projected alongside a set of more concrete, but ill conceived, operational proposals destined to fail. In the 1960s, coarser American GIs are said to have responded to the CIA's 'hearts and minds' project with the suggestion, no doubt clouded by the influence of marihuana, that 'if we have the Vietnamese by the balls, their hearts and minds will follow'. As we know, the might of the US Army, the USAF blanket bombings of the countryside and the mining of Haiphong harbour, the deployment of napalm and the defoliant 'agent orange' all failed to secure the Americans' desired outcome.

Despite an explicit denial, Etzioni's communitarian views are clouded too – in his case by the mist of time as he gazes back to an America that never really was the 'we society' he so fondly imagines. It is not that Americans of Etzioni's ilk should give up the war against the effects of poverty and inequality, but they should recognize and register more clearly those effects for what they are. Of course, not all of America's or the West's problems are the effects of inequality and there is, in any case, no real prospect of social equality on the political horizon. Far from it. The immediate need is to bring forward and implement policies to try to tackle the worst effects of poverty; to recognize the corrosive effect of inequality in a way that communitarians fail to do, and to work towards the construction of a political ideology that would begin to tackle social problems constructively. This would be to take a step towards the 'decent society' that communitarians fervently desire for Americans and for the peoples of other societies. But Etzioni and his friends cannot muster assets approaching anything like those commanded by the US military and the CIA, and their war machine explicitly eschews the backing of any established political party. In fact, Etzioni's only real asset is the media arm of the 'teledemocracy' he claims to despise. In *The Spirit of Community*, in his television appearances, and in the pages of the quarterly journal *The Responsive Community: Rights and Responsibilities*, Etzioni's appeal is to a middle-American sentimentalism that probably *does* want to listen but is confined within the ghetto of its own community interests, deafened by the scream of its burglar alarms and the clanging of the security gates which defend the new out-of-town housing estates.

The social problems that communitarians such as Etzioni identify, and the idea of 'moral revival' that they want to promote, are not confined to the West as is sometimes suggested. Reviewing Alexander Solzhenitsyn's *The Russian Question at the End of the Twentieth Century* (1995), Geoffrey Hosking notes that (like Etzioni) Solzhenitsyn 'wants a moral revolution, one of self-limitation'. Hosking concludes with the observation that 'Solzhenitsyn has raised absolutely the right questions, but in his answers I would like to see less vague moral teaching and more concern about practical solutions to the agon-isingly difficult problems Russians face today' (Hosking, 1995). Much the same could be said of Etzioni's 'answers' to the problems faced by Americans today.

Towards the dawn of the new millennium, sometimes different but nonetheless difficult problems face Russians, Americans, Africans, Canadians, Britons and the peoples of the other European counties East and West, as well as those of Australasia and the Pacific rim; and especially the new China as it emerges from its most recent era of self-enforced isolation. All around the world, much of the focus is on the question of economic development – but there is also a grow-ing recognition that attention also needs to be paid to environmental, social and political conditions, rights and responsibilities. Arguments over rights, community and citizenship almost always involve discus-sion of the role of education. Whilst education for citizenship and political education are important, and can play a significant role, it is wrong to regard education as some kind of panacea. There *is* an emphasis on education in this book, but this should not lead readers to assume that its contributors or editors are unaware of the vital importance of factors which lie outside of the sphere of influence of education and education systems[7].

NOTES

1. See especially Talcott Parsons (1935, 1938, 1949, 1951, 1952, 1959 and 1964), and Parsons and Shils (1962).
2. A discussion that would do justice to the question of identity is outside the scope of this chapter, but see Gilbert in this collection. I have also dis-cussed the question elsewhere (Demaine 1996).
3. Also see Miliband (1994) and Turner (1990 and 1993) for further discussion.
4. See for example, The Citizenship Foundation (1995) and other recent material.
5. By the end of 1995 there were indications that Conservatives might move further down the path laid down by the new right. Media reports suggested that the Conservative Party might propose to end local authority funding of schools in its manifesto for the general election to be held in 1996 or 1997 (see, Webster, P. and Charter, D. (1995). Media reports suggested that John Major was late for a photo-call for heads of state at the United Nations 50th birthday party in New York in October 1995 because he was embroiled in argument with his colleagues in England over the matter.
6. The notion of 'stakeholding' is a further, and more promising, development of this theme in Labour Party thinking. The notion was introduced into popular political debate after this book was finished. However, the idea of

stakeholding, in relation to education and training policy, is discussed in a forthcoming book, *Education Policy and Contemporary Politics* (Demaine, 1997, London: Macmillan).

7.   I am grateful to Lorraine Culley, Harold Entwistle, Elizabeth Kingdom, Ruth Lister and Ken Tyler for their helpful comments on an earlier version of this chapter. I take sole responsibility for its final form and content.

2 Gender and Citizenship Rights

Elizabeth Kingdom

Despite its pervasiveness, the presentation of political positions in terms of rights discourse – understood as the official ideology of liberalism – has been subjected to wide-ranging critiques: left, right and feminist. Two critiques of rights discourse have attracted critical feminist attention. The first is the communitarian criticism that rights discourse is divisive as between human individuals. The second is the new republicanism criticism that rights discourse is an obstacle to participation in democratic politics.

Both communitarianism and new republicanism offer political discourses which are attractive to feminists. Communitarianism recognizes the social connectedness of human beings which feminists have emphasized and promotes the neglected values of caring and mutual support. New republicanism gives political expression to the interconnectedness and interdependence of human beings. It defines members of the political community as citizens committed to the values of active participation and constantly renewed dialogue for the determination of the common good. New republicanism reworks rights discourse for the promotion of social rights and citizens' rights which advance equality and social justice but which are inseparable from the political values of active citizenship, civic duty and responsibility.

Yet feminists have argued that 'community' is a political chameleon which has the capacity for excluding women from democratic politics, and, to the extent that the new republicanism retains an uncritical conception of how the concept of citizenship operates in contemporary politics, new republicanism is itself an obstacle to radical democratic politics. These critiques have led some feminists to construct a new republicanism allied to a politics of difference. On this view, feminist democratic politics gives no political priority to the oppression of women in general, nor to social groupings based on gender. For those radicals concerned with practical politics, however, this new republicanism and its politics of difference appear to constitute an obstacle to feminist democratic politics and also to the possibility of engagement with practical policy issues, such as the devising of a national curriculum. But the politics of difference need not result in political paralysis, nor need it involve the wholescale abandonment of rights discourse. On the contrary, the new republicanism and its politics of difference require the constant review of political alternatives, including strategic decisions on the use of rights discourse.

COMMUNITARIANISM

Communitarianism identifies communities as the social units which, by promoting the values of justice, equality and fairness, care and cooperation, can serve as pockets of resistance to the dehumanizing effects of much contemporary politics, in particular the pervasiveness of rights discourse. Proponents of communitarianism typically reject the political discourse of rights on the grounds that it is a key ideological support of the politics of individualism (Sandel, 1982). This individualism is in turn castigated for its defence of a form of politics which promotes solitariness and selfishness and which trivializes the values of cooperative living and mutual aid (Glendon, 1991). Accordingly, rights discourse encourages the resolution of interpersonal conflicts in the law courts by reference to the rights of parties as individuals rather than by reference to the responsibilities of persons in a complex set of relationships (Regan, 1993).

The Communitarian Vision

Communitarians propose to remedy this overemphasis on the discourse of individual rights neither by discarding the discourse nor by supplementing it with a discourse of group rights (Thornton, 1990, p. 259). Rather they identify rights as the product of a community which promotes a vision of individuals as mutually supportive and as the product of social institutions designed to further the ethics of caring and cooperation. Mary Ann Glendon, for example, argues for the refinement of rights discourse, the disease of American politics, through invoking what she sees as a more venerable tradition of rights. That tradition is the one consonant with the values of justice, welfare and human dignity as articulated in the Preamble to the US Constitution. She discerns these values in persisting discourses of community which are found 'around the kitchen table, in the neighbourhood, the workplace, in religious groups, and various other communities of memory and mutual aid' (Glendon, 1991, p. 174). Similarly, Milton Regan invokes older notions of duty, interdependence and collective responsibility to develop a discourse for family law which undermines law's preference for constructing persons' legal identities through contract law and which aids the pursuit of intimacy. In Regan's preferred discourse, individual rights arise out of the definition of members of families in terms of their status and role as husbands, wives, and parents (Regan, 1993, p. 2). In his view, status discourse strengthens the relational and situational ethic favoured by feminists, rather than the traditional male emphasis on separation and independence (Regan, 1993, p. 184).

Community as Oppression

Glendon and Regan both express their communitarian ideals in terms of a vision for the future. What they also have in common is the invocation of the past for the development of their communitarian alternative to the contemporary political malaise. It is precisely this invocation of the past that provides the central theme of Derek Phillips' devastating analysis of the historical communities which are typically proposed as models from which contemporary communitarians should draw their inspiration: post-colonial America, the medieval kingdom, the Greek polis. Phillips reveals in scrupulous detail the discrepancy between the social realities of such communities and the ideologies of community, and he reaches this conclusion:

> Communitarians [such as MacIntyre, Sandel, Taylor and Bellah] emphasize the peace and harmony of earlier times and places, while I see even more domination, subordination, exploitation, and human suffering than surrounds me today. So, while I share much of their disenchantment with life in the modern age, I reject their idealized portrayals of the past. If those were the good times, Lord protect us against the bad. (Phillips, 1993, p. 195).

A recurring theme of Phillips' analysis is the inferior status of women in all these communities. Indeed, the capacity of communitarianism for anti-feminist politics is a major element in the work of even those feminists who might have been drawn to its claimed values of mutual responsibility and human interconnectedness (cf. Frazer and

Lacey, 1993). For example, Marilyn Friedman considers communitarianism a perilous ally for feminism, because of the way in which it typically invokes communities such as families, neighbourhoods and nations that have harboured social roles and structures which have been oppressive of women (Friedman, 1992, p. 103). Precisely the same criticism can be made of Glendon. Her vision of the future is conveyed in disturbingly nostalgic terms, with no reference to the massive sociological literature damning as sites of women's oppression the very communities she cites with approval. Similarly, Regan's advocacy of the resumption of status in family law skates over the feminist critique of status as typically supporting unequal roles for husbands and wives in marriage (Kingdom, 1994, p. 142).

Yet the attraction of the ethics of community persists, and, as John Holmwood has argued persuasively, communitarianism can take conservative, pluralist and socialist forms (Holmwood, 1993, p. 100). For example, Friedman herself investigates the possibilities of friendship and the stereotypical urban community as examples of non-oppressive communities. Further, 'community' can be located in the discourse of republicanism which is dedicated to the development of those forms of citizenship which can accommodate all minorities.

NEW REPUBLICANISM

Margaret Thornton proposes that 'republicanism is the constitutional expression of communitarianism' (Thornton, 1990, p. 250). In this chapter, the term 'new republicanism' follows Emilios Christodoulidis' characterization of new republicanism, with the concomitant resurgence of interest in citizenship, as a theory about the self-determination of community (Christodoulidis, 1995, p. 12). New republicanism too has a critique of rights discourse. Like communitarianism, new republicanism has focused on the unacceptably individualistic politics of rights discourse. For example, Richard Bellamy shows how a moral theory based exclusively on rights does not encourage acts of supererogation or charity (Bellamy, 1993, p. 67). Bellamy also argues that rights-based forms of citizenship are essentially passive and anti-political, because far from protecting the individual against the state, rights strengthen the state and reinforce the concentration and centralization of power (loc. cit., p. 68).

For feminists, too, rights-based forms of citizenship have a problematic history, occasioning the general claim that women have often been excluded from the enjoyment of citizens' rights. This exclusion has been theorized in two main ways. First, Sylvia Walby documents how women have been excluded de facto and de jure from the enjoyment of citizenship rights. She points to how women have not enjoyed the right to make their own medical decisions, and to how married women did not acquire the right to own property or the right to vote until well into this century (Walby, 1994, pp. 378–9). Secondly, Carole Pateman has argued that women's inability to enjoy citizenship rights has never been a simple matter of excluding them from the citizen body. Rather, women have been both included and excluded on the basis of the same characteristics. They were excluded on the basis of their capacity for motherhood and they come to be included as men's subordinates through that same capacity (Pateman, 1992, p. 19). Similarly, Ursula Vogel argues that, typically, men's citizenship rights and obligations in relation to the state have been 'direct', whereas women's have been articulated through their relationships with others as dependants, carers, and providers of services (Vogel, 1991, p. 77).

Responsible Republicanism and Social Rights

A typical response to new republican critiques of rights discourse has been to rework the concept of rights, sometimes by combining rights and duties, sometimes by substituting social rights, with a view to promoting citizens' more active participation in democratic politics. For example, Suzanna Sherry argues for avoiding the limitations of the crude discourse of citizens' rights by focusing attention on the conditions under which rights are exercised. The effect of that displacement, Sherry maintains, is to link rights with responsibilities:

> If what is important is not that one has a right to vote but that one is able to (and does) use it wisely, we have moved our vision of citizenship from rights alone to rights and duties, or rights and responsibilities (Sherry, 1995, p. 132).

Sherry is concerned that the critique of rights should not involve their being abandoned, and she argues that it is education that provides 'the bridge between selfish, rights-bearing individuals and their deliberative republican community'. For Sherry, 'one can reconcile rights and republicanism only by suggesting that a republican citizen needs an education that will enable her to exercise both the rights and responsibilities of citizenship' (ibid.). This reconciliation of rights and responsibilities provides Sherry with the cue to detail the contents of a republican education.

Similarly sympathetic to feminist critiques of citizen rights, Fred Twine argues that human agents are socially embedded and mutually interdependent. He claims that an emphasis on the social rights of citizenship is an antidote both to the limitations of individual rights discourse and to the exclusion of women from citizenship rights (Twine, 1994). Twine argues that social rights to well-being should be based not on workers' rights acquired through participation in the wage labour market, because of the adverse effect on women of such welfare schemes (cf. Lister, 1995, pp. 17–20), but on citizens' rights. Twine is impressed with the potential for social justice of Basic Income schemes under which the social right to a citizen's income is not predicated on participation in the paid work market.

Gendered Citizenship

Feminists have argued that within citizenship discourse it is not only rights that are covertly gendered. For example, Iris Marion Young offers a feminist critique of the gendered basis of the concepts of duty, impartiality, and rationality characteristic of republican thinking. She shows how they support the preservation of the concept of the unity of the civic public into which republican man enters. Young argues that these concepts are invariably contrasted with those of affectivity, sentiment and desire, and that, in so far as women are thought to exemplify those qualities, they will be excluded from full citizenship rights (Young, 1987, p. 60–63).

On Young's analysis, the ways in which Sherry and Twine rework rights discourse leave untouched the covertly gendered concepts of new republican thinking. For the mere juxtaposition of rights and duties, and the substitution of social rights for individual rights preserves the main features of what Barry Hindess has termed the 'realization thesis'. This thesis, which Hindess ascribes to T. H. Marshall, is that citizenship is 'a set of civil, political and social rights that have been more or less adequately realized in the democratic societies of the modern West' (Hindess, 1993, p. 19). Hindess challenges this thesis both on the grounds that it underestimates the effects of major economic inequalities on the enjoyment of rights and that it misrepresents the way in which ideas such as citizenship and rights – and, one might add, in the case of Sherry and Twine, duties and social justice – are deployed in contemporary political discourse.

Hindess' political point is that the realization thesis encourages the expectation that the perfecting of already existing democratic structures is largely a matter of renewed effort, or of a change of emphasis from one political principle to another, or, in the case of gender politics, of simply alerting feminists to the need to reveal the imperfect workings of the concept of citizenship.

On this critique, both Twine and Sherry attempt to strengthen citizenship rights by adding in new political ideas, as if these new ideas could have the effect of materially improving citizens' capacity to participate in democratic politics. Hindess' critique is also a warning to feminists, such as Pateman, who take an over-simple view of how the concept of citizenship can function. He argues that 'the significance of the principle of citizenship in Western political discourse does not [as Pateman appears to argue] ensure that men and women will be treated unequally. The point is that it contains elements that could be used either way' (Hindess, 1993, p. 33). To support Hindess' thesis here, one might cite Bryan Turner's observation that the sociology of education has shown that there will always be a discrepancy between government policies promoting equal opportunities in education and the actual social outcomes (Turner, 1994, p. 163). A clear illustration is Joan Scott's brilliant case study of how preoccupation with an over-simple view of the adversely gendered nature of access to university history departments — a form of the realization thesis — conceals the sheer variety of the female academics' experiences. In fact, Scott's study is an antidote to a an over-simple reading of Hindess' critique. For the logic of Hindess' argument is not merely that the principle of citizenship may result in men and women being treated equally or unequally but that it may have effects which either defy or do not exhaust analysis in terms of a gendered grouping.

It is the recognition of non-gendered forms of inequality and oppression that leads Iris Marion Young to question the feminist construction of citizenship discourse, including that of rights discourse, as predicated on the distinction between female and male virtues. Accordingly, she widens her form of new republicanism to include forms of oppression other than those experienced by women. Yet even Young's form of new republicanism has had a mixed response from proponents of radical democratic politics. Chantal Mouffe, for example, is sympathetic to Young's claim but she is uneasy at Young's concept of 'group differentiated citizenship'. Mouffe argues that it is predicated on the existence of groups which have already been formed, such as Native Americans, and may on that account be unreceptive to the appearance of new social groupings (Mouffe, 1992, p. 380). For Mouffe, new republicanism has to be allied with the politics of difference.

NEW REPUBLICANISM AND THE POLITICS OF DIFFERENCE

In the new republican literature, Christodoulidis notes, the emphasis has been shifted from 'rights' and individualism to active participation in the political (Christodoulidis, 1995, p. 177). So, for example, whilst Mary Dietz acknowledges the political value of defending individual freedom and equality, she counsels feminists against the deployment of the vision of the citizen as the bearer of rights, on the grounds that it is inseparable from the notion of democracy as equivalent to the operation of representative institutions of capitalist market society (Dietz, 1992, p. 67). Similarly, Mouffe has argued that the defence of acquired rights is a serious obstacle to the achievement of equality (Mouffe, 1988, p. 100).

Radical Democratic Politics

For Dietz and Mouffe, essentialist theories of politics, whether in the form of liberal democratic politics or politics which is predicated on the interests of pre-existing groups, such as women or Native Americans, have serious limitations for radical democratic politics. Whilst not opposed to feminist politics, they envisage a radical democratic politics in which gender is not a pertinent category, in which the feminist politics of difference would be displaced by an undifferentiated politics of difference. As Dietz puts it:

> A truly democratic defence of citizenship cannot afford to launch its appeal from a position of gender opposition and women's superiority. Such a premise would posit as a starting point precisely what a democratic attitude must deny – that one group of citizen's voices is generally better, more deserving of attention, more worthy of emulation, more moral, than another's. (Dietz, 1992, p. 78)

Similarly, Mouffe resists essentialist analyses of political agents as possessing a single identity, such as their gender, or their being differently abled. Instead, she argues, citizenship is a political principle which supports multiple and constantly changing identities and which persistently subverts existing and evolving forms of domination (Mouffe, 1992, p. 372).

Political Paralysis?

Some participants in the new republicanism debates are clearly disturbed by the implications of this type of politics of difference for political activity. For the eradication of any discourse, including rights discourse, which privileges specific moral or political principles or which gives priority to specific political groupings, would appear to lead to political paralysis. For example, Bryan Turner acknowledges that the language of citizenship, including rights discourse, has quite simply not included women (Turner, 1994, pp. 157–8) but he is concerned that postmodern critiques of politics and culture appear to be incompatible with the development of democratic political institutions, such as the imposition of national standardization by a high culture and a national curriculum, policies which he sees as compatible with the democratic thrust of modern citizenship norms (loc. cit., p. 166). *A fortiori*, Turner could identify the new republicanism and its politics of difference as an obstacle to the development of any feminist democratic politics which could operate within the framework of prevailing state politics. On this view, new republicanism and its politics of difference provide no political principles or analyses which permit the determination of consistent policies and the calculation of strategies, in particular for feminist politics.

STRATEGIC INTERVENTIONS

Both Dietz and Mouffe are alert to this critique. Dietz anticipates the criticism that she has collapsed feminist consciousness into democratic consciousness, but she points to how the feminist movement has been informed by democratic organization and practice and argues that this recent history is one valuable resource for the democratization of politics (Dietz, 1992, p. 78). Similarly, Mouffe argues that the anti-essentialist theorization of the multiple forms of women's subordination is not an obstacle to feminist democratic politics but a condition of it. That is because the democratic project requires a perspective which is predicated on the diversity and multiplicity of ways in which relations of power and political subjects are constructed (Mouffe, 1992, p. 372).

Developing a comparable politics of difference, Anna Yeatman insists that postmodernism involves not the abandonment of the values of contemporary democratic institutions but a deconstructive involvement with them. For example, Yeatman argues that an appeal to universal values such as rationality is typically a mechanism for closing off debate and for the silencing of voices. In her concluding analysis of the politics of assessing home and community care needs, Yeatman shows how the postmodern emancipatory vision can introduce the principle of irresolvable difference into decision-making processes and thereby destabilize dominant constructions of power. Yeatman is not proposing that such destabilization leads to the discovery of a political solution. Rather, it provides the space for reflection on new political practices and for the refinement of 'strategic interventions' (Yeatman, 1994, p. 122).

Strategising Rights

Yeatman's analysis reintroduces the question of the deployment of rights discourse, both through the notion of a deconstructive involvement with the values of contemporary democratic institutions and through the contention that this process requires reflection on strategic interventions. For rights are undoubtedly a major component of the value discourse of modern democratic institutions and, whilst it does not follow that rights discourse should remain undisturbed, the calculations surrounding strategic interventions may well have to include an assessment of whether to deploy rights discourse in the interests of progressive politics. Here again, Twine's work is of interest, for his purpose is not simply to redefine rights so that they can be adduced in support of a social vision of citizenship in which 'each must be the defender of the citizenship rights of all', a social vision which would be consonant with that of Dietz and Mouffe. He is also concerned to refine a discourse of social rights which can inform specific policies, such as Basic Income schemes, which he sees as crucial to the new citizenship.

Now, there is no doubt that the discourse of social rights is a familiar one, and one instantly recognizable (if not approved) by politicians. In this respect, then, Twine's deployment of social rights discourse has a relatively easy entrée into contemporary political debates, and constitutes a good example of how, if rights discourse is to be deployed for progressive politics, it has to be converted into realizable strategies (cf. Kingdom, 1995). On the other hand, the limitations of Twine's realization thesis raises the question of whether some other way of making his policy recommendations might not be more effective. A revealing comparison with Twine's position is provided by the way in which the Commission on Social Justice, henceforth CSJ, debates the feasibility of a Citizens' Income, a Basic Income. In its report, the CSJ has as its starting point only the briefest outline of the values of social justice. They comprise 'the equal worth of all citizens, their equal right to be able to meet their basic needs, the need to spread opportunities and life chances as fairly as possible, and finally the requirement that we reduce and where possible eliminate unjustified inequalities' (CSJ, 1994, p. 1). From then on, CSJ makes only the most fleeting of references to rights, concentrating instead on the strategies which their opening statement requires. Here, then, CSJ deploys rights discourse as little more than a signal for the development of a policy research programme (cf. Kingdom, 1996) in which the pros and cons of a Citizen's Income are debated in the light of economic and political feasibility.

My argument here is not that CSJ entirely escapes the problems of the realization thesis. Indeed, Hindess might argue that its concept of social justice is just as vulnerable to that critique as rights discourse. But I put forward the report of the CSJ as a concrete illustration of deconstructive involvement with a pervasive political discourse. The report gives rights discourse minimal recognition, using it instead as an impetus for policy-making, thereby largely avoiding the problems of rights discourse for purposes of progressive politics.

CSJ's minimal reliance on rights discourse shifts attention away from preoccupation with how more and more citizens can enjoy more and more rights. Instead, it encourages an approach in keeping with the new republicanism allied to a politics of difference, namely reviewing as many alternative ways of formulating social issues as possible. For example, its first five priorities for the revitalization of the UK education system are: universal pre-school education, an attack on inadequate basic skills, ending the distinction between education and training, a minimum training investment by all employers, and a new and fairer expansion of higher education (CSJ, 1994, p. 122). All the goals identified by CSJ are linked to costings and funding strategies. The sixth priority is a 'Learning Bank' to extend to every adult the opportunity of learning throughout life (ibid.). Here, however, CSJ frankly admits that at the moment the Learning Bank exists as a concept only, thereby opening up debate at the level of political discourse. For whilst educationists sympathetic to radical politics may applaud the goal of lifelong education, they may well resist the discourse of a Learning Bank and an Individual Learning Account (CSJ, 1994, p. 144). For even if the language of credits is already with us, that is no argument for extending what might be called the monetarization discourse.

CONCLUSION

For those participants in the rights debate who are impressed with the political limitations of rights discourse, there is a strong temptation either to abandon rights discourse or to incorporate it into a discourse, such as new republicanism, which gives greater emphasis to different political principles, such as civic duty or social justice. What I have argued in this chapter, however, is that theoretical problems with new republicanism require that it be allied to a politics of difference, and that this politics of difference need not induce political paralysis. Rather, the new republicanism allied to a politics of difference requires the constant review not only of realizable political alternatives but also of the political discourses in terms of which those alternatives are theorized. Under present political conditions, I have suggested, the discourse of social rights, whether in conjunction with other political principles or not, may have its uses for progressive politics but there is no need for it to have pride of place. Further, in the case of CSJ, where rights discourse is not given political priority, its minimal status encourages the development and critique of new political principles and concepts.

3 Identity, Culture and Environment: Education for Citizenship for the 21st Century

Rob Gilbert

Education for citizenship has become a key concern for educational policy and debate in the advanced economies of the English-speaking world, where education systems and agencies have produced reports, curriculum guidelines, and school programs in surprising number. From the United Kingdom come parliamentary inquiries and national curriculum statements (Commission on Citizenship, 1990; National Curriculum Council, 1990); in the United States agencies are producing guidelines and statements of national standards for education for citizenship (Bahmueller, 1991; Center for Civic Education, 1994); and in Australia, the source of this chapter, the national parliament has conducted three important inquiries, the most recent leading to a major national curriculum development initiative (Senate Standing Committee, 1989, 1991; Civics Expert Group, 1994).

This work signals not only the importance of the idea of citizenship in the education pantheon but also the significance of the present historical conjuncture in focusing attention on citizenship, and on education programs to promote it. While it is dangerous to generalize too far, it seems that common influences on these developments are the continuing need to promote the legitimacy of present systems of government in the face of increasingly diverse political constituencies and institutional privatization, and the fear that cultural and economic globalization is threatening the core identity and cohesion of the nation-state.

These fears are usually expressed as concerns about apathy among citizens and lack of motivation in schools. The Australian Senate inquiry into active and informed citizenship (1989) quoted findings of attitudes among young people of confusion, cynicism, indifference and an unwillingness to become involved in the formal political process. The UK Commission on Citizenship states that 'Our society is passing through a period of change and we are concerned that without our realizing it, we could lose some of the benefits of living in the relatively free and open society which we have inherited.' (Commission on Citizenship, 1990, p. xv). The US Center for Civic Education (Bahmueller, 1991, p. 3) notes the low voting rate among Americans and the 'widespread disengagement of citizens from the responsibilities and rewards of involvement' and a 'lackadaisical acceptance of their own apathy and inertia'. These comments direct attention to questions of motivation to citizenship and education for citizenship, and this will be a central concern of this discussion.

The implications for citizenship of cultural and economic change in the postindustrial global environment are important issues in education for citizenship and the associated questions of motivation. This chapter reviews aspects of the renewed interest in education for citizenship in the context of these aspects of global change. It briefly surveys major strands in the current concept of citizenship and assesses their relevance to contemporary global change. The argument is that current concepts of citizenship pay insufficient attention to a crucial aspect of the debate for education: the issue of identity and its implications for motivation to citizenship. This then becomes the chief concern of the paper, and the issue of motivation for citizenship in the present world context is explored in a number of educational contexts.

APPROACHES TO CITIZENSHIP: LIBERAL INDIVIDUALISM

Citizenship is a broad, complex and contested term, and programs in education for citizenship vary with the notion of citizenship which underlies them (Leca, 1992; Oldfield, 1990). The following discussion traces two major strands in the concept of citizenship which have characterized traditional democratic debate: liberal individualism and more communitarian approaches. From these broad strands a number of specific emphases have developed, with their own implications for the needs and desired capacities of citizens, and hence for education.

Oldfield (1990) identifies liberal individualism as the source of the most influential concept of citizenship in Britain and the United States, where citizenship is a status implying individuals' rights of sovereignty over their lives:

The function of the political realm is to render service to individual interests and purposes, to protect citizens in the exercise of their rights, and to leave them unhindered in the pursuit of whatever individual and collective interests and purposes they might have. Political arrangements are thus seen in utilitarian terms. To the extent that they afford the required protection for citizens and groups to exercise their rights and pursue their purposes, citizens have little to do politically beyond choosing who their leaders are to be. One of the rights of citizens within this framework is the right to be active politically: to participate, that is, in more substantial ways than merely by choosing political leaders. Because it is a right, however, citizens choose – on the assumption that they have the resources and the opportunity – when and whether to be active in this way. It is no derogation from their status of citizen if they choose not to be so active. (p. 2)

Oldfield points out that a major advantage of liberal individualism and the rights-based account is that it does not postulate any one conception of the good life. It sets out the procedures, rules and institutional framework which allow individuals to pursue their own visions of the good life, including some provision for minimum levels of welfare and access to allow those deprived of the relevant resources to participate. Based on the philosophy of the autonomous and responsible moral agent, there is no requirement in this view for any commitment to the collective other than to respect the autonomy of others, and to maintain the system of rules and institutions within which individuals can strive to attain the good life. The emphasis is on the political system as a guarantor of individual freedoms.

A good example of this approach is the view of the UK Commission for Citizenship that citizenship refers to 'the separate role of individuals as citizens within the political or public community, and the rules that govern it' (1990, p. xv). The procedural emphasis is classically illustrated in the Commission's statement that 'We consider that citizenship involves the perception and maintenance of an agreed framework of rules or guiding principles, rather than shared values' (1990, p. 13). This definition leads the Commission expressly to exclude the economy and the family as spheres of relations and experiences relevant to citizenship, and to focus on rules (rather than experience, practice or well being) as the essence of citizenship. The educational prescriptions that flow from this focus primarily on the skills required for participation in this institutional framework of rules, determined by the role of the individual citizen in the political system:

> The Commission regards the element of acquisition of skills as crucial to the success of the citizenship theme; young people should leave a democratic school with some confidence in their ability to participate in their society, to resolve conflict and, if they oppose a course of action to express that opposition fairly, effectively, and peacefully. These skills within school may involve, for example:
> - the capacity to debate, argue and present a coherent point of view
> - to participate, for example, in elections
> - taking responsibility by representing others, for example on the School Council
> - working collaboratively
> - playing as a member of a team
> - protesting, for example by writing to a newspaper or councillor or a local store.
>
> The development of social, planning, organisational, negotiating and debating skills is a major part of this theme. (Commission on Citizenship, 1990, p. 104)

The emphasis on skills and procedure, albeit restricted to the confines of the school, is a classic indication of the liberal individualism at the heart of this proposal. Note that in this view citizens should be armed with the skills to express their opposition to a course of action, but not necessarily to propose a course of action. This is consistent with the individualist view that citizenship is primarily about defending one's rights rather than, for instance, working to transform economic, social or political arrangements. Also, there is nothing here about substantive rights or common values which would assist citizens in deciding what course of action should be opposed. The commitment to individual autonomy in the liberal individualist view places this beyond the role of the state in promoting citizenship.

This concept of the citizen, citizenship rights, and the relation of the citizen to the state is deeply embedded in democratic theory and practice, and is a major plank of popular political thought in English-speaking representative democracies. However, it is not without its problems. The first is that it is not a purely individualist argument, since it requires that all members of the community, or at least a majority of them, share the commitment to individual autonomy and are sufficiently committed to it to support the institutions it needs to operate. Second, it follows from this that the individualist position requires that people be motivated to work together to operate such a system. If the price of freedom is eternal vigilance, then some means must be found to sustain the vigilance.

Third, the liberal individualist commitment to rights has led it to a point where the atomistic individual is no longer an adequate model for the holder of rights. The rights which accrue to the individual in the modern state are not only negative rights (freedom from imposition of various kinds) but also, and increasingly, positive ones (freedom of access to various personal, social, political and economic goods), and the extension and development of such rights quite simply outreach the capacity of individualism to encompass them. Rights are increasingly extended to minorities and other groups as collectives and not as individuals, and are justified in terms of normal expectations of levels of wellbeing in particular societies. Liberal individualism then is not a pure form, but rather a strand in a complex web of arguments, policies and practices which go beyond references to the rights and properties of individuals.

Finally, the proviso that the individualist ethos needs to be combined with a welfare orientation to ensure all individuals have access to the system implies obligations to fellow citizens that ultimately undermine the basis in self-interest. Liberal individualism then is inadequate in its own terms, and is not sufficient to encompass the elements of citizenship which characterize current debates.

COMMUNITARIAN APPROACHES TO CITIZENSHIP

In most policy debates and prescriptions for practice, the focus on individual rights is combined with a more communitarian approach, and this forms the second major strand of the concept of citizenship. Just as people identify themselves as members of families, communities, nations, they also recognize, to varying degrees and in varying ways, obligations implied by these memberships. In this view, citizenship implies membership of a community entailing a juridical status which confers formal rights and obligations, such as equality under the law, the right to vote, paying taxes or otherwise contributing to the social and economic welfare of the community. The concern is for the extent to which these are safeguarded in law and government, but also whether citizens practise these formally established rights and obligations. The balance between rights and obligations, and the nature and extent of the obligations vary, but the key characteristic of citizenship is the idea of community membership and what that implies for shared values, interests and obligations.

Oldfield (1990) labels this strand the tradition of civic republicanism, in which citizenship is not only a status, but an activity or a practice, so that not to engage in the practice is not to be a citizen. The important educational implication of this strand is that citizens in the civic republican view need to be supported in practising citizenship. They need to be empowered to practise it through access to resources such as knowledge, skills, information and welfare; they need the opportunity to practise it through decentralization of political and economic power; and they need to be motivated to practise it. Civic republicans therefore are concerned with ensuring that citizens can and do contribute to the practice of citizenship, including fulfilling their obligations as members of the political community.

Promoting obligations is more difficult than promoting rights of self-interest, and this strand of citizenship often carries a tone of austerity and moralism:

> Civic republicanism is a hard school of thought. There is no cosy warmth in life in such a community. Citizens are called to stern and important tasks which have to do with the very sustaining of their identity. There may be, indeed there ought to be, a sense of belonging, but that sense of belonging may not be associated with inner peace and, even if it is, it is not the kind of peace that permits a relaxed and private leisure, still less a disdain for civic concerns. (Oldfield, 1990, p. 6)

The great difficulty in promoting this view of citizenship (and this is a key issue for educators who have generally been given the responsibility for doing it), is how to motivate people to the communitarian commitment. The common strategy is to say that it is actually in people's individual interests to be so committed, since such a commitment is necessary to support the social contract which guarantees individuals the right to autonomy and privacy. In other words, the instrumental argument for the communitarian view justifies itself by resorting to liberal individualism, and becomes a derivative of it.

A stronger base for the communitarian argument, and a potentially important source of ideas for the motivation problem, is the notion of identity based on what people share with other individuals. Traditional statements of the civic republican view have emphasised patriotism and loyalty as simultaneously the sources of citizen identity and the motivation to practise citizenship. However, the civic republican view holds that human beings will not choose this level of agency and form of consciousness unless they are educated into it, but that they would choose it if they could know everything in advance. (Oldfield, 1990, p. 153) This paternalistic position is justified in the argument that it is aimed at producing free and autonomous moral beings.

Criticisms of the communitarian approach relate especially to this paternalism, and the associated argument that, in promoting a version of the collective welfare, communitarian prescriptions may be simply the imposition of the identities and interests of some over others. An example of such an approach is Janowitz's (1983) call for the formation of civic consciousness through patriotism developed in forms of national service. Janowitz sees that schools can teach the nation's political traditions and how government institutions operate, and develop 'essential identifications and moral sentiments required for performance as effective citizens' (p. 12). However, schools cannot form the bonds between citizens which create in them the obligation to perform the duties of citizenship unless they include some form of military or civilian service. This can only be done by 'immersing them in a social setting that emphasizes work and service in the context of symbols of national (or community) identification' (p. 169). Janowitz mentions environmental conservation projects, assistance in the control of natural or man-made disasters, and educational and social work programs as the type of activities which might develop the affiliation with the social which citizenship requires. At the level of national affiliation, of patriotism, Janowitz advocates national service as the key to the development of civic obligation.

Communitarian approaches are not always so overbearing, but they do share the problem of how to define and develop the shared commitment to some collective interest. However, as we have seen, and contrary to some claims, the liberal individualist approach also requires a similar commitment. In this sense, the two strands have a common interest in finding a base for commitment, a solution to the motivation problem.

A common emphasis of the civic republican view focuses on citizenship as a set of moral and social virtues required for practising and sustaining a democratic ideal. An interesting example is Heater's concept of citizenship in which citizens need to understand that their role entails status, loyalty, duties and rights 'not primarily in relation to another human being, but in relation to an abstract concept, the state'. (Heater, 1990, p. 2) He traces the idea and practice of citizenship from its origins in the Greek city state through its manifestations in the age of revolutions, 19th century nationalism, liberalism and socialism, to its consolidation in the modern nation state. This grand narrative, notwithstanding its diverse episodes and tenuous continuity, is held together by the idea of citizenship, a concept whose power derives from 'identity and virtue'. (p. 182)

This identity is based on social reciprocity and common interests, which may themselves be based on a sense of tradition, ethnicity or way of life, and heightened by systems of beliefs, ceremonies and symbols. Citizenship is one amongst many identities an individual will feel, but it is distinguished by being necessary for moral maturity, and by its potential to moderate the divisiveness of other identity feelings – gender, religion, race, class and nation: 'citizenship helps to tame the divisive passions of other identities' (Heater, 1990, p. 184). In Heater's view, history, 'a society's collective memory' (p. 184), plays a special role in citizenship identity, along with nationality and fraternity. Equally, the cultural togetherness of nationality and the collaborative sense of purpose in fraternity bind people to a common identity.

Heater identifies loyalty, responsibility and respect for political and social procedural values as the key virtues of citizenship. Loyalty is an emotional attachment to an institution, land, a group or a person, and a belief in the values which the object of loyalty stands for. It is closely linked to identity through the sense of fraternity. The good citizen also has a sense of responsibility to take positive and supportive actions, and understands and accepts legal duties and moral obligations.

In setting out his educational prescriptions, Heater specifies three main objectives. First, he suggests knowledge of the history of citizenship, associated laws and institutions, and the primary value concepts of identity, loyalty, freedom, rights, duties, justice, representation. Second, teachers should stimulate a predisposition to be interested in public affairs, and committed to the values of citizenship, including those listed above as well as fairness and altruism. Finally, there should be an emphasis on intellectual skills and skills of judgment, empathy, communication, participation and action.

Heater's scheme is typical of the civic republican approach to citizenship. However, Heater acknowledges that the common identity on which citizenship rests is threatened by a series of tensions:

the division between an emphasis on individual freedom and social duties and obligations; the antithesis between the private and the public citizen; the difficulties of incorporating a complex society into a coherent relationship with a unitary polity; and the conflicting demands of state and world citizenship. (p. 284)

PROBLEMS OF INDIVIDUALISM AND COMMUNITARIANISM: IDENTITY AND MOTIVATION

We have seen that neither the individualist nor the communitarian approach is adequate in its own terms. The individualist prescription must rely on some communal commitments for its existence, and developments in the concept of rights are making the individualist view of them increasingly untenable. Similarly, the communitarian view often finds itself resorting to arguments of individual self-interest as its justification.

However, both approaches share drawbacks which have important implications for education. The first is their abstractness from the complex experiences of everyday life. The restriction of the individualist approach to the formal mechanisms of public politics limits its usefulness, since it excludes consideration of important areas of human experience, both public and private. Similarly, the communitarian approach emphasizes abstract ideals of nation or community to which people are to be committed in their public role as citizens, and tends to be preoccupied with notions of nationhood and loyalty, again taking for granted the significance of these commitments at the level of everyday personal experience.

The great gap in these views is the lack of systematic attention to people's personal experience in their everyday lives, including the workplace and private life, and how the abstract elements of citizenship are related to these spheres. This is especially significant in view of the growing acceptance of identity politics, the political work of movements which organize around sexuality, gender and ethnicity, where political activity involves a 'process of making and remaking ourselves' (Brunt, 1989, p. 151):

> Identity politics expresses the notion that individual and collective identities – race, gender, sexual preference, class background, and so forth – thoroughly infuse all political preferences and visions. ... subject positions take precedence over, say, ethics in

giving form to political beliefs. As such, they fundamentally depart from the universalizing tendencies of citizenship-based politics; for practitioners of identity politics, particularities not only matter, they are the stuff of which political thought is made. (Kauffman, 1990, p. 10)

Identity politics sees the socially-defined personal and interpersonal realms as the most important site of power relations ('the personal is political'), and its practitioners 'tend to focus more heavily on individual and group self-transformation than on engaging with the state' (Kauffman, 1990, p. 10). In this sense, identity politics is the direct opposite to the Commission on Citizenship's focus on rules. Similarly, identity politics has little interest in the abstractions of loyalty to and identification with the state. In identity politics the concern is much more for how people experience power relations in their everyday lives, and how their sense of themselves and their relations with others is given meaning. Taking political action, participating in the political process in all its diversity, becomes a matter of self-construction, reflection and expression with others who share similar commitments.

The significance of these issues for motivation is that if people are told that citizenship is unrelated to work, family and other elements of their everyday experience as persons, they might justifiably doubt its value. Similarly, if educators try to promote citizenship ideals and involvement without considering its personal significance for people in their everyday lives, students are unlikely to accept them.

In addition to abstractness, a second problem in the procedural emphasis of the individualist approach and the emphasis on virtues and ideals of the communitarians is a lack of the substance which lies at the heart of the real attractions of citizenship, that is, the broad range of entitlements which accrue to citizens. The classic modern concept of citizenship established by T. H. Marshall (1964) at least had the benefit of recognizing the civil, the political and the social spheres of citizenship. In the modern world, while all three are important, it is the third which holds the greatest potential for citizens of the developed nations. Here the chief concerns relate to the equitable distribution of access to normally expected levels of wellbeing. Evidence for this lies in the surveys which show that British citizens place the social rights to minimum standards of living, medical care, work and education at the forefront of the rights of citizenship (Johnston Conover, Crewe and Searing (1990), quoted in Commission on

Citizenship, 1990, p. 6). Yet the focus on procedural rights and national sentiments in the main strands of citizenship discussed here excludes the material base of much of the value of citizenship for people in their daily lives.

Finally, it must be doubted that either the individualist or the communitarian views as rendered here are viable responses to the social, economic, political and cultural changes which are sweeping the world. The Western world is in a process of fundamental change which goes to the heart of the individual–society relationship in which the concept of citizenship has developed. Generally described as a move from a modern to a postmodern society, this change provides the background to any discussion of the relationship between citizenship and personal experience and will be taken up here.

A CHANGING GLOBAL CONTEXT: POSTINDUSTRIALISM, GLOBAL CULTURE AND ENVIRONMENTAL RISK

Postmodernity is difficult to define, but any attempt to characterize contemporary society and culture must acknowledge the speed of change in traditional patterns of social and cultural formations and their significance for politics and citizenship. The information age and its superhighway, changes in the production and dissemination of knowledge, and changing political cultures are important aspects of these changes (Gilbert, 1992). In economic terms, globalization, deregulation, privatization and post-Fordist production interfere with the contractual relations of state and corporation which have underpinned the economic significance of nationhood. The consequences for employment, regional economies and labour/management relations are in the direction of less stability over time, greater movement over space, and a general threatening of the old certainties of the economic system. The precariousness of the cults of the market and individual enterprise can be seen as a threat to any historic compromise or social contract between citizens and the economy.

The postmodern economy has fragmented the experience of production, and at the same time heightened the significance of consumption. While politics has in the past relied on a formal public rationality, 'the new consumerism on the other hand is all about floating visual images, pleasures and impossible dreams' (Mort,

1989, p. 169) – emphasising a private sphere in which people find solace and satisfaction in getting and spending. Citizenship as entitlement becomes central to this issue, as does the relationship between civil and political rights on the one hand and social welfare rights on the other, since the principles of equality which drive political citizenship raise challenging questions when applied to the economic sphere.

Related to these changes is the growth of the information society. The information revolution is among the most pervasive forms of social change experienced by the present generation. In the advanced capitalist economies, information workers (including computer manufacturing, telecommunications, mass media, advertising, publishing, accounting) comprise more than half the workforce. Central among these is the growth of the culture industries, especially in the English-speaking world, where the international market for film, television, music, sport, and the promotional trappings that go with them are leading to a standardization of the everyday cultural experiences of millions across the globe. The implications of these developments for identity and attachments to the nation can only be speculated about, but they cannot be passed off as insignificant.

Further, the growth of consumption as central to people's experience of the economic, and of the mass media and informationalism as the dominant mode of the cultural, are increasingly closely related:

> From spiralling prices on the international art market to the legitimation of consumer culture, even in the Eastern bloc, and the role of PR and image in hyping everything from global brands to green issues and government policies, all the evidence points to the collapse of any firm line between 'culture' and 'commerce'. (Hebdige, 1990, p. 19)

Some commentators see these developments as major threats to democracy itself. For instance, Wexler argues that in such a situation, individual identity is decentred, diffused and fragmented. Since societies are equally fragmented, the base for the individual–society contractual relation (on which both liberal individualism and communitarianism rely, albeit in different ways), no longer exists. The capacity of the individual mind to locate itself in history is lost, replaced by the mass media and its images, especially television, which now constructs the network for social relations, but in a form much less stable than before.

Telepolitics and network news, mass audience soaps, consumerism, the production of demand through the manipulation and consumption of images, increasingly fragmented occupational structures and work patterns – these are conspicuous features of the information and consumer societies. Wexler takes up the implications of this 'semiotic society' for individual identity, since 'identity dynamics, like knowledge, are different in the semiotic society', and if citizenship is to survive as a meaningful term, 'it will have to be recreated within this new social, class, and psychological reality' (p. 171). Wexler is pessimistic about how this trend can be reversed, what possible alternatives can arrest the power of the semiotic society.

Finally, economic and cultural change are accompanied by environmental changes, a range of consequent hazards, and a social framework built on the need to contain risks. The significance of this 'risk society' is, according to Beck (1992), that the hazards and risks know no national boundaries, and that their effects are not distributed on class lines. Nuclear, chemical and genetic technology developed on a global scale in supra-national corporations is not controllable in traditional national terms. It also produces dissensus on the value of progress. However, citizen concern is stimulated by media reports of international disasters like Chernobyl, threats to the ecosphere from depleted ozone and the greenhouse effect, and images of 'skeletal trees or dying seals' (Beck, 1992, p. 119).

An important outcome of these concerns is the flourishing environmental movements, and organizations like Greenpeace and green political parties parallel the movements of identity politics. Lash and Urry (1994, p. 297) argue that environmental concern has led people increasingly to view humans as part of nature, and become less committed to conquering or dominating it. People are thought to have special responsibilities for nature, partly because of their unprecedented powers of global destruction. They also have such responsibility because of the particular human capacity to act reflexively, to project environmental degradation, and see the need for behavioural change.

Further, environmental concern leads to a view of nature as global or holistic, a perception promoted by the media which have generated an imagined community of all societies inhabiting one earth. Finally, the notion of the rights of future generations to a sustainable future and a life in a quality environment is an important addition to the rights debate.

The significance of environmentalism is that environmental concerns, movements and politics raise new considerations for citizenship. They give material substance to the notion of global citizenship, offer important forms of political expression, introduce new concepts of rights, and, as illustrated by the Brundtland Report's title *Our Common Future* (World Commission on Environment and Development, 1987), are the basis of shared values and experiences in the material contexts of daily life. As a result, environmentalism raises the prospect of a citizenship firmly based in experience, and one which is more communal than individualism, and more material than communitarianism. The potential for motivation in environmental citizenship is therefore very strong.

Making sense of the world and our place in it is not achieved through rational abstract ideas of the state, but by reflecting on the realm of everyday experience and how it constructs our sense of ourselves. If schools wish to find the answer to the motivations of young people towards participation, not to mention the broader notion of citizenship, then they need to understand how the experiences of the young and their social location are represented to them by the cultures in which they live and those which they construct themselves. They also need to show that citizenship can be about the very concrete experiences of the everyday, and that global change can be seen and acted on at the local level.

Two areas illustrate what such an education for citizenship might entail: the experience of citizenship entitlements and action in the cultural and environmental spheres of everyday life. The following discussion reviews examples of education in these spheres as models for a more effective education for citizenship.

EDUCATION FOR CITIZENSHIP AND CULTURAL POLITICS

The political importance of the cultural lies in its increasing dominance as a form of life in the postmodern society, but for educators it also has a special significance for the clients of schooling: the cultural sphere is the sphere of the young. The youth culture industries are among the most widely penetrated by the postmodern society and its media forms. For some, like the UK Commission, this is a threat to the nation. For others, like Wexler, it threatens any form of community identity. However, others see in it new possibilities for a politics based in these cultural forms themselves.

Willis, for instance, argues that what organization and protest has been generated by youth has drawn from 'an enormous reservoir of informal passion and energy and a sensuous hunger for access to and control of usable symbolic materials, their means of production and reproduction, as well as cultural assets and spaces necessary for their exercise' (Willis, 1990, p. 144). The 'proto-communities' that result from the serial and random contacts of popular culture do have the capacity to identify the influences that shape young people's private powers and those of others, a consciousness of a common culture as an arena of choice and control. 'The possibility of connecting with these, and interconnecting them is the promise of the politics of the future' (p. 147). Youth culture is the arena where citizenship and identity can be connected in ways that are clear, concrete, and mutually supporting.

> The starting point I'd suggest for any politics of identity is the issue of 'representation': both how our identities are represented in and through the culture and assigned particular categories; and also who or what politically represents us, speaks and acts on our behalf. These two senses of 'representation' alert us to the whole areas of culture and ideology as we live it and as it is lived and directly experienced by us. They help us think how we both 'make sense' of the world and get a sense of our 'place' in it – a place of many, and increasing, identities. (Brunt, 1989, p. 152)

A useful example lies in the project reported by Cohen (1990) which developed a course in photography as a form of social and personal education for students in a school-work transition program. Seeking a form of 'really useful knowledge', Cohen and his colleagues chose an apprenticeship model of pedagogy, combining learning on the job from skilled practitioners with the social relationships of co-worker which such a paradigm makes possible. This was not an 'apprenticeship in its traditional patriarchal form, or confined purely to the techniques or craft of photography', but was 'a wider process of social and cultural mastery over the process of representation' (Cohen, 1990, p. 3). Cohen chose a cultural studies perspective for the educational connections it provided between cultural theory and political consciousness, and between technical and political education.

By producing photographic exhibitions of the nature of work, the transition process and their personal biographies, Cohen's students explored the tensions between the official and unofficial versions of transition, and the 'autobiographical grammars through which these positions are lived and given meaning' (p. 7).

One project involved a group of mostly black girls in a community care course which explored the pressures from family, school and work which were channelling these girls into a traditional servicing role. In other work the issue of gendered transitions was developed in a project on the position of women in popular music. Working with a girls' band trying to make the transition from amateur to semi-professional status, students explored the links between cultural practice and political and economic structure.

> The practical difficulties of combining their musical interests with having to earn a living by other means, the desire to 'make it' on the music scene without exploiting their femininity either ideologically or commercially, the excitements and anxieties of 'doing a gig', the construction of a group image, the pain and sweat of getting it all together, these were some of the themes which the girls addressed in their collective self-portrait. (Cohen, 1990, p. 9)

The project sought to focus on the cultural practices which 'positioned boys and girls subliminally (and asymmetrically) within various fields of "personal" discourse centred on the youth question' (p. 9). Cohen notes that the popular cultures formed around computers, video, photography, and stereo illustrate how technologies can be transformed by the social relations of their use. Private home consumption combines with the public discourse of the forms, styles and practices of the media, but it is also true that 'the enlarged reproduction of dominant imagery is potentially interrupted by new facilities for do-it-yourself culture' (p. 17). In all of this there is the development of the ability to decode the ideological messages of the culture industries, major potential sites of employment of the 'new' working class.

The important features of the project are its concern that students were able to analyse critically the ideological messages in the way transition to work is constructed in official policy, institutional practices and the commonsense assumptions of their own milieu; the opportunity to re-present the process of transition from their point of view, and to relate it to an exploration of their own personal biographies; the recognition that cultural practices are sites of economic and other forms of power, linking with gender, race and class concerns; and that the practice of representing these insights itself involves mastering the technology of cultural forms as well as their political and economic significance. The project shows how cultural politics can link to civil, political and social forms of citizenship, where students consider their entitlements and how they can maximize their access to them.

Cultural politics is a necessary element of citizenship in the semiotic society, for interpreting and producing the meanings through which experience is represented becomes an important dimension of citizenship rights, along with those of contract and personal rights, political participation and welfare. However, this expressive form of entitlement in the cultural sphere inevitably connects with other spheres and their corresponding forms of citizenship. If rights of access to cultural expression are to be realized, the civil, political and social rights of traditional citizenship are also necessary. These in turn cannot be applied separately from particular kinds of economic organization. Both corporate capitalism and state socialism are too singular, closed and hierarchical to foster such a range of rights. To sustain the conventional forms of citizenship, and to extend them to the cultural sphere, participation and power sharing in economic life should be seen as parallels to the conventional entitlements of membership, more so than the traditional focus on legal rights and parliamentary politics would allow.

EDUCATION FOR CITIZENSHIP AND ENVIRONMENTAL POLITICS

In discussing his curriculum development work with the World Wildlife Fund and the United Kingdom Global Environmental Education Programme, John Huckle (1987a, p. 147) opens by citing the ubiquity in everyday life of the fast food chains:

> Fast food has become a staple of the young generation. It is sold in an environment where the decor, atmosphere, and uniforms are designed to stimulate excitement and advertised with images which promise everything nutritious, convenient and desirable.

Yet the resource costs of wasteful packaging, of disposing of litter, and of clearing land for the beef industry are not part of this consumer consciousness. Nor are the social and economic costs of the low-wage regime on which it is based, or the health risks involved in eating as a form of image-making rather than nutrition. Huckle's curriculum project *What We Consume* (Huckle, 1987b) takes up these relations by showing the connections among economic production and distribution, power, social structure and culture and ideology through an educational strategy based on political literacy (Porter, 1983). Huckle's work demonstrates the close connections among popular culture, a consumer economy, environmental quality and power in the everyday experiences of the young, and how these experiences provide a fertile ground for curriculum work – an excellent example of the approach to education for citizenship advocated here.

Environmental politics is, for many of its practitioners, a form of identity or lifestyle politics, where people construct their identities in a sense of oneness with the world, and through a shared experience with others in environmental social movements. Petra Kelly of the German Greens wrote of the spirituality surrounding green politics, in which 'one's personal life is truly political and one's political life is truly personal' (quoted in Spretnak and Capra, 1985, p. 52). The commitment of young people to environmental movements such as Greenpeace, and the remarkable proliferation of environmental organisations of all kinds is telling evidence of their potential for citizen involvement.

Environmentalism can be seen simply as a technical process whereby problems are addressed with the increasingly sophisticated scientific knowledge at our disposal – what Slocombe (1987) describes as 'environmentalism as plan'. As such, environmentalism has few implications for citizenship, as environmental problems are no different from other problems of economic and technological development. On the other hand, Slocombe recognises a second stream of 'environmentalism as goal', where problems become matters of changing human value systems and world views. Gough (1989) notes that this ecological consciousness can be seen as a new paradigm of thought, while Robottom and Hart (1993) point to the increasing significance of what Skolimowski (1981) described as an ecophilosophy, an emerging world view which has had a profound effect on the environmental movement, and through it on public consciousness itself.

Ecophilosophy is distinguished from conventional philosophy by its orientation to life rather than language and to commitment and political awareness rather than objective detachment and neutrality. It is holistic and global rather than analytical and reductionist, and concerned with wisdom and judgment rather than information and abstract systems thinking. While traditional philosophy is based on dualisms which oppose mind with matter, persons with things, ecophilosophy sees human existence as part of nature. This ecological view of human existence explains ecophilosophy's concern for co-operation, collaborative action and a communal approach to social organization and welfare. Each person's inextricable role in the web of life means that everyone has a direct responsibility for the environment, an obligation that cannot be passed off to experts. In all these ways, ecophilosophy is approaching the status of a new foundation for citizenship, a new basis for a common sense of shared goals and responsibilities. The difference from earlier ideals of citizen obligation, such as nationalism and other forms of communitarianism, is that the environmental consciousness is a material fact of our everyday existence. This salience in experience gives it a powerful potential for motivating citizens to action.

The significance of these developments for education for citizenship lies in their translation into a concept of education for the environment. This is distinguished from education about the environment, where the emphasis is on knowledge of ecology and other environmental concepts and information, and education in the environment, in which field studies are the main focus. Fien (1993, p. 59) defines education for the environment as one which 'provides opportunities for students to participate actively in maintaining and improving the environment through the critical appraisal of environmental situations and issues, the development of an environmental ethic and the understanding, motivation and skills to act on their values and commitments'.

Environmental education is becoming increasingly important as a site for integrating social, economic and political learning, and examples are reported worldwide. Of particular interest are those in the Third World (Briceno and Pitt, 1988), Russia (Corcoran, 1994), and Hong Kong (Wong, 1994), where environmental politics is related to international economic and political power in ways not always so obvious in the West.

Curriculum work in environmental education in Australia offers numerous examples of education for citizenship. The Earth Education movement is spreading across many schools, as are water quality monitoring programs (Greenall Gough, 1990). Robottom and Hart (1993) describe a participatory research project on environmental health in which a youth network, formed as a consultative group for local government, became members of a participatory action research team studying environmental and health issues. Greenall Gough and Robottom (1993) report a school program where students monitoring water quality revealed high levels of pollution in a popular beach. Using Freedom of Information legislation and the local media, students triggered a series of important responses. The issue was taken up by state and national media, local organizations like the surf-riders association, a local health centre and the State Rural Water Commission, and other schools. Ultimately, the local Water Board was requested by the State Minister for Environment and Planning to improve sewage treatment facilities.

The summary of this experience is a powerful advertisement for environmental education as education for citizenship:

> The changes in community consciousness stimulated by the activities of Queenscliff High School staff and students brought about a major redistribution of resources aimed at environmental protection...There were changes in the ways certain sectors of the community related to other sectors of the community. There was criticism of conventional wisdoms: for example that the government agency's authority in respect of water management need not and should not be questioned. And there was the realization that individuals can act collectively to shape society in a way which recognizes, but is to some extent independent of, the constraining influences of traditional hierarchical bureaucracies. (Greenall Gough and Robottom, 1993, p. 313)

In seeking solutions to the problems of motivation for education for citizenship, the success of programs like these, and of environmentalism in general, provides food for thought. As a crucially important aspect of human existence in the twenty-first century, environmental quality is becoming a major component of citizen and government concern. As a source of new ideas and experience of citizen action and shared commitment to common goals, environmentalism is developing as a central strand of the concept of citizenship itself. Education for citizenship and education for the environment ultimately become indistinguishable.

CONCLUSION

Contemporary global change requires an extension of the concept of citizenship into the spheres of cultural expression, economic production, and environmental sustainability. To engage students in these spheres, educational programs must focus on entitlements in the various discourses and experiences of everyday life, showing the connections among them, and the need to deal with life experience in its essential connectedness. In this way citizens are empowered to understand change, form alliances and develop strategies for the future. Such a politics follows the pattern of articulation argued by Laclau and Mouffe (1985, p. 165) in which political struggle becomes a process of 'the displacement into new areas of social life of the egalitarian imaginary constituted around the liberal-democratic discourse'. As a result, the rights of liberal individualism, the ethos of communitarianism, and the shared sense of common destiny of environmentalism can be interwoven into a concept of citizenship more appropriate to present circumstances.

An education which promotes this view of citizen entitlements would not be distracted by calls for loyalty to the symbols of hierarchical economic or political power, or to the abstract ideals of a past golden age, however well intentioned. Education for citizenship must focus on concrete principles of rights and the practices of political action. Since the power of cultural expression is to some extent already accessible to youth, and plays an important role in their understanding of self and others, the incorporation of a political economy of the cultural into the concept of citizenship is an important part of this strategy. Similarly, the power of environmentalism for young people and their images of the future is a fertile area for developing the skills and commitments of citizenship. Such studies could further show the value of conventional forms of citizenship in civil and political rights, and the need to extend these more fully to the social and economic spheres.

Education for citizenship must address the problems of political participation in ways that acknowledge the characteristics of contemporary global change. By focusing primarily on the liberal rule of law and its institutions, or on an abstract concept of a unified community as competing versions of the citizenship ideal, conventional approaches cannot connect with the chief concerns or experiences of young people in a postindustrial, postmodern age. To motivate students to citizenship, education for citizenship must connect to their developing identity, their sense of what is important to them. The political economy of culture and the environment are potentially powerful means to this end.

4 Civic Education, Democracy and the English Political Tradition
Wilfred Carr and Anthony Hartnett

The powerful still do not favour the cultivation among the lower orders of the skepticism and critical intelligence that is valued among their betters...The decline in investment and support for public education in this country at the moment is... a vindictive rather than a prudent economy. At stake is more than a hundred years of adventure beyond the mere basics, a span in which schools ...have tried to make people independent thinkers capable of participation in the democratic process and of deciding what the future of their own society shall be like... We must now find ways of ensuring that a defensive, and more apprehensive, establishment in the context of a contracting economy does not make a critical education an education reserved for privilege. (Stenhouse, quoted in Plaskow, 1985)

The National Curriculum, like many of the educational reforms in England since 1979, has altered and restructured the entire framework within which educational debate takes place. For teachers and other involved in education, it has snuffed out the energy and space in which to develop serious alternatives, by enabling the New Right to capture the key educational concepts of 'quality', 'standards', 'discipline', 'testing' and 'achievement'. Even the recent effective opposition to an elaborate and byzantine system of assessment is likely to lead to a greater concentration on 'basics' and to more traditional pencil-and-paper tests, both of which the New Right wanted from the start.

These characteristics of debate about the National Curriculum raise a wider issue about how educational debate has developed since the mid-1970s. During this period, educational debate has become atomized and de-contextualized so that issues such as 'citizenship' are talked about as if they existed in a social, political and historical vacuum. What passes for serious debate about the nature and purpose of education for citizenship does so as if issues of power, status

64

and wealth could be disregarded; as if politics, ideology and institutional traditions were not important; and as if wider issues concerning such central notions as democracy, justice, equality, and freedom could be ignored. It seems to be assumed that 'citizenship' can be plucked out of the air and talked about as if England in the 1990s was already a fully developed democratic society: almost a delightful 'Eden, a demi-paradise... set in... a silver sea': a nice mixture of classical Greece, medieval solidarity, Victorian respectability, and modern industrial affluence. But, of course, it is none of these things, and any educational debate which assumes that this is how things are is bound to fail to grapple with the complexities of English education at the end of the 20th century. In this essay we take citizenship as an issue and use it to illuminate the quality and characteristics of educational and political discussion and debate. To do this we first connect citizenship to wider issues in political and social theory; and secondly, we locate views about citizenship within the English political and educational traditions.

CITIZENSHIP, POLITICS AND DEMOCRACY

'Citizenship' and 'citizens' are distinctively 'un-English' and have the smell of the continent about them. The English traditionally talk about being loyal subjects of the Queen (Johnson, 1985). However, recently, and relatively suddenly, the word 'citizenship' has been constantly on the lips of politicians, academics and educators from both the New Right and the New Left. Hugo Young, writing in *The Guardian* a few years ago, explained this situation in the follow way:

> Something is rotten in the state of Britain, and all the parties know it... The buzz word emerging as the salve for this disease is something called 'citizenship'... Somewhere out there is an immense unsatisfied demand for it to mean something. But it needs to become much more than a word. (Young, 1988)

Explanations of 'what is rotten' in Britain, and hence of the 'disease' for which citizenship is prescribed as the cure, have varied. For some, the call for citizenship is a belated response to the steady drift towards narrow individualism. For others, it is a reaction to the dismantling of the welfare state, the erosion of local democracy and the increasing power of the state. But whatever the reasons for putting citizenship on the political and educational agenda, the demand for it to 'mean something' remains unsatisfied. 'It needs', in Hugo Young's words, 'to become much more than a word', particularly if we are to begin to think about education for citizenship and about the kind of curriculum provision this entails.

Discovering what the concept of citizenship actually means is more difficult than it sounds. The reason why this is so is that citizenship is a paradigmatic example of an 'essentially contested concept' – a concept whose very meaning is itself the subject of intense controversy and conflict between rival social and political groups (Gallie, 1956). Citizenship is a 'contested' concept in the sense that the criteria governing its proper use are constantly challenged and disputed; such disputes are 'essential' in the sense that arguments about these criteria turn on fundamental political issues for which a final rational solution is not available. To concede that citizenship is a political concept whose meaning has always been, and still is, 'essentially contested' is not to say that the concept is so elastic that it can mean whatever anybody wants it to mean. Contested concepts always have some uncontested common core which provides an understanding of the general ideas they express and helps to clarify the substantial points of disagreement that rival and conflicting interpretations of its meaning incorporate.

One way of identifying the common core of any essentially contested concept is to look to its history. As with so much else, the origins of the concept of citizenship are to be found in Athenian democracy, so that its current meaning must, however, tenuously, be connected to the meaning it had in ancient Greece. In the earliest systematic analysis of the concept, Aristotle defines a citizen as 'someone who participates in public affairs'. Although in the Athenian *polis* the right to participate in public affairs was restricted to a small minority of the general population, citizenship nevertheless marked the emergence of the idea that man (but not woman) was 'a political animal' who could adequately fulfill himself only by sharing in the common life of a political community. For Aristotle man was, by nature, *homo politicus* whose very being was constituted and affirmed through political activity. Citizens did not understand themselves as private individuals with certain legal rights but as free and equal participants in a political order developing and realizing their human capacities by making and obeying laws within the framework of a common life and on the basis of the common good.

The story of the eclipse of the Greek ideal of citizenship is no doubt very complex and very difficult to tell (Heater, 1990). It will, in part, require some explanation of why, in modern western democracies, the role of the citizen has been transformed by a division of labour between an 'active' political elite of full-time rulers and a 'passive' political majority who only participate in politics by casting votes in periodic elections. But what such a story will also reveal is how the history of the concept of citizenship is a history of social struggle and political conflict in which, and through which, its original Greek meaning has been gradually changed. These changes are analysed in some detail by T. H. Marshall who is now generally regarded as offering the most authoritative formulation of the meaning of citizenship in modern industrial democracies. His definition of citizenship is worth quoting at length:

> Citizenship is a status bestowed on all those who are full members of a community. All who possess the status are equal with respect to the rights and duties with which the status is endowed. There are not universal principles that determine what those rights and duties shall be, but societies in which citizenship is a developing institution create an image of ideal citizenship against which achievement can be directed. The urge forward along the path thus plotted is an urge toward a fuller measure of equality, an enrichment of the stuff of which the status is made, an increase in the number of those upon whom the status is bestowed... Citizenship requires a direct sense of community membership based on loyalty to a civilization which is a common possession. It is a loyalty of free men endowed with rights and protected by a common law. Its growth is stimulated by the struggle to win those rights and their enjoyment when won. (Marshall, 1950)

The obvious attraction of Marshall's definition is that it makes 'membership of a community', 'rights' and 'duties' definitive features of citizenship without stipulating how 'membership' is to be determined or what the specific rights and duties of citizens should be. Who are to be 'full members of the community'? Who are to be excluded? What kind of rights should citizens have? Is participation in the exercise of political power a right or a duty? Are the duties of citizenship absolute? It is the different and often conflicting ways in which these questions are asked and answered that give rise to rival and incompatible account of what citizenship actually means.

What Marshall's definition also recognizes is that these questions cannot be answered by appealing to any absolute standards. Rather, our sense of what the appropriate rights and duties of citizenship should be is always changing and evolving under the impetus to make available to all a status previously limited to a privileged elite. Our present understanding of citizenship is thus the result of past struggles and organized protests (such as those of the Chartists and the Suffragettes) on behalf of social groups who were denied a full degree of legal, social and political equality. In this sense, citizenship is the dynamic historical process of social transformation through which the demand for great social justice and a more egalitarian social order has been gradually promoted and realized.

For Marshall the three key stages in this historical process have been the sequential evolution of civil, political and social rights over the past 250 years. Civil rights refer primarily to those legal rights – such as the freedom to own property and freedom and justice before the law – which were established for some groups by the end of the eighteenth century. Political rights – particularly the right to vote – were extended in the nineteenth and twentieth centuries. Social rights – such as the right to a minimum level of health care and economic security – were finally conceded in the post-war establishment of the Welfare State.

For Marshall, the modern concept of citizenship is counter-posed to social class and the civil, political and social rights that have emerged have served both to modify 'the worst defects of economic inequality' and to make 'modern capitalist systems and liberal polity more equal and just, without revolutionary activity' (Held, 1989). Marshall was also aware of the connections between these rights: of how, for example, the extension of the political right to vote led to improved civil rights for trade unionists, which in turn led to better social rights for ordinary workers. He also highlighted the fragile and contingent nature of these hard-won rights and of the central role of political struggle in their achievement. For Marshall, citizenship rights were always the outcome of 'struggle against hierarchy in its traditional feudal form, struggle against inequality in the marketplace, and struggle against social injustice perpetuated by state institutions. Rights had to be fought for, and when they were won they had to be protected. At the root of these processes was (and is) the delicate balance between social and political forces' (Held, 1989).

Because Marshall's account of the development of citizenship has achieved such authoritative status, it is unsurprising to note that the National Curriculum Council's guidelines on education for citizenship are influenced by both his definition of citizenship and his formulation of civil, political and social rights. What is suprising is that, in the document containing these guidelines, social rights are virtually ignored and no reference is made to the Welfare State at all (see National Curriculum Council, 1990b). Even more remarkable is the fact that the document repeatedly refers to 'the responsibilities and rights of citizens in a democratic society' without ever clearly explaining what these responsibilities and rights are, or how the notion of the democratic citizen is to be understood. Yet in the absence of some such explanation, the key terms used in the document – terms such as 'participation' and 'democracy' – remain vacuous. Although the document declares that the 'the aim of education for citizenship is to establish the importance of positive participative citizenship' (p. 2), its reluctance to address unavoidable political questions about the participative role of citizens in a democracy means that the guidance given to schools remains ambiguous and unclear.

That these questions are both unavoidable and political stems from the fact that the 'liberal democracy' of the United Kingdom is an amalgamation of both 'liberalism' and 'democracy' – two political traditions which, because they are based on different political values, give rise to internal tensions about how the concepts of democracy and citizenship are to be understood (MacPherson, 1977). It is a commonplace for political theorists to explain these tensions by constructing analytical 'models' which encapsulate the core principles, key features and basic assumptions which different ideas and arguments about democracy tacitly presuppose (Held, 1987). One of these models – the 'moral' model of democracy – is intended to accommodate a broad range of democratic theories ranging from the 'classical' theory of ancient Greece to the 'direct democracy' of Jean-Jaques Rousseau (1968) and the 'developmental' democracy of John Stuart Mill (see Acton, 1951). It also includes the more modern 'participatory' theories of political theories such as MacPherson (1973) and Pateman (1980). Table 4.1 below summarizes its main characteristics.

In this model, democracy is 'moral' in two senses. First, it is itself a moral way of life intrinsically constituted through fundamental human values. Democracy is thus not just a political system but a political expression of the values of self-fulfillment, self-determination and equality – values constitutive of the kind of society in which autonomous individuals can fulfill themselves by freely and equally determining the public good. Second, democracy is 'moral' in the sense that it prescribes the moral principles to which any society

Table 4.1   The moral model of democracy

Core Principles:
Democracy is an intrinsically justified form of social life constituted by the core value of political equality. It is the way of life in which individuals are able to realize their human capacities by participating in the life of their society. A democratic society is thus a society whose citizens enjoy equal opportunities for self-development, self-fulfillment and self-determination.

Key Features:
Democracy is a moral ideal and, as such, is never fully achieved. It requires continuously expanding opportunities for the direct participation of all citizens in public decision-making by bringing social, political, industrial and economic institutions under more genuine democratic control.

Main Assumptions:
Human beings are essentially political and social animals who fulfil themselves by sharing in the common life of their community. Since involvement in the life of the community is a necessary condition of individual development, all should participate in deliberations about the good of their society. Any distinction between rulers and ruled is a distinction in degree rather than in kind.

Social Conditions:
Democracy can only flourish in a society in which there is a knowledgeable and informed citizenry capable of participating in public decision-making and political debate on equal terms. It thus requires a society in which bureaucratic control over public life is minimal and in which decision-making is not treated as a professional expertise.

which claims to be democratic should conform. At such, it provides a moral basis for evaluating the social relationships, political institutions and cultural practices of any society that seeks to give expression to democratic values and ideals.

The conceptions of democracy which fall under the second model of democracy – the market model – do not claim to be 'moral' in either of these senses. Indeed, on this model, which includes 'elitist' (Schumpeter, 1976), 'pluralist' (Dahl, 1985) and 'neo-liberal' (Hayek,

1976) theories, any suggestion that democracy is a moral ideal is rejected as unrealistic, impractical, misleading and illusory. This model can be represented diagrammatically as follows:

Table 4.2 The market model of democracy

Core Principles:
Democracy is justified extrinsically as the political system which is most instrumentally effective in securing the core principle of individual liberty. By providing a method for selecting political leaders which curtails an excess or abuse of political power, it helps to protect the freedom of individuals to pursue their private interests with minimal state interference.

Key Features:
Democracy is a value-neutral descriptive concept and its achievement is synonymous with certain empirical conditions. These include: regular elections, universal suffrage, the existence of rival political parties, a representative system of government, a centralized political leadership, a free press and an independent judiciary.

Main Assumptions:
Human beings are primarily private individuals who form social relationships in order to satisfy their own personal needs. They thus have no obligation to participate in political decision-making and most ordinary people have no desire to do so. A rigid distinction is, therefore, made between an active elite political leadership and the passive majority of ordinary citizens.

Social Conditions:
Democracy flourishes in an individualistic society with a competitive market economy, minimal state intervention, a politically passive citizenry and a strong active political leadership guided by liberal principles and circumscribed by the rule of law.

What unites the different views of democracy incorporated in this market 'model' is their claim to offer a realistic understanding of democracy based on detailed empirical studies of how modern democratic societies actually work. What these studies claim to show is that the essence of democracy is not its allegiance to a moral ideal but its method of selecting between competing political elites for the right to exercise power. What these studies also claim to show is that most of the population of modern western democracies do not possess the knowledge or expertise that positive participation in political decision-making requires. Democratic freedom is thus not the positive freedom to participate in political decision-making but the negative freedom to pursue one's private interests with the minimum of state coercion or control.

The fact that these two models of democracy have been presented as two isolated and independent models should not obscure the extent to which they may, in reality, merge and overlap. Attention has been drawn to them only because they allow the formulation of some basic questions about what education for citizenship involves. In what different ways is the notion of 'education for citizenship' understood in 'market' and 'moral' democracy? What are the curriculum and pedagogical implications of such differences? What, in a 'moral' and in a 'market' democracy, would education for citizenship actually involve?

Since, in a 'moral' democracy, the status of citizenship is only acquired through exercising the rights and duties of citizenship, citizenship means participating positively in a collective effort to reshape society in ways that will preserve the existing rights of citizens, enhance the possibilities for their practical realization and develop new ways of making them more widely available. Clearly, citizens can only participate in this process if they are not so economically or socially deprived that their civil and political rights cannot be adequately exercised or enjoyed. This means that, in a 'moral' democracy, the state has some obligation to redistribute the wealth of society in a more egalitarian way than a free market economy would naturally allow. Hence, the social rights embedded in the institutions of the Welfare State are essential to minimize those social and economic inequalities which are incompatible with the civil and political equality that positive participation requires.

Although in a 'moral' democracy the maintenance of certain political and welfare institutions is necessary, it is not in itself sufficient. For citizenship to flourish, there must always be a critical tension between the ideals and values in terms of which the rights and duties of citizenship are defined and the dominant institutions which make provision for their practical enactment and realization. It follows from this that 'education for citizenship' presupposes a critical understanding of the limitations of its own contemporary institutional definition. It also follows that an education for citizenship requires a specific political education which will bring pupils to an historical consciousness of how present citizenship rights were achieved, how they became embedded in the legal, political and social institutions of the modern democratic state and how these institutions may now be functioning in ways which preserve, rather than prevent, the kind of inequalities and injustices they were originally established to eliminate. But, in addition, 'education for citizenship' will also require a 'general education' to meet the needs of citizens engaged in the common life of the community. Feinberg defined 'general education' as:

> those forms of instruction primarily intended to further social participation as a member of the public through the development of interpretive understanding and social skills... It is that component of education that prepares students for a common life... General education, as education for participation in a public, ideally implies a community of equals, active partners engaged in a process of self-formation. (Feinberg, 1983)

In a moral democracy, the task of cultivating in pupils the knowledges, skills and attitudes necessary for this kind of public participation is the only way of providing an education which enables them to fulfil their status as citizens. It requires a curriculum which fosters those forms of critical and explanatory knowledge which allow pupils to reappraise existing social norms and reflect critically on the dominant social, political and economic institutions of contemporary society. Pedagogically, it requires participatory rather than instructional teaching methods in order to cultivate the skills and attitudes which democratic deliberation and participation require (see Gutmann, 1987).

What conception of citizenship is endemic to a democracy in which *homo economicus* takes preference over *homo politicus* and in which the notion of the market is assigned a central place? In a 'market' democracy, citizenship is invariably interpreted in ways which emphasize responsibilities rather than rights and thus is closely associated with law-abiding behaviour, service to the community and national loyalty. In such a democracy, civil rights – particularly those associated with individual liberty and property ownership – tend to have an elevated status and the egalitarian thrust of social citizenship is rejected on the grounds that it creates precisely the kind of state-dependency and second class citizenship it originally promised to eliminate. From this perspective, citizenship is extended, not by the extension of social rights, but by creating a 'property-owning demo-cracy'. Only the expansion of 'popular capitalism' can free citizens from the stigma of social security and their reliance on the bureau-cracies of the Welfare State (see Hayek, 1976).

The kind of 'Education for Citizenship' appropriate in such a society will be very different from that which a moral democracy requires (see Tarrant, 1989). For example, since political apathy and ignorance are endemic in a market democracy, 'education for citizen-ship' will have a marginal status in the curriculum corresponding to the marginal status of politics in the lives of individuals. For the most part, political education would combine an uncritical know-ledge of how the institutions of government work with passive sociali-zation into the *status quo*. Since a market democracy prizes factual knowledge and vocational skills over social awareness or critical reflection, the political role of 'general education' would not be seriously entertained. Those curriculum subjects which provoke open discussion about the processes and institutions of the modern democratic state – subjects such as social studies and economics – will be systematically neglected and the role of subjects such as his-tory and literature in preparing pupils to participate in the social life of their community will be minimized. In a modern market democ-racy 'education for citizenship' must not only depoliticize general edu-cation; it must also depoliticize the concept of citizenship itself (Feinberg, 1983).

Which of these two conceptions of 'education for citizenship' are currently being endorsed? To answer this question it is necessary to understand the historical traditions of English education in which contemporary understanding of education for citizenship is unavoid-ably embedded. And to do this it is necessary to connect contem-porary questions about citizenship and education to the political, contexts and structures out of which have they emerged.

CITIZENSHIP AND ENGLISH POLITICAL AND EDUCATIONAL TRADITIONS

The 19th century climate in which England developed its state schooling system and its modern political traditions was one of immense social change and economic growth. During this period England became urbanized, suburbanized, secularized and partially democratized. Between 1861 and 1901 income per head of population more than doubled. Britain led the world in finance, trade and industry. It was, 'the forge of the world, the world's carrier, the world's shipbuilder, the world's banker, the world's workshop, the world's clearing house, the world's entrepot' (Connell, 1950). These economic factors meant that England was a liberal, market-dominated society long before it became democratic. Political rights, in the limited sense of extending the franchise, came extremely slowly during the 19th century and were not fully completed until 1948. England, and the United Kingdom, did not have a major political event like the French or American revolutions which forced onto the public agenda a statement of the rights and duties of a citizen. There was (and still is) no equivalent of the American Declaration of Independence and no written constitution.

Between 1832 and 1948 the electorate was gradually extended first across class barriers and then across gender barriers. Each new group that entered the formal political arena had to do so on existing terms. This resulted in a peculiarly British view of 'the public' as 'all those people whom the state and its Establishment wish to address or acknowledge as their own' (Johnson, 1985). In English usage the public often means 'polite society' and raises issues about the membership of 'respectable, polite and responsible' groups. This usage can be seen in the label 'public schools' (those for the children of the wealthy) and 'public libraries' which were for the respectable and literate classes. The judgment about whether or not individuals are members of 'the polite, responsible, or respectable' is made by 'one's betters'. Until 1884 it excluded the entire working class and women; until 1918 it still excluded the bottom half of the working class. In contemporary debate it probably still excludes the poor, trade unions, and various minority groups. This view of the 'public' is encapsulated in Margaret Thatcher's famous phrase, 'Are they one of us?'.

All of this has important implications for the notion of citizenship. The slow and subtle move from an aristocratic society to a formally modern democratic society meant that the old characteristics continued. In particular, a hereditary royal family with (until recently) symbolic power and popular support; an unelected second chamber – the House of Lords; and a secretive and hierarchical culture which has only partly accepted the idea that democracy should influence the whole range of public life and the operation of public institutions. Given this historical background, it is easy to see how the 'market' model of democracy fitted English society like a glove on a hand,

and how the impact of democracy could be contained and limited to regular elections for competing groups of politicians.

These political traditions were made even more important by the way in which the state educational system has developed. Until the mid-19th century, England lacked a strong motivating drive to take an interest in education. Unlike America or France, it had not had a revolution which required a serious public debate about the role of citizenship in the modern state. Uniquely, it had industrialized without a state-run education system. During the 19th century it exported rather than imported people and therefore lacked the American problem of turning immigrants into citizens. The complex religious issues which arose in, for example, Scotland and the Netherlands did not produce, in England, the Calvinist pressure for literacy; and it seemed as if the religious issue could be resolved by doing nothing for as long as possible (Wardle, 1976).

All this meant that England was, by international comparisons, exceptionally slow to develop a national system of schooling. When it was eventually established, in the second half of the 19th century, the schools were not for the children of citizens, with full political rights, but largely for children of the 'lower orders', many of whom still did not have a formal vote. By 1850, when Holland, Switzerland, Germany and the northern states of America virtually had universal education, England had barely half the age-group in school. In the same way, when England instituted state secondary schooling in 1902 it was '100 years after Napoleon created the lycées and almost as long since the USA and the German states created public elementary schools' (Green, 1991). In the same way higher education was only gradually extended and still remains the preserve of a minority. This failure to see the connection between political advance and educational provision effectively inhibited the development of an 'educated public' which is so vital to the construction of a democratic citizenry and replaced it with the notion of a 'public' which is exclusive, selective and respectable.

These tendencies towards preserving aristocratic and feudal elements in a supposedly democratic society have been supported and increased by key characteristics of the English educational system. For example, there has never been an English 'system' of education as such. Rather it has evolved in a fragmented, voluntarianist and uncoordinated manner. Educational reform, like the political changes which often precede it, has always been preoccupied with the partial and the specific: to limit and constrain change to the minimum required and to do it as cheaply as possible. Higher elementary schools, grammar schools, comprehensive schools and the polytechnics have all, in their time, been agents of modernization and democratic advance. But they have had to be assimilated into a structural framework in which the 19th century citadels of exclusion and exclusiveness – public schools and the ancient universities – remained hardly touched by democratic and egalitarian ideals. State power has rarely been used to shift the debate onto the complex issues of citizenship and education. Instead, a great suspicion of the state has allowed *voluntarism* to flourish through the 19th century religious societies, the endowed school movement, the public schools and the grammar schools. These have been the socially and politically acceptable educational mechanisms and institutional frameworks through which structural inequalities could continue to flourish, be reinforced and be legitimated. The explicit 19th century assumption that social class should determine the type and quality of education that children are given has, in the 20th century, been replàced by the assumption that innate individual differences in children's ability should be the selective mechanism for making distinctions between and within schools. In the twentieth century 'meritocracy' has replaced aristocracy as the new agency of exclusiveness and exclusion.

A second, and related, characteristic of the English education is its obsession with differentiating, grading, sorting, classifying, and testing pupils from an early age. In Turner's phrase it is a 'sponsored' system rather than a 'contest' system (Turner, 1961). This means that the most deserving rather than the most able win the prizes; that talent has to be identified early; that the criteria for defining talent are beyond serious public debate; and, perhaps most importantly, that too much talent is a sure sign of falling standards. It also means that the questions about how citizens should be educated is always subordinated to questions about the sort of education appropriate for different sorts of people. This leads, quite easily, to different sorts of schools, curricula and pedagogy for different groups of people.

Just as the middle class, the upper working class, women, and the lower working class had to wait to get the vote, so their children had to wait patiently to be invited into the great English educational institutions of the sixth form and the university. Incredibly, until the mid-1960s, the vast majority of children were publicly excluded, at the age of 11, from most opportunities to pursue higher education and upward mobility. When in 1965 a Labour government tentatively proposed to end this educational apartheid the Prime Minister (Harold Wilson) had to say that the real aim was 'a grammar school education for all'. As E. P. Thompson has shown, although the excluded groups did not always follow the paths set out for them, the fact that the paths were *there* is an important aspect of English culture and history (Thompson, 1968).

A third important characteristic of the English education system is the critical and continuing role played by elite schools and institutions, particularly public schools and the ancient universities. As Stone argues, the 'nineteenth-century English Public School was (and still is) a highly successful device for the preservation in an industrialized society of aristocratic values, institutions and distribution of power and wealth' (Stone, 1969). These schools were, and are, the educational equivalent of the rotten boroughs of the 19th century where privilege and status could, and can, be bought on the open market. In England, unlike many other societies where the main purpose of private schools 'is to satisfy minority and mainly religious groups', they 'provide an intensive education for the children of the upper middle class' and give 'far better access to positions of influence, power and affluence than do other schools' (Green, 1991). Not only do such schools get various economic and taxation advantages; they also subvert the state system by generally ensuring that their criteria and standards become the criteria and standards by which state schools are judged.

Given these political and educational traditions, it is easy to understand why England has no tradition of taking citizenship seriously. It has separate educational institutions for leaders and led, and often separate curriculum, pedagogy and assessment for each of these groups. Its political traditions are based on an extremely limited model of democracy and its view of the 'public' is exclusive and excluding and quite different from the 'educated public' that is a precondition for a fully democratic society. In this situation it is hardly surprising that England has no tradition of asking the right questions about citizenship at the level of serious political discussion and that vacuous rhetoric continues to replace the hard task of re-examining educational provision in the light of the requirements of a fully democratic society. Nor is it surprising that education and schooling in England, far from reducing the impediments to citizenship, have magnified, legitimated and fossilized them.

THE NEW RIGHT'S SOLUTIONS

Between 1979 and 1993 the Conservatives won four general elections and their educational policy was increasingly influenced by the ideas and rhetorics of the New Right: allowing the 'market' to be the key mechanism for distributing educational resources and making market forces the levers of social and cultural change. In doing this, the New Right achieved four important successes. Firstly, they captured and took over an educational vocabulary of the 'best words' (Knight, 1990). These included *excellence, quality, core subjects, traditional, discipline, standards, examinations, parents, freedom, market, choice,* and *local autonomy.* These could be counter-posed with 'bad' words such as *equality, experts, expertise, educationists, militant teachers, loony left councils, ill-discipline, falling standards, progressive education, anti-racism, anti-sexism, local bureaucrats, political indoctrination* and many more. What Ball (1990) calls the 'discourse of derision' uses these 'best' and 'bad' words in a repetitive, but politically effective, manner.

Secondly, by a use of rhetoric, evidence, and story-telling they reconstructed a golden past for education. In that golden age enormous opportunities existed for the working class (via grammar schools and especially the sixth form); educational standards were high because everyone could read, write and do their sums; schools were centres of discipline and order; and teachers knew how to teach through whole-class formal pedagogy. Teachers led the children forward to real learning. The curriculum was made up of 'proper' subjects (like Latin) and assessment really tested children through formal examinations with pencil and paper. Selection and differentiation ensured that children were taught in a way which reflected their abilities and needs and there was no nonsense about mixed-ability teaching. The New Right established the view that all new developments had to be judged and evaluated against this traditional golden age. If changes did not measure up they were discounted. Through these techniques and processes the New Right constructed an alternative view of the past to that presented by what it called 'the educational establishment's' view.

Thirdly, the New Right created by hard work, imaginative use of language and the use of the media, a new, populist form of discourse based on pamphlets, the 'findings' of its think-tanks and common-sense language. This discourse was not directed at educational experts or teachers but at parents and voters. Finally, during the 1980s and 1990s, when the Conservative Government had to face the awkward question of what to do about education, the New Right was ready with ideas and proposals which could become policy almost overnight. What had, in the 1960s and 1970s, seemed to be bizarre, poorly thoughtout policies that appeared to be more at home in the saloon bars of Conservatives clubs were now to be translated into government policy. During the 1980s, New Right ideas and prejudices became a 'counter-reality' to the complexities of what was actually happening (and what had happened) in schools. and provided an essential resource to the years of Conservative rule.

The Conservative Party in government has, with considerable help from the New Right, altered the general discourse about education so that it reflects their vocabularies, concerns, claims and aspirations. Through Acts of Parliament they have made substantial changes to the policy framework within which education takes place; and they have altered in radical ways the consensus about education which they inherited. They have moved the debate about education away from serious public debate about its political and cultural role, and replaced deliberation, evidence, argument and contestation with ideological assertion and unexamined political prejudice. They have ensured that educational policy has been shifted towards creating their vision of the good society and, through a combination of managerialism, centralization, and bureaucracy they have asserted the importance of authority and the strong state. In short, through devolution, opting-out and market forces they have reasserted the critical role of the neo-liberal intellectual tradition in which the notion of citizenship is of minimal significance.

Educational policy making, is, of course, a lot more complex than politicians sometimes think and its outcomes and unintended consequences are often more important than its officially stated aims. As Bowe, Ball and Gold (1992, pp. 19–23) suggest, there are at least three arenas in the process of policy formation. Firstly, there is the 'context of influence' where 'public policy is normally initiated'. Particularly important here are the various think-tanks, and official and unofficial advisers to politicians, as well as senior individual civil servants. Secondly, there is the 'context of policy text production'. Here, Bowe, Ball and Gold give the examples of Acts of Parliament and official commentaries on these texts. They further suggest that these texts will often be internally contradictory and will often be produced as a result of 'struggle and compromise'. Thirdly, there is 'the context of practice'. This refers to yet another potential arena for conflict, contestation and compromise: the particular schools, educational institutions and local authorities where policy is enacted. As Rizvi and Kemmis put it, 'people who have to participate in (or 'implement') a programme will interpret it in their own terms, in relation to their own understanding, desires, values and purposes... In short, all aspects of a programme may be contested by those involved in a programme, moreover a programme is formed and reformed throughout its life through a process of contestation' (quoted in Bowe, Ball and Gold, 1992, p. 22).

What this means is that any official policy for education for citizenship will not interpret itself, and the way in which schools make sense of such a policy will be conditioned by discussions conducted between teachers on the basis of their own educational values and in relationship to the structures of meaning and understanding within which they work. But since 'citizenship' and 'democracy' are both essentially contested concepts, such discussions will always be marked by contestation, and conflict about the meaning of the concepts in terms of which the discussion proceeds. Should such discussions adopt the prevailing 'market' concepts of citizenship and democracy? Or should they involve critically examining and revising those concepts in the light of some fundamental educational values and democratic ideals? Is 'education for citizenship' *itself* a political right of all future citizens in a democracy, and, if so, how is this entitlement to be met? It is precisely because citizenship is an essentially contested concept that such questions cannot be settled prior to questions about how any education for citizenship should be implemented. To force schools to 'deliver education for citizenship' on the basis of some prior stipulative definition of 'what citizenship is' is merely to deprive citizenship of its indispensable political dimension.

In the conclusion to his book on citizenship, Derek Heater wrote:

> Disagreement is rife about what citizenship means and consequently about the educational processes most appropriate to support citizenly status, role and qualities. This cannot be a satisfactory conclusion. At best, it leads politicians and educationalists into semantic confusion; at worst, young citizens are being fobbed off with only a portion of that whole citizenship which should in fact lay at the heart of their life as social beings. (Heater, 1990)

Schools can only be confident that their pupils are not being 'fobbed off' in this way, if they are encouraged to provide the curriculum and teaching space in which the essential contestability of citizenship can be protected from a political climate which increasingly requires such space to be closed. The only kind of civic education which can prepare citizens for life in a fully democratic society is one which acknowledges *both* that the meaning of citizenship is perennially the subject of contestation, *and* that it is through this process of contestation that the relationship between the citizen and the state is being continuously redefined. In this process, the political and educational agenda of the New Right will, like any other, have to be confronted, argued against and assessed. Indeed, in educational institutions committed to developing an education for citizenship which speaks to a fully democratic society, the conception of citizenship which the New Right seeks to impose will not be allowed to define and constrain what is to be taught and learned but will itself be treated as a legitimate subject for critical discussion and open debate[1].

NOTE

1.   These themes are discussed further in Carr and Hartnett (1996), *Education and the Struggle for Democracy* (Buckingham: Open University Press).

5 Education for Citizenship and the National Curriculum

Ken Fogelman

Throughout Europe citizenship education has been the subject of increasing concern and debate in recent years. The reasons for this are numerous, including concern about low levels of participation in local, national and European elections; concern about the perceived rise of intolerance, xenophobia and racism throughout Europe; particular concerns about some young people and their apparent alienation and marginalization from the mainstream of society; the need for an understanding of and an informed debate on the development of the European Union; and consideration of the role of education in preparing young people for participation in the newly democratic countries of Eastern and Central Europe.

For such reasons, the Council of Europe has played a particularly active part in taking the debate forward, holding a number of conferences and courses (see, for example, Edwards, Munn and Fogelman, 1994), and supporting the proposed establishment of a European Centre on Civic Education in Warsaw. Similarly, the European Commission's Phare and Tacis Democracy Programme specifically includes 'Civic Education' among the areas of activity which it will support.

However, developments in citizenship education in Britain have been largely independent of these international considerations. Indeed, citizenship education in our schools is far from being a new idea. Batho (1990) has described the teaching of civics and citizenship since Victorian times; and there was particular activity in the 1930s, motivated by concerns about the spread of totalitarianism (for example Hubback, 1934; Association for Education in Citizenship, 1935; also see also Edwards and Fogelman, 1991).

More recently, but before the introduction of the National Curriculum, there were several initiatives with regard to specific topics or activities which might now be seen as coming under the general heading of citizenship education, although that term might not have been used at the time. These included community service and involvement (for example, Preecy and Marsh, 1989), political awareness (for example, Stradling, 1975) and education for democracy and human rights (for example, Starkey, 1991; Stradling, 1987).

The response of schools to such ideas was variable. A survey of secondary schools in 1989, carried out on behalf of the Speaker's Commission on Citizenship, took place at a time when schools would have been aware that citizenship education was under discussion and on the agenda of the National Curriculum Council, but prior to the publication of the guidance documents described below. At this time almost all responding schools reported some involvement in community or citizenship activities and stated that some classroom time was given to citizenship studies. On the other hand, overall school policies were rare, content and approaches were very variable and often limited to particular age groups or ability levels; and the general impression was that citizenship education was dependent on the enthusiasms of individual teachers rather than any coherent school policy (Fogelman, 1990 and 1991a).

CITIZENSHIP EDUCATION AS A CROSS-CURRICULAR THEME

It might have been expected that this picture would change with the introduction and, for a while, promotion of the ideas of the cross-curricular themes, by the National Curriculum Council. These first appeared in *Circular Number 6* (National Curriculum Council, 1989), which described three aspects of cross-curricular elements: dimensions, skills and themes. This was subsequently elaborated in *Curriculum Guidance 3: The Whole Curriculum* (National Curriculum Council, 1990a), which identified:

- *dimensions:*
  a commitment to providing equal opportunities for all pupils
  preparation for life in a multicultural society
- *skills:*
  communication
  numeracy
  study
  problem solving

personal and social
information technology
- *themes:*
economic and industrial understanding
careers education and guidance
health education
environmental education
education for citizenship

It is important to emphasize from the outset that the themes were not part of the National Curriculum. Although *Curriculum Guidance 3* does contain the statement, 'It is reasonable to assume at this stage that [the themes] are essential parts of the whole curriculum', elsewhere it is stated that they are 'by no means a conclusive list'. In several places it is emphasized that it is for schools to decide how the themes might be tackled. Above all, the themes, unlike the core and foundation subjects of the National Curriculum were not, and never became, part of what schools were required to teach by statute and regulation.

Curriculum Guidance 3 was followed by five further guidance documents, one on each of the themes; the final one was *Curriculum Guidance 8: Education for Citizenship*. Although once again there was much emphasis on the content being a 'framework for debate' and not a 'blueprint or set of lesson plans', the guidance offered was quite detailed and consisted of three elements: objectives, content and activities. Objectives were further subdivided into:

- knowledge (of the nature of community, roles and relationships in a democratic society, the nature and basis of duties, and responsibilities and rights);
- cross-curricular skills (essentially as listed above from Guidance 3);
- attitudes;
- moral codes and values.

For the content, eight 'essential components' were outlined, each accompanied by areas of study and some suggested activities:

- the nature of community;
- roles and relationships in a pluralist society;
- the duties, rights and responsibilities of being a citizen;
- the family;
- democracy in action;

- the citizen and the law;
- work, employment and leisure;
- public services.

There is much which can be debated about this framework – its completeness, the clarity of some of the terms, the lack of an international perspective, and the underlying concept of citizenship which it appears to assume (see, for example, Bottery, 1992). Nevertheless, it remains the clearest and fullest description of a possible curriculum for citizenship education which has been offered to date.

THE SPEAKER'S COMMISSION

At broadly the same time as the guidance documents were gestating in the National Curriculum Council, the Commission on Citizenship was deliberating, and produced its report in 1990. Although it did not have the formal status of the National Curriculum Council, the political origins of the Commission, the patronage of the Speaker of the House of Commons, and the eminence of many of its members led to considerable publicity surrounding its report and recommendations, and it has thereby influenced the development of citizenship education in schools. It is also possible that its influence was more direct, as it did submit evidence to the National Curriculum Council at the time when *Curriculum Guidance 8* was in preparation.

The Commission was concerned with what it termed 'active citizenship' throughout the community, but a substantial proportion of its recommendations addressed educational issues and implications. In some respects its approach was distinctive from that of the National Curriculum Council. For example, it did accept the challenge of attempting a definition of citizenship, drawing mainly upon the approach of Marshall (1950) and his distinction among the civil, political and social elements of citizenship. Secondly, the Commission did adopt a more international perspective, specifically by recommending that the study of citizenship should take account of the main international charters and conventions to which the UK is a signatory.

In other respects the Commission's approach was not dissimilar to that of the National Curriculum Council. It recommended that citizenship should be part of every young person's education, and it offered a description of citizenship education as including understanding the rules; the acquisition of a body of knowledge; the development and exercise of skills; and learning democratic behaviour through experiences of the school as a community.

CURRICULUM MODELS

The Commission's evidence to the National Curriculum Council included a brief discussion of the place of citizenship within the curriculum, noting the potential links with subjects such as English, History and Personal and Social Education (PSE). Similarly, Duncan Graham, in his Foreword to *Curriculum Guidance 8: Education for Citizenship* wrote that, 'Elements of [citizenship education] can and must be taught through the subjects of the National Curriculum and other timetabled provision, enriched and reinforced by being woven into the wider work of the school in the community'.

Curriculum Guidance 3 had, in fact, suggested a number of ways in which the cross-curricular themes could be approached. These included teaching through other subjects (or 'permeation'), but also separate timetabling, teaching through PSE, and long-block timetabling (for example, activity weeks). Subsequent publications have developed such ideas further and offered more detailed models. Several chapters in Edwards and Fogelman (1993) discuss the links between citizenship education and core and foundation subjects. Indeed the case is made that every subject provides opportunities for citizenship education. Fuller consideration of more general approaches to cross-curricular planning can be found in Morrison (1994).

In the context of an overcrowded curriculum, at least prior to the Dearing review (see below), the permeation model was probably the most realistic approach for schools to adopt, if they chose to address the cross-curricular themes at all. However, it does present a formidable challenge for planning and ensuring coherence and progression in the experiences of an individual student. Morrison (op. cit.) and Edwards and Pathan (1993) do describe some techniques for auditing and monitoring the provision of the themes.

It is relevant to note that within Europe this country is relatively unusual in not having some version of citizenship education with a regular place in the school timetable. Many countries have a long tradition of civics education as a school subject. This includes countries in eastern and central Europe, where the debate is now not about whether there should be citizenship education, but how to transform it to be appropriate to new circumstances (see Edwards, Munn and Fogelman, op. cit.).

THE PRE-DEARING RESPONSE

Without doubt, the publication of the National Curriculum Council documents stimulated the development and production of a wide range of excellent materials for schools. Some of these were produced by established organizations which perceived how educational activities which they wished to promote could be justified by the ideas of citizenship education (some organizations even changed their names to include the word 'citizenship'). Just a few examples of what is now available include: Children's Society (1991); UNICEF – Save the Children (1990); Rowe and Thorpe (1993); Lloyd et al. (1993).

What is less clear is the extent to which such materials are being used in schools. The only systematic evidence on the schools' response to the themes comes from a survey of secondary schools carried out by Whitty et al. (1994), which was concerned with all five themes. They found that those themes which had already been well established in schools, i.e. health education and careers education, continued to be much more prominent than the other three. About 70 per cent of schools surveyed had specific policies in these two areas, and in many schools they were treated as separate subjects or taught through PSE. A third or fewer had policies for the other three themes, and they were more likely to be taught, if at all, through other subjects.

Although the data are not directly comparable with the earlier Fogelman survey, the general impression must be that there had been little progress in the implementation of the themes, including citizenship education. It has continued to be the case that while some schools are enthusiastic, others have had to give this issue lower priority than the many others with which they have had to cope in the last few years.

THE DEARING REVIEW

That schools had had difficulty with, or had chosen not to give their attention to, the cross-curricular themes is hardly surprising, given the difficulties which were becoming apparent in the National Curriculum. As the Programmes of Study worked their way through the schools from 1989, it was increasingly recognized that they were over-prescribed and over-large. Eventual recognition at the political level led to the establishment of a review, its report (Dearing, 1994), and new regulations in 1994.

The Dearing Report made no mention of the cross-curricular themes as such, nor of citizenship education. This is not surprising, given its remit to simplify and reduce the National Curriculum. On the other hand, one of the main thrusts of the report and its subsequent implementation has been the intention to reduce the requirements of the National Curriculum, at least up to the age of fourteen, to occupy only 80 per cent of the timetable. Decisions on the use of the remaining 20 per cent are to be at the discretion of the school.

It remains too early to judge what the impact of this will be. First, it must still be an open question as to whether the intentions of the Dearing review will be fulfilled – whether schools will find that the newly defined National Curriculum does in fact account for only 80 per cent of the available time. Secondly, if this is the case, schools will have to decide how best to use the 20 per cent. Some may decide to give space for the subject matter of citizenship education and the other cross-curricular themes, but the pressures of assessment and league tables may lead others to devote additional time to the core subjects.

WHERE NOW?

More optimistically, there have in the meantime been other influences to encourage schools not to overlook the importance of citizenship education. For example, among the recommendations of the National Commission on Education (1993) is that from Key Stage 2 citizenship should be part of the compulsory core curriculum, together with English, maths, science, technology and a foreign language. The report states that 'We consider the teaching of citizenship of great importance. We define the subject in a broad way to concern the relationship between individuals and the world they live in. It relates not only to this country but to the European Community and the world as a whole. It concerns the institutions of democracy and the rights and responsibilities of individuals in a democratic society; the creation of wealth; the role of public and private employers and voluntary organizations; and the opportunities which people have to shape or play a creative part in the life of the community.'

Of course, the National Commission does not have any official status – though its influence might be expected to increase if there is ever a change of government – but its list of the content of citizenship education reproduced above demonstrates how the issues of citizenship education remain relevant and important; and they would be recognized as such by a government of any complexion.

This is further reinforced by a body whose existence is more official – OFSTED. Sections 5.5 and 7.7 of the Framework for Inspection of Schools reflect the responsibility which the 1988 Education Act places upon schools to 'promote the spiritual, moral, cultural, mental and physical development of pupils at the school and of society' and to 'prepare pupils for the opportunities and experiences of adult life'. They set out the criteria for the inspection of spiritual, moral, cultural and social education and also of equality of opportunity, welfare and guidance, many of which correspond directly with the objectives of citizenship education. Not surprisingly there are difficulties in the operationalisation of such concepts, and tensions about the relative emphasis given to evaluating outcomes, i.e. children's development, as against the processes by which these are fostered. The complexities have been recognized by OFSTED by engaging in an extra stage of consultation on these issues (OFSTED, 1994). Nevertheless, it is clear that schools will in part be judged by their policies and activities in these areas.

BEYOND THE FORMAL CURRICULUM

This chapter has been about citizenship education within the curriculum and its relationship with the National Curriculum. However, it is important to note that the ideas of citizenship education have substantial implications for other aspects of school life. This is not the place to do more than indicate those very briefly.

For example, there are issues about the nature of our schools and the atmosphere or ethos within them. If citizenship education is in part about promoting such values as tolerance and understanding, what models do our schools provide in this respect? What example is given by the relationships within the school – among students, among teachers, and between teachers and students? Do they consistently encourage respect for other points of view? Are systems of discipline and rules based on recognition of rights and responsibilities, or can they sometimes appear arbitrary and irrational? Also, what opportunities do schools provide for young people to develop and practise the skills of participative citizenship? Are there, for example, school councils, or other structures, through which students can influence important decisions in a meaningful way?

Similarly, do schools foster links with and understanding of the local community? Are there opportunities for students to work with the community, for example with the elderly or with younger children? If so, are they supported by adequate preparation and follow-up so that this experience is integrated with other parts of the curriculum? There are also pedagogic implications. These are not a matter of stark alternatives in teaching methods, but many of the objectives of citizenship education do seem to imply, for example: a greater emphasis on group teaching as against whole class teaching; more collaborative and co-operative approaches; greater use of student projects and other student-led activities; more use of resources outside the classroom.

In this context, it must be recognized that citizenship education deals with many issues which are controversial, which are contestable politically or morally. This places particular demands on teachers, who must be able to handle open debate and conflicting views in a sensitive way. This is partly a matter of their specific skills, but also very dependent on the context within which they are working – within their school, but also more widely. Citizenship education can only be effective if those attempting it have the confidence and support of politicians and the wider community.

6 Literacy, Citizenship and Education

Kenneth Levine

The principle that all the capable adult members of a democratic society should be able to read and write was a major consideration in the framing of the Education Acts of the 1870s which established universal basic education in Britain. Since most contemporary theories of citizenship, ranging from the commonsensical through to the systematically philosophical, continue to presuppose (albeit sometimes implicitly) adult literacy, educationalists have been able to treat it as an uncontested objective in schooling. The major official reviews of school English, including Newbolt, Bullock and Kingman, have consequently been mainly preoccupied with framing or defining a syllabus that, together with other ingredients, will maximize pupil attainments in reading, writing and spelling. At this point, though, the consensus has tended to fall apart. While the reassuring rhetoric of such reviews tends to imply that the abiding concern of all interested parties is to select approaches and materials of undoubted educational effectiveness, on more than one occasion the process of drawing up the syllabus for English has become professionally divisive and politically contentious. Indeed, for an extended period in the early 1990s, the English syllabus became a political football at the end of an especially muddy and bruising contest in which the sides continued to struggle conscientiously without knowing where the ball was, who belonged to which side, or whether the referee was still on the pitch.

It would be wrong to see the politicization of school English as simply the product of recent party political battles and the manoeuvring for supremacy between successive Secretaries of State and teachers' unions. By 1840, thirty years before the advent of state education, the kinds of basic training in literacy available to the working class and their children in Britain had already differentiated along recognizably political lines. On the one hand there were the Sunday schools, factory schools and the institutions set up by the Anglican National School Society (among many other similar societies) which offered reading and writing embedded in a syllabus and daily regime designed to instill piety, discipline and obedience, and which provided a route that led to the assimilation of 'respectable' cultural forms in school, work and worship. At the other pole lay the private venture schools, the corresponding societies, the ale house and coffee-house reading rooms, self-help and casual instruction which offered learners much greater continuity with the oral traditions and culture of the manual working class and which tended to reinforce values of autonomy, community solidarity and political dissent.

The recent hurly-burly over school English appears at first sight to have centred mainly on teaching methods and course content, that is, on the means of delivering literacy in schools. In the background, however, there is also a muted and somewhat limited debate over the functions of reading and writing in contemporary society. A brief but significant discussion about this appears at the start of the Kingman Report and the topic is also raised directly by some of the polemicists who have sought to redefine the context for English studies. In this debate over the ends of literacy, two distinct conceptions of the way it relates to citizenship can be discerned. In what I will term Citizenship 1, the mastery by children in schools of a common written and spoken language and their appreciation of a shared literary heritage expressed in that language are taken to be important ingredients in the creation of a sense of national identity. A shared language and literary tradition are also taken to generate a centripetal and stabilizing force within an increasingly turbulent cultural environment. In Citizenship 2, on the other hand, literacy has a broadly instrumental and practical character, covering tools and concepts designed to facilitate a general understanding of the political sphere. Such an understanding begins with but goes beyond the assimilation of factual and historical information about institutional mechanisms and political processes that marked the 'British Government and Constitution' tradition. It encourages a critical understanding of political discourses and the articulation and analysis of pupils' own political thinking. Citizenship 1 and Citizenship 2 are not simply grander and lesser versions of the same thing but are, in key respects, in opposition. Citizenship 1 rests on the prior possession of a common language and the capacity to use it to recognize and to respond to the national cultural heritage. This appreciation allows citizens to participate in symbolic celebrations of unity (including political rituals) which are thought to produce, in a Durkheimian manner, a sense of national membership and belonging. In contrast, the citizen acquires information and analytical techniques in Citizenship 2 which are taken to be the prerequisites of meaningful participation in political life. Any subjective sense of membership that results from this participation is contingent and could well centre on a social class or an ethnic or single issue group in a way that reduces, rather than promotes, an identification with the nation as a whole.

This chapter has two main contentions. First, the current National Curriculum for English, despite the lip-service paid to the linguistic dimension of democracy in the Kingman Report, comprehensively fails to deliver on the Citizenship 2 front. No systematic attempt has been made in its provisions to deal with any significant aspect of political life or to promote seriously the often invoked ideal of active citizenship. Indeed, the syllabus for English in schools is vulnerable to general criticism on the grounds of its extreme remoteness from the everyday practical language tasks and language difficulties encountered by adults which, by and large, it ignores completely and leaves for the attention of basic skills and adult literacy classes. The second contention is that in their treatment of Standard English (SE), the Kingman Report and the subsequent National Curriculum proposals fall seriously short on Citizenship 1 grounds. There is a failure to appreciate both that a multi-ethnic society will tend to be a multi-lingual society, and also that this imposes a political obligation not simply to tolerate but actively to encourage and support linguistic diversity. In paying lip-service only to highly selected aspects of linguistic diversity, the citizen rights of linguistic minorities have been endangered and the seeds sown of future social resentments and antagonisms.

In developing these contentions, Section Two unpacks the various goals literacy has been taken to serve in technologically advanced and politically centralized societies. Section Three examines in some detail the relevant assumptions and arguments of the Kingman Report which gave the National Curriculum Council's proposals for English much of their intellectual and linguistic legitimation. The fourth section discusses the significance of SE in the light of multicultural education and changes in the nature of access to the printed word. The final section considers the ways in which a more integrated and explicit language and literacy policy could assist the exercise of social and civil rights in Britain.

LITERACY AND THE CITIZEN

There are four main 'civic' roles that have been attributed to literacy and these can be identified in a preliminary way as follows. First, as noted above, some of the political philosophies underpinning parliamentary democracy have identified literacy as paramount among those characteristics of an educated electorate that will maximize the effectiveness of the franchise. Only a public that can read the press and understand policies and political events, it is assumed, is equipped to participate actively and effectively in democratic politics. This view, which is commonly expressed in parliamentary democracies today, portrays mass literacy as a collective good that helps to ensure that the public understand the basic principles and issues of democratic politics. It is worth remembering, however, that in other settings, including several American states in the nineteenth century, literacy has been a formal prerequisite for individuals to obtain the franchise. In the American case, the underlying objective was to create a test that minimized the political participation of European immigrants who did not have English as their native language (Bromage, 1930). Although the aims were partisan and tactical, it was possible to legitimate the device by claiming that literacy in English was an essential and necessary condition for full participation in American politics. In this first role, then, literacy is conceived as an intrinsic ingredient in citizenship, generally in Citizenship 2 terms.

A second role played by literacy stems from the mode of operation of bureaucratically organized institutions in modern nation-states (including central and local government administrations, and judicial, health and welfare agencies) which rely extensively on written transactions and records. Although, historically, written bureaucratic procedures were adopted in Britain in the embryonic branches of the central administration largely for efficient internal communication, such agencies come over time to relate to their wider publics principally through the written channel. This process can, for example, be seen at work in the Inland Revenue which has gradually been shifting towards a greater and greater reliance on self-assessment and form completion by taxpayers along the lines established by the Internal Revenue Service in the United States of America. Although the outcomes of this general consequence of bureaucratization are variable, depending on the institution or function concerned, a potential result of shifting the burden of processing written transactions onto the citizen is the restriction of the individual rights of those people who are not able to handle (often) highly technical documents. If, for instance, some of the information necessary to make a successful claim for a welfare benefit is only available from leaflets, and if the claim itself entails a lengthy application form, prospective claimants with limited literacy will necessarily be disadvantaged. One official defence is that those who have such difficulties are always free to enlist assistance, but such assistance is rarely truly 'free' and will usually entail a loss of privacy. Within this role, written communication is simply a 'convenient' means adopted by bureaucracies for the execution of their business and literacy is not formally required for entitlement to rights or benefits themselves. However, since it may be a barrier to the effective exercise of formally enshrined citizen rights and benefits, an inability to exploit literacy for this function, as in the first role, detracts from Citizenship 2.

The third role relates to employment. In advanced economies, paid work, which is an increasingly necessary precondition for the exercise of a range of social and political rights, has become premised on literacy. The rising proportion of jobs which stipulate some kind of educational or vocational qualification as an entry requirement are screening recruits for literacy by proxy. Additionally, however, most employers of unskilled and semi-skilled manual labour on a medium or large scale insist on basic literacy from job-seekers, whether or not the jobs in question actually entail reading or writing[1]. Literacy is often 'tested' by such employers via a requirement that job-seekers complete application or other forms on the spot during a personnel department interview. Such procedures may be justified in the employing organizations in various ways. One common justification invokes Health and Safety legislation which places various burdens on employers to inform staff of safety rules and requirements (Atkinson and Papworth 1991, p. 51). Employers claim that written circulars and public notices are the only way that they can demonstrate that they have fulfilled their legal obligations. In its employment role, literacy is again clearly in the Citizenship 2 category and it appears to be in the course of a long-term transition from a contingent to an intrinsic status.

Finally, in a fourth role, literacy is regarded as the major means through which individuals gain access to their national history and cultural heritage, and familiarity with history and heritage is, in turn, widely perceived to foster an (arguably) desirable and necessary minimum identification with the nation and national interests. It is this objective, more than any other, that has defined the overall shape of National Curriculum English and has determined the manner in which the study of language has been associated with the appreciation and criticism of English literature. This is clearly Citizenship 1 territory.

The most important element enabling this civic role is the extensive support provided within the educational system for Standard English (SE), the discourse variant required in public examinations and used both in school textbooks and the bulk of the literary canon to be studied, as well as in nearly all communications between 'official' agencies and the citizen. The inculcation of a standard language was recognized from the outset of public education as a key means by which the lower social strata could be incorporated into a unitary culture in its broadest sense (Crowley, 1989). Since then, the education system has not simply reinforced SE as the authorized form of discourse for a wide range of educational activity and public communication; it has been the most powerful agency actively engaged in standardization.

A corpus of written materials is, of course, always needed in the process of teaching reading and writing. The selectors of this corpus are in the position of being able to include work which is not merely linguistically appropriate for pupils' current stage of linguistic development but which represents ideas, values and ideologies that they consider to be 'appropriate'. For many hundreds of years, training in literacy in Britain was based on materials which had a religious character or reflected religious themes and moralities. With the advent of mass public education, religion was given its own place in the curriculum and was replaced by an 'English' slot that was occupied in part with the study of representative work from the English literary tradition, a canon of appropriate authors whose work represented, in Arnold's famous phrase, '... the best of what has been thought and written'. While the composition of the canon is necessarily always contestable (and frequently contested), the celebration of a literary tradition of any kind itself reinforces such 'political' themes as historical continuity, a culture shared by all and national (or ethnic) achievement and excellence. The next section discusses the way these literacy functions were dealt with in the influential Kingman Report.

THE KINGMAN REPORT

The Kingman Committee into the Teaching of English Language was appointed early in 1987 with a brief from the Secretary of State for Education, Kenneth Baker, to recommend a model of spoken and written English that could be used in teacher training and to consider how far it could also profitably be taught to pupils at different stages of development. Although the committee's brief studiously avoided the word 'grammar' ('knowledge about language' was the chosen euphemism), it was widely believed at the time that ministers were responding to pressure from the traditionalistic wing of educational thinking who had long been campaigning for the teaching of grammatical correctness to be rescued from the neglect into which it had allegedly fallen and restored to its rightful place at the centre of English studies. The composition of the committee guaranteed that these preoccupations would be aired. In addition to teachers, academic linguists and miscellaneous 'great and good' public figures, it contained, in the words of Professor Brian Cox, a committee member who, as chief editor of the influential Black Papers on Education published between 1969 and 1977, had himself earned a reputation as an educational conservative, 'traditionalists of an older generation such as Peter Levi, Professor of Poetry at Oxford, and Patrick Kavanagh, a poet whose conservative views were well known from his regular column in *The Spectator*' (Cox, 1991, p. 4). Cox subsequently chaired the working party that produced the detailed National Curriculum proposals for English, thereby providing an element of continuity between 'theory' and legislation. In the event, the committee resisted some of the more extreme dogmatisms that were in circulation and published a report that deeply disappointed the far right which had wished it into existence. Nevertheless, Kingman embodies some serious flaws. This section is concerned specifically with its attempt to relate the teaching of English to the uses of literacy in adult social life, while a subsequent section deals with the Report's thinking on SE.

Kingman had been given a surprisingly open-ended mandate to produce an authoritative statement about the socio-linguistic background to, and purpose of, English studies in schools. Most of the Report is devoted, naturally enough, to an examination of the way language functions in the context of the developing faculties of the school pupil, leading up to the recommended age-related attainment targets. In an early section, the broad objective of school English is defined as being '. . . to enable and encourage every child to use the English language to the fullest effect in speaking, writing, listening and reading' (Department of Education and Science, 1988a, p. 4). Only in Chapter 2, which attempts to explain why this starting point is 'axiomatic', are the functions of language in the adult social world explored at any length. In a paragraph in which the word 'democracy' and its cognates are repeated three times, it is made clear that the primary function of teaching English is to facilitate citizenship and to enable adult social and political participation:

> People need expertise in language to be able to participate effectively in a democracy. There is no point in having access to information that you cannot understand, or having the opportunity to propose policies which you cannot formulate... A democratic society needs people who have the linguistic abilities which will enable them to discuss, evaluate and make sense of what they are told, as well as to take effective action on the basis of their understanding. The working of a democracy depends on the discriminating use of language on the part of all its people. Otherwise there can be no genuine participation, but only the imposition of the ideas of those who are linguistically capable. As individuals, as well as members of constituencies, people need the resources of language both to defend their rights and to fulfill their obligations. (Department of Education and Science, 1988a, p. 7)

The paragraphs that follow identify additional roles for literacy in adult life. The first of these is what could be termed 'practical life support', that is, the use of literacy in connection with every day matters such as tax returns, mortgage agreements and installation manuals (referred to collectively by Kingman as the 'carpentry of life'). The third role identified is in employment, but here the Report says little beyond the sweeping assertion that linguistic competence is required in any job.

The fourth function is to support 'social identification and membership' and it is at this point that Kingman introduces the importance of Standard English (SE). A distinction is drawn between primary social groups which will be able to retain and exploit a variety of dialect usages, and secondary groupings, up to and including the nation and the world communities, in which communication via the standard language is 'indispensable'. We return to this point in the next section.

The fifth function assigned to literacy is to facilitate adaptability and change. Here the Report clearly has in mind the way in which a proportion of the workforce in an advanced economy requires periodic formal retraining, but it also mentions the new forms of 'public' literacy embedded in electronic technologies like broadcast media and computers.

Kingman identifies these various functions by working back from the extensive penetration of written communication into the texture of modern life to construct a conception of 'literacy' that is framed by, and thus automatically supports, all these activities, transactions and relationships. The argument is essentially this: many socially important activities involve reading and writing; literacy entails mastery of reading and writing; therefore making children literate will enable them to accomplish many socially important activities as adults.

An obvious flaw in this syllogism is that literacy is simply one ingredient, and invariably a minor ingredient, in the kinds of adult accomplishment that Kingman seeks to facilitate. As far as the 'carpentry of life' is concerned, there are people who will possess relatively high levels of literacy and can read and apparently fully understand a technical manual as a text, but are nevertheless unable to implement its instructions (simply because the task of installation or assembly necessarily entails non-linguistic skills and knowledge). On the other hand, although a low level of linguistic competence is generally perceived by the highly literate to be a very severe handicap in everyday matters, many of the individuals concerned have developed compensatory techniques and substitute skills that minimize any practical inconvenience (Levine, 1986, p. 118).

Kingman is, however, correct in identifying literacy and its absence as playing an important role in the employment process, but it does so in several distinct ways. As was noted in Section 2, literacy is incorporated within the educational credentials which are prerequisites for nearly all jobs in the skilled manual and non-manual sectors of the labour market. Less obviously, job seekers for manual work who have literacy problems may be at a disadvantage to the extent that they conduct a less comprehensive search, possibly relying more on word of mouth for finding openings than job seekers who are able to scan newspaper advertisements and Job Centre vacancy boards, as well as using word of mouth information. However, *pace* Kingman, there are relatively few jobs in any employment sector where proficiency at listening, speaking, reading and writing are the only requirements, independent of any substantive knowledge, personal characteristics or experience. Once again, Kingman oversimplifies the part literacy plays in adult transactions and relationships.

Finally, while literacy may widely be judged to be an extremely useful asset in the conduct of political life, it is hyperbolic to imply, as Kingman does, that linguistic knowledge and competence, in and of themselves, can facilitate genuine participation and prevent the hegemony of the 'linguistically capable'. The latter highly optimistic assumption is thrown into greater relief by the failure of Kingman to include any explicitly critical function in the catalogue of adult uses based on school English. As a variety of influential linguists and social theorists have repeatedly pointed out, language is a leading medium through which power relations in society are articulated. Hierarchical aspects of social relations are partly embedded in linguistic differences and conventions and, as the concluding section of this chapter suggests, knowledge about language can assist in revealing its ideological and legitimating roles.

One serious problem, then, with Kingman's approach is that it encourages inflated expectations of what can be achieved on the basis of one part of the school curriculum. In addition to the adult objectives discussed above, Kingman identifies the ways English language instruction can encourage far-ranging personal, social and aesthetic development in children. Admittedly, the nature of the Committee's task licensed the promotion of a positive public image for the subject, but no English syllabus could possibly deliver so much across so wide a front. The degree of overstatement has proved harmful because it sponsors the development of a syllabus which promises pupils too much and makes teachers responsible for too much.

A further problem derives from Kingman's failure to specify the relationship between the four fundamental linguistic activities and the uses of language in adult life. In a note of reservation to the Report from Professor Widdowson, this failure to spell out the details of a vital connection is highlighted very clearly. He regrets the failure to analyse how

> different aspects of development nurtured in school actually prepare the pupils for the uses of language in the adult world. Adult purposes are said to determine the degree of competence in the four language skills to be aimed at by pupils. How then is the achievement of these degrees of competence in the four language skills to be put into correspondence with the four aspects of language development? None of these questions is addressed. (Department of Education and Science, 1988a, p. 77)

None of the main documents produced in the subsequent implementation process came near to dealing with Widdowson's question and the concern to respond to the realities of adult language use gradually slips from centre stage in National Curriculum English to make only occasional fleeting appearances from the wings.

While they preferred to avoid the term, it is clear that the Committee understood 'literacy' to mean the possession of a core of linguistic skills which are a necessary condition for carrying out almost any adult activity. There is an underlying issue here of whether mastery of any set of purely linguistic skills can be the basis of competent performance of the communicative element in adult roles (as suggested by the concept of 'functional literacy'). This kind of 'autonomous' model of literacy has been forcefully criticized by Street (1984) whose work emphasizes the impossibility of identifying abstract linguistic skills which will have fixed outcomes independently of the structural and cultural environment in which written activities and transactions are always embedded.

More serious, however, than this particular conceptual weakness is the dramatic failure of school English, following Kingman, to deal systematically with the 'carpentry of life' (despite the latter's emphasis on its significance). The proposals contained in English for Ages 5 to 16, a crucial part of the implementation of Kingman, mention the importance of extending the range and diversity of texts studied by including authors who are not part of the traditional English canon (Department of Education and Science 1989), but the conception of 'text' is still implicitly restricted to works of recognizable literary merit. The proposals devote 10 paragraphs to the relations between English language and literature and 17 paragraphs to those with drama, but non-literary forms of writing are alluded to only in passing. The storm over the composition of the canon of suitable authors for school study has distracted attention from the fact that any fiction canon, however catholic in conception, will completely exclude the kind of texts which many adults find most problematic – invoices, employment contracts, summonses, final demands, divorce papers, hire purchase and tenancy agreements, insurance policy fine print, letters from professional advisers. The abiding concern with 'imaginative' writing is inconsistent with the emphasis on giving pupils a greatly enhanced knowledge about the mechanics of spoken and written language in general, and with certain attainment targets which mention non-literary materials (see, for example, Reading Attainment, Target Level 5). It seems clear that if pupils do gain experience in school with completing application forms, or drafting complaints, or filling in tax returns, or wrestling with technical documentation, it is unlikely to happen in the English timetable slot.

The same strictures could be applied to the study of political writing which appears, judging from its neglect, to have been regarded as a sensitive or possibly restricted area. The Attainment Targets mention the capacity to differentiate between statements of fact and opinion (for example, Reading Attainment, Target Levels 5 and 6), while Level 9 refers to the recognition of differences of presentation in news stories in the press and on television. The possibility of using specifically political materials is not excluded by the proposals for English but neither is it explicitly encouraged. There is no reinforcement of the potential utility to teachers of using published political debate (or even Hansard) as class texts which would raise so many of the presentational issues with which the Attainment Targets at the higher levels are concerned. There is no encouragement for the discourse analysis of other political messages, advertising and propaganda. This failure to encourage within English the critical and linguistic analysis of political argument and debate sits very strangely alongside the bold and repeated protestations about the linkages between literacy and citizenship with which the Kingman Report begins.

THE DEBATE OVER STANDARD ENGLISH

In the 19th century, there was scholarly agreement that 'national character' was reflected in a language. Far from adopting the stance of neutral technical observers of language behaviour, linguists were keen to draw out the implications of their understanding of the cultural dynamics of the English language for such issues as national unity and patriotism. By the middle of the century, when dialectology began to systematize, the idea of the 'Queen's English' came into prominence. It was a phrase which had appeared in print as far back as the 16th century, but its academic role in the 19th was to define an abstract form of the language which was distinct from any of the regional dialects and with which they could all be compared. The Queen's English also set up a conceptual association between native speakers of English and citizenship. By associating political rights and duties with the medium in which they were inscribed, it offered a potential principle of selection for assigning those rights and duties to living persons. It also invited a respect and protection for the linguistic sphere which mirrored that already established for the political. In other words, the Queen's English provided an extremely serviceable symbol of nationhood (Crowley, 1989, pp. 129–131).

The idea of a standard dialect or standard language was an early conceptual development from Queen's English. In its initial forms, it combined the meaning of non-local, that is, a language variant indifferent to the speaker's birthplace and residence, with the sense of standard as prestigious, an ideal whose emulation guarantees social acceptance. Subsequently, there have been many shifts in the meaning of SE and repeated reinterpretation of its cultural significance, all of which are documented in detail by Crowley (1989).

The source of the high social standing of SE has been a particularly disputed issue. A recent discussion of SE by a linguist specifically concerned with its implications for education characterizes it technically in terms of the intersection of a language dialect and a language diatype (Stubbs, 1986, p. 87). Put simply, according to this view, SE is the variant characteristic of a particular kind of user employing language for specific purposes. It is a social rather than a geographical dialect that developed historically from the language of the royal court but spread widely beyond London to become the variant typical of the educated middle classes (largely because of the power and social influence of its original users). Such a dialect lent itself to standardization because it was used frequently for a variety of written, formal, public functions (though it was not, and is not, restricted to these functions), and these uses have further reinforced its prestige. The agents of standardization were originally book editors, proof readers and dictionary compilers, but as we argued above, the education system itself is the most powerful contemporary force for standardization of written English through the activities of examiners, curriculum designers, school teachers and teachers of English as a foreign language.

There is some agreement among linguists that SE is primarily a matter of grammar, vocabulary and spelling rather than pronunciation, and it is accepted that SE can be spoken in a range of accents. There is an extensive overlap between the features of SE and non standard (NS) variants (partly because users alternate between the two in different situations) and this makes it difficult to identify concrete linguistic patterns that are unambiguously SE. In fact, Stubbs' approach is to define SE negatively via syntactic features which are distinctively NS. Among these features are the regularization of irregular verbs and reflexive pronouns ('we was', 'hisself'), multiple negation ('I didn't do nothing') and the use of 'ain't' as a negative form of 'be' and 'have' (Stubbs, 1986, p. 89).

This approach to SE cannot be represented as commanding universal support from linguists, but it does reflect mainstream theoretical assumptions and it has a large body of empirical research on English usage in its support. It has, however, been represented as insidiously egalitarian by some educational commentators. One of the older generation of right wing protagonists, John Honey, presented a radically different view on SE in his 1983 pamphlet, *The Language Trap* (1983). This polemic helped to politicize SE and contributed to the climate out of which Kingman later emerged. The main targets of The Language Trap were linguists and fellow travellers who subscribed to what Honey termed the 'theory of functional optimism' (Honey, 1983, p. 3), the thesis that all languages and language variants are adequate, and equally adequate, to their users' needs. The details of his case against a collection of linguists including Chomsky, Labov and Trudgill are not important here. Honey argued, however, that a result of their work was the diffusion of a mistaken relativism, the 'new orthodoxy in socio-linguistics' (1983, p. 17), which has undermined the attempts of parents, teachers and employers to enforce standards of 'good English'. In Honey's view, any reluctance to correct non-standard usages leads to the trap of his title. NS variations put their users at a distinct social disadvantage in a cultural environment in which textbooks and examinations are based on the standard variant and in which '. . . there is a long-standing and now overwhelming association, right across British society, between the use of the grammar, vocabulary and idiom of SE and the concept of "educatedness"' (Honey, 1983, p. 19). Honey argues further that support for non-standard language varieties will necessarily result in a reduction in the capacity of users to communicate outside their local group or subculture (p. 22). He quotes with approval the conclusion of the American, David Laitin, that '. . . speaking the language of the state is often the critical condition enabling the citizen to participate in the political arena of that state', and goes on to suggest, 'If . . . - whether we like it or not, the 'language of the state' in Britain is Standard English, then any action which impairs the ability of any future citizen to communicate adequately in that medium is an act of political emasculation . . '. (p. 24).

Honey is certainly correct in one of his central arguments, namely that success at almost any stage of the education system, as presently constituted, requires the individual to possess or develop a facility with SE (p. 20). Indeed, since education is the institutional system that has played a leading role in defining and standardizing SE, this is hardly surprising. Honey, however, then overplays his argumentative hand by producing a sustained attack on all educational reinforcement of NS language forms. He suggests that since SE is a marker of membership of a respected social grouping or subculture, any encouragement of NS variants is likely to further disadvantage the social and ethnic minorities that tend to use them. He alleges that many immigrant parents are, in fact, very hostile to their children retaining dialect features (p. 33) and he finds the promotion of dialect to assert ethnic identity 'illogical' because it can only result in a handicap for the individual in educational and job market competition (pp. 26–7). There is a little, very lukewarm, acceptance of 'mother-tongue' instruction for immigrant children 'at an early stage in their schooling' (p. 31), but in the main, Honey systematically questions the value and necessity of educational reinforcement of any and all linguistic deviations from NS (including British regional dialects, Caribbean patois, West African English and Black English Vernacular). Additionally, throughout *The Language Trap*, Honey repeatedly hints that use of NS English is likely to be a direct intellectual handicap and a brake on the individual or group's intellectual development (see particularly, pp. 18–19).

In *English Our English*, a pamphlet published in 1987 by the right-wing Centre for Policy Studies, John Marenbon picks up several of Honey's themes. The spectre of the 'new orthodoxy' again looms large but the later work contains an even greater emphasis than Honey on the desirability of correctness for correctness's sake. Marenbon rejects the view that SE is simply one (prestigious) dialect of English among many, preferring to characterize it as a repository of 'English culture at its highest levels'. He writes that the '... differences in capacity between modern standard English and the modern dialects of English are even more striking than those between Chaucerian and modern English', and also that 'dialects of English reflect the much more limited range of functions for which they have traditionally been used' (1987, 22) It is claimed that while 'dialect is always changing', SE is slow-changing: this contrast is important because Marenbon believes the consequence is that 'it is never clear exactly which of the constructions that a dialect-speaker is using are grammatical and which are not, because it is never clear exactly which dialect he is speaking, or how consistently he is intending to speak it'. (1987, 25) Everyone conversant with SE, however, instantly knows what is correct and what is not, what register a word belongs to, and when departures from recognized norms are being used to achieve rhetorical effect and nuance.

The sense of 'grammatical' used in the last quotation is, of course, a survival from an era of traditional prescriptive grammar where the motive was to establish 'correct' ways of speaking and writing. Such usages are incongruent with the contemporary understanding of grammar and dialect shared by all serious modern linguists under which all users of any dialect have no option other than to employ a grammar, irrespective of any subjective intention to speak 'consistently'.

In Marenbon's anxiety to dispose of the theory of functional optimism (he recognizes Honey's target but does not employ his terminology), there is a rather desperate casting about for illustrations of the superior capacities of some languages. He argues, for instance, that both 18th century English and SE are grammatically and syntactically superior to either Anglo-Saxon or Chaucerian English for the representation of abstract arguments. (It would be instructive to learn how Marenbon would propose to test such a tortuous hypothesis.) In the course of justifying the retention of Latin as the basis for understanding English grammar, he asserts that SE 'has been formed through the centuries by its contact with Latin' (1987, 38). This and other claims made about SE throughout *English Our English* are inconsistent with its characteristics as conventionally recognized by linguists.

Everything that Marenbon attributes to some inherent linguistic superiority of SE, and especially its cultural prestige and what he takes to be its intellectual superiority, is in reality a reflection of its greater degree of standardization. Any dialect standardized to an equivalent degree would have the characteristics Marenbon believes are uniquely enshrined in SE. Marenbon seems ignorant of the fact that many users switch between SE and NS dialects in different settings and for different functions, recognizing and applying quite different norms in each case.

While the Kingman Report was careful to distance itself from the kind of extreme opinions about SE developed on the political right by polemicists like Honey and Marenbon, it nevertheless championed its educational importance in a forthright manner. It states very clearly that pupils have a right to acquire SE and schools a duty to enable them to do so. SE is '... the language we have in common' and is a necessary element in the process by which '... adults move from localized speech communities into a wider world' (Department of Education and Science 1988a, 14). The Report goes on to argue that since there are no serious alternatives to SE for interregional and international communication, it merits a central place in National Curriculum English.

While there is certainly a good deal in favour of this position, Kingman advances it for the wrong reasons and tends to draw the wrong inferences from it. The main problem that confounds Kingman is a social perspective from which it is necessary to disregard or downplay ethnic and class differences and their impact on language patterns and uses. One expression of this is the repeated failure to acknowledge the fact that SE is itself a class dialect used by a national elite. The Kingman Report takes the view that SE is standard because it is written down (Department of Education and Science 1988a, 14) but it would be more accurate to say it is standard because it was the dialect of a strategically located social class who exercised an early monopoly over publication.

Another misconception is the suggestion that there are no conventions for writing NS dialects whereas in reality it is simply that the conventions that exist are generally not familiar beyond, and sometimes even among, the speakers of that particular dialect. A sense of unfamiliarity was one of the reasons that lay behind some 1994 Booker Prize judges criticizing the Glaswegian of James Kelman's winning novel, *How Late it is, How Late*, as 'inaccessible'. As a direct consequence of a novel written in Glaswegian winning a prestigious literary award and thereby gaining a national readership, the orthographic conventions of Glaswegian will become known more widely and a small step towards the standardization of Glaswegian will have been taken. The existence of small bodies of published dialect poetry and fiction is a further indication that the problem of non-recognition is economic rather than linguistic, involving principally limited access to the means of publication.

The Kingman Report has little to say about the relationship between English and other mother tongues spoken by children starting formal schooling. Cameron and Bourne point out that the Secretary of State's notes of 'Supplementary Guidance' to the National Curriculum working group on English indicate that 'English should be the first language and medium of instruction for all pupils in England' (quoted in Cameron and Bourne, 1989, p. 16). This restriction of the principle to England rather than Britain reflects the terms of the

1967 Welsh Language Act which made bilingual educational provision possible and granted Welsh 'equal validity' within the borders of Wales. The existence of territorial boundaries for England and Wales permits English and Welsh to be treated as the 'natural' tongues of residents in these regions. This contrasts with the absence of any similar formal recognition conceded to speakers of ethnic minority languages such as Punjabi or Gujarati who are permanently resident in Britain but who cannot identify a 'home' territory. Cameron and Bourne suggest that the inevitable implication of such a differential is that ethnic minority languages are assigned an 'alien' status because they are seen to be the result of 'a historical accident and a territorial aberration, a temporary occupation of someone else's space' (Cameron and Bourne 1989, p. 17). This unequal treatment in terms of legal recognition is reinforced by the educational marginality of language support for children from ethnic minority groups. The arrangements for funding this support have traditionally signalled its status as extraordinary and discretionary. It is significant, for instance, that Section 11 funding for projects for children whose first language is not English has come from the Home Office. Recently, however, funding has been transferred to the Department of the Environment's Single Regeneration Budget for promoting urban renewal (*Times Educational Supplement*, 1994, p. 1). As well as being a straightforward cut in educational resources, it is symptomatic of an unwillingness by central government to accept that support for languages other than English is a legitimate call on the mainstream Education budget.

We are now in a position to understand why it is that the New Right and many traditionalists have adopted SE as a rallying point. It has represented to them a bastion against a miscellany of social and cultural developments which they regard as wholly undesirable. As with many previous attempts to purify the language of 'barbarous' elements, the empirical realities of linguistic usage are ultimately less centrally of concern than what 'language' in the abstract is taken to represent. Thus, one typical motivation for 'purification' is the denigration by proxy of the social groups held to be responsible for linguistic pollution. From the discussion above, it is clear that immigrants and the educationally unsuccessful are explicit targets for the traditionalists. Another motive is the belief that a standard language makes a direct contribution to social order and discipline. John Rae, ex-Head of Westminster School, drew precisely this parallel in a newspaper article which connected the alleged contemporary failure to observe linguistic rules and the prevalence of crime and other infractions of rules of conduct (Rae, 1982). This point of view only expresses in a more extreme form the fundamental conviction under-pinning most of the 'radical' views discussed above that the 'rules' of natural languages possess a moral authority and are not just descrip-tive norms inferred from observations of usage.

LITERACY AND LANGUAGE POLICY

This chapter set out to identify some of the limitations in the way the linkages between citizenship and literacy have been understood in current educational thinking and translated (or not translated) into policy. We have seen that the current English syllabus falls short of delivering some of its formally stated objectives on the citizenship front. We have noted the marked failure of the syllabus to address the literacy requirements of the adult citizen confronted with the increas-ingly technical documentation generated by powerful public and private bureaucracies. This failure is magnified by the reluctance of curriculum planners to encourage the examination of materials relat-ing to political life. Although the Kingman Report appears to argue the case, it has not yet truly been accepted in government circles that schools are the place where the foundations for modern Citizen-ship 2 should be laid (despite a widespread recognition that cynicism and political disenchantment are rife among young people). Political literacy, understood not just in terms of a formal appreciation of con-stitutional niceties and institutional mechanisms, but as a toolkit for active participation in the democratic process, has barely a foothold in the curriculum, and as things stand at present, it is not just English but the whole of the National Curriculum that is glaringly deficient in providing such a toolkit.

One of the factors that hampers the educational promotion of Citizenship 2 is the continuing emphasis on studying, criticizing and producing fictional and 'creative' writing, leaving school English still effectively dominated by Citizenship 1 objectives. Although literary criticism has an important and entirely legitimate place at the centre of English studies, it has limited the scope for the introduction of other kinds of important material. A place needs to be found, for example, for those newer varieties of discourse and media analysis which are able to deal, among other things, with the ideological dimensions of texts and broadcasts. It may be, however, that the continuing furore over how the canon of recommended authors should be composed will, in the long term, help to sow the seeds of doubt over whether school English can in fact serve as a source of Citizenship 1 and reopen in a fundamental way the question of political education in schools.

One theme in the Kingman Report that has undoubtedly been translated into concrete practice is the central place given to SE. The debate over SE has a variety of different implications which need to be clearly distinguished. There was a danger during the 1980s that SE would be hijacked by right-wing ideologues determined to harness it to Citizenship 1 objectives – the celebration of a comfy Merrie England version of English history and heritage which was successfully resisted by Kingman and the Working Groups. Although the origins and nature of standard languages remain somewhat mystical in Kingman, a pre-eminent position for SE is defensible on both educational and Citizenship 2 grounds. A familiarity with SE is unquestionably a vital ingredient in overall adult communicative functioning, given SE's domination of the written channel in contemporary Britain. However, this policy can be misrepresented and misinterpreted as the equivalent of 'English monolingualism'. That is, laying the case of Welsh to one side, promoting proficiency in spoken and written SE has been accepted as the overriding linguistic objective of schools. The position of mother tongue literacy in NS dialects and in other languages is relegated to the residual efforts of families and ethnic communities themselves, often unsupported from central or local educational budgets. This situation is unsatisfactory and has consequences that diminish the citizen rights of ethnic and linguistic minorities.

After the struggles over the National Curriculum, educationists in Britain are now deeply suspicious of all new initiatives. The system is riven by a variety of internal conflicts, each associated with its own agenda, which together generate a high degree of inertia, hampering desirable change and adaptation. In the face of this situation, it is doubtful that the political will and commitment at present exists to deal in a root and branch manner with the difficulties outlined. Nevertheless, one expression of such a commitment and a positive step towards the implementation of remedial policies would be the adoption in Britain of a broad language and literacy policy that sets targets and guidelines that extend beyond education (and are therefore not 'owned' by any single department of government). Such a policy would help to forge links between the now largely separate literacy worlds of school English, adult literacy in a community education context, adult basic education in a vocational skills context, English as a second language literacy, and mother tongue literacy schemes. It could also be the basis for the establishment of standards for clarity and simplicity in the production of written public communications and underline a place in schooling for a non-partisan training in critical citizenship. Australia, a multilingual and multi-ethnic society which, despite differences in scale and in the precise mix of languages and groups, bears comparison to Britain, introduced a National Literacy Strategy in 1990 (Lo Bianco, 1990). Among the many positive features of this strategy are, active literacy in English for all by the year 2000 (Lo Bianco, 1990, 3.3); a recognition of the rights of ethnic minorities to literacy in their mother language unprejudiced by the status of English as the national language (2.4, 3.1, 3.2); responsibility for promotion and support for 'active' literacy vested not only in education but in agencies including central and state governments, community groups, employers and trade unions (4.1); support for forms of literacy which enable '... a critical appraisal of current sociopolitical arrangements as an important tool of empowerment' (5.1.2); the use of plain English and reader-friendly public documents (5.1.22).

Many of the objectives of the Australian literacy strategy are ambitious and, as with many similar statements, precise funding commitments are absent. For the list of objectives just cited, however, Britain provides a negative contrast in as much as the articulation by government of appropriate principles and targets, as well as the commitment of adequate resources, are absent.

NOTE

1.   As part of the Basic Skills at Work Programme funded jointly by the Department for Education and the Employment Department, a series of surveys were conducted in the early 1990s which enable a picture to be constructed of the basic skills requirements in the 15.6 million manual, personal service, sales and clerical/secretarial jobs in England and Wales. The results indicated that no reading was required in about 11 per cent of manual jobs (reading was defined as the 'ability to read and understand text in the form of letters, written instructions, manuals, notes, orders, etc.'). About the same percentage had no need of writing (defined as the ability to 'write accurate letters, notes, reports or messages'). The evidence also pointed, however, to a rising demand for basic skills, especially in larger establishments, resulting from the adoption of new methods of

work organization (including especially the adoption of quality assurance standards and the application of information technologies). See Atkinson and Papworth (1991), Atkinson and Spilsbury (1993), and Atkinson, Spilsbury and Williams (1993), especially 2.3.1 and 2.3.2.

7 Ethnic Minorities, Citizenship and Education

Sally Tomlinson

Nations are political units, created by governments of particular territories and peoples, but an important part of nation building involves laying claim to a unique national identity (Smith, 1986). Claim to a national identity is usually based on the assertion of a common ancestry and a shared history and is often accompanied by the exclusion of 'others', who have been conquered, colonized or otherwise subordinated. Debates over 'who belongs' to a particular nation with a national identity and citizenship rights are not purely theoretical. People are prepared to die in pursuit of their claims to be recognized as citizens of particular territories, and national majorities are prepared to use all strategies, including violence, in attempts to exclude minorities from citizenship rights. The question as to how far membership of a British national identity with full citizenship rights will ever be fully offered to those of 'non-white' ethnic backgrounds in Britain is still an open one[1]. Migrants of African, Caribbean and Asian origin and their descendants still have a struggle to exercise their political, civil and social citizenship rights. The white majority still seems determined to reject non-whites as equal citizens within the British nation, and the view of black British scholars is that a 'black British' or 'Asian British' identity is still not part of an acceptable image of post-imperial Britain (Gilroy, 1987, Goulbourne, 1989). Heater's suggestion that citizenship in the Western liberal tradition presupposes that 'citizens and the state are mutually respectful and supportive' (Heater, 1990, p. 97) has never been a situation that ethnic minorities in Britain would recognize. Instead, there is both a political and cultural resistance by the white majority to the conjunction of being black or Asian and British.

This chapter briefly examines the politics of exclusion of ethnic minorities over the past forty years, from a 'citizenship' which has itself been changing. This process has been accompanied by anxiety over a changing 'British'[2] national identity on the part of the majority society. It discusses the way in which the education system, through a school curriculum still permeated by residual Victorian beliefs in

114

white superiority, has helped sustain a resistance to the idea that ethnic minority groups can be included within the national identity and exercise full citizenship rights. It also questions whether education can influence non-rational ethnocentric beliefs in white superiority and the implications of minority exclusion from recognition as both British and European citizens.

THE POLITICS OF EXCLUSION

There has been political resistance from both the left and the right to the idea that former imperial subjects and their children should be accepted as part of the British nation, and despite the election of four black MPs to Parliament in 1987, many politicians still do on occasions present immigrants and minorities as being a threat to the nation, rather than part of it. The conjunction made in Victorian Britain between race and nation is still apparent in the presentation of the British nation as biologically and culturally exclusive and monocultural. Phrases such as 'This Island Race' and 'this bulldog breed' vividly convey the ideal of the nation as belonging to white people (Gilroy, 1987) and right-wing nationalist parties use the bulldog and the Union Jack as symbols of this exclusiveness. The concept of national belonging not only at times excludes non-whites but also uses militaristic and patriotic metaphors of war and invasion to describe immigrant minorities:

> The enemy within, the unarmed invasion, alien encampments, alien territory, new commonwealth occupations, have all been used to describe the black presence in this way. (Gilroy, 1987, p. 45)

The post-war Conservative position centred round the belief that all British citizens, of whatever colour, had equal rights before the law, although during the 1950s this was contested and Winston Churchill considered the possibility of using a 'keep Britain white' slogan in the 1955 General Election. In the 1960s Enoch Powell began what Rich (1986) has described as a populist quest against the Commonwealth and the search for a new English identity. His anti-immigration speech in April 1968 aroused extreme racist reactions. He received nearly 65,000 letters of support, 4000 white dockers went on strike in his support and marched to Westminster proclaiming 'Back Britain, not black Britain'. A long-term result of Powell's views has been a heightening of race consciousness in Britain and the reiteration of the idea that non-whites could somehow be 'repatriated', and he has never abandoned his view that the actual presence of non-white minorities constitutes a 'menacing' threat that will inevitably lead to civil discord (Powell in Lewis, 1988). When Prime Minister, Mrs. Thatcher also presented the idea of the British nation as a superior, imperial power, resistant to alien cultures, and the 1982 Falklands War provided an opportunity to assert patriotic white imperialism. At a Conservative Party rally following the end of the Falklands War Thatcher asserted that 'There were those who would not admit... that Britain was no longer the nation that had built an Empire and ruled a quarter of the World... well, they were wrong.' (Thatcher, 1982). At the same time a Sunday Telegraph article was assuring the world that 'if the Falkland Islanders were British citizens with black or brown skins... it is doubtful whether the Royal Navy or Marines would be fighting for their liberation' (Worsthorne, 1982).

There is, however, no single Conservative Party position on the place of minorities within the nation and some have voiced concern over the attempted exclusion of minorities by influential politicians. The first Chairman of the Commission for Racial Equality, himself a former Conservative MP, wrote in 1987 that:

> It is lamentable that in eight years as Prime Minister Mrs Thatcher has not made a single speech denouncing racialism and discrimination and encouraging the work of justice and harmony. (Lane, 1987)

A major recognition behind such lack of political leadership was that electoral success has always been enhanced by assertions that foreigners, immigrants and alien cultures have swamped British values and by the continued presentation of non-white minority groups as not part of the national identity. In 1990 Minister Norman Tebbitt proposed a 'cricket test' – the loyalty to Britain of people of Asian origin should be judged by the national cricket team they support (The Times, 1990).

Some socialist and left-wing groups have however often excluded ethnic minorities and their cultures, despite ideologies of the 'brotherhood of man' and universal human rights. The Labour Cabinet of Harold Wilson had accepted by 1965 that sympathy for 'immigrants' was a vote-loser (Crossman, 1979). A Labour Home Secretary introduced an Immigration Control Act in 1968, and the socialist writer Raymond Williams analysed English working class resentment of 'unfamiliar neighbours' (Williams, 1965). The Labour MP David

Blunkett, Shadow Minister for Education in 1994, has written about 'the crisis of cultural identity for us, the white British, half-Christian majority' (Blunkett, 1987).

Liberal individualism has, in the twentieth century, provided a basis for social reform and the acquisition of social and welfare rights. Roy Jenkins's 1966 speech extolling 'equal opportunity and cultural diversity in an atmosphere of mutual tolerance' came to embody a national goal for a liberal democracy (Jenkins, quoted in Rex and Tomlinson, 1979, p. 41). However, liberally-minded social, community, and educational workers, attempting to create one nation out of a predominantly antagonistic white majority and increasingly vocal non-white minorities, have occasionally come under attack from all sides, being derided as 'do-gooders' or as part of a 'race relations industry'.

There has been, during the past thirty years, an uneasy political resistance to the acceptance of non-white ethnic minorities as equal citizens whose cultures and histories should be respected, but who are also part of the British nation. Politicians prefer to present minorities as scapegoats for social and economic ills, as responsible for inner city decline and problems of law and order. Few public figures have been willing to take a lead in asserting that ethnic minorities do share a British national identity and are entitled to equal citizenship rights.

THE CHANGING CONCEPT OF CITIZENSHIP

In 1950 T. H. Marshall argued that the existence of a welfare state and social benefits made common citizenship a more important basis for allegiance than old style 'class solidarity' (Marshall, 1950). Common entitlements and rights bound citizens together. Those studying the incorporation of immigrant minorities into this concept of citizenship found, however, that there was conflict and resistance – over employment and educational opportunities, housing and social benefits, on the part of a post-war British working-class, who had themselves 'won' trade union and welfare rights and who resented the competition for scarce resources, posed by the minorities (Smith, 1977; Rex and Tomlinson, 1979). Rex and Tomlinson, in their 1970s study of the relations between minorities and the majority society, pointed to the complex interrelation between the British class structure and the social structure of Empire, which made it unlikely that immigrant minorities would be able to 'join' the majority society as equal citizens. They asked how far minorities did actually enjoy the same rights as their white fellow workers and how far the attainment of equal rights was compatible with the maintenance of ethnic group identity. They concluded that by the 1980s, and despite three Race Relations Acts designed to reduce levels of discrimination, the heightened antagonism of whites to ethnic minorities and the actual structural and cultural position of minority groups made it almost impossible for minorities to benefit equally from the common citizenship envisaged by Marshall (see Jones, 1993). Although many individuals from ethnic minority groups made successful lives and a small black and Asian middle class was emerging, by the 1980s it was possible to identify a minority underclass.

The erosion of the welfare state and the disappearance of employment opportunities has, in the 1990s, placed many white people in an underclass position. The gradual removal of welfare rights and entitlements, together with low wages, has eroded the idea of common citizenship rights and there is currently much anxiety as to what holds together all classes and groups as citizens. A commission on citizenship, set up in 1989 and chaired by Lord Weatherill, former Speaker of the House of Commons, attempted to change the concept of citizen from the Marshall view of citizens as individuals with civil rights and entitlements to 'active' citizens who would intervene politically, both locally and centrally, to improve the quality of life in the society generally. The active citizen was defined as one who pays taxes, votes, is involved in local community affairs, and companies could also be 'good citizens' responsible to their employees and shareholders (Institute for Citizenship Studies, 1994a). Both the Commission and the Institute for Citizenship Studies which was set up in 1992 to implement the Commission's report, were concerned to clarify the legal position – entitlements, duties, obligations – of 'British citizens' and clarify citizenship arrangements that pertain in Britain and Europe (Institute for Citizenship Studies, 1994b).

The Commission's concept of an active citizen does not, however, in any way address the real position of a citizenry divided along class and ethnic lines, in which the white majority increasingly scapegoat minorities as responsible for unemployment and scarce social resources. In addition, the 1990s are seeing once again a resurgence of racist theories of minority intellectual inferiority (Murray and Herrnstein, 1994). The theories are likely to be promulgated with enthusiasm, some by fascist political parties, as is the case in some European countries (Lieven, 1992). Such theories have surfaced at various times during the twentieth century, being likely to emerge whenever there is anxiety over 'who belongs' within the boundaries of the nation.

A CRISIS OF NATIONAL IDENTITY

Explanations for the intensity of political and popular resistance to the acceptance of former colonial subjects and their descendants as equal citizens of the United Kingdom must be grounded in the history of the British Empire, colonial expansion and Imperialism. The consequences of rule over large numbers of non-white people led during the nineteenth century to a variety of rationalizations for economic and political exploitation. Victorian discussions of 'race' helped to develop a complex collection of pseudo-scientific theories portraying non-whites as everything from 'savage and bestial figures' to 'helpless beings in need of missionary protection' (Rich, 1986, p. 12). The liberal evangelical movement which had achieved the abolition of slavery gradually gave way to a more powerful racial hostility based on economic exploitation, and the incorporation of Darwin's ideas of biological hierarchies led to the development of social Darwinism and claims of a genetic white British superiority over non-white races. Lloyd (1984), an historian of Empire, wrote that by the 1860s British popular opinion regarded 'the Empire's black and brown subjects as natural inferiors'. The idea of a blood brotherhood of white nations was propagated by Victorian eugenicists (Murray, 1905) and the populist idea of 'our kith and kin' survived into the war of independence in Zimbabwe in the 1970s. At the high point of Empire the Anglo-Saxon 'race' was presented as the world's superior group: biologically, economically, politically, linguistically and culturally superior to colonized and non-Anglo-Saxon 'races'. The strength of Victorian beliefs in white racial and cultural superiority has persisted through the ending of colonialism, and still strongly influences the perception of 'who belongs' to the British nation and who does not. The white majority in Britain selectively holds on to remnants of Victorian beliefs in order to sustain a narrow, parochial and intolerant view of who should be included within the boundaries of a national identity.

Those who view the national identity from the point of view of the former colonized have pointed out that as Britain completes a translation from imperial status and ruler of colonies to national status with a dwindling influence on world affairs and an uncertain European future, there is something of a crisis of national identity. Hall (1988) has suggested that in the long post-imperial period the white British are attempting to reconstitute an image of themselves by defining who is not British and those defined as non-white are automatically excluded. Continuing to believe in stereotyped images of inferior cultures and peoples is not a good way to construct a national identity which can be acceptable in the modern world, but Hall has further suggested that it is only by doing this that the British 'know who they are' (Hall, 1988). The Committee of enquiry into the education of ethnic minority children, chaired by Lord Swann (Department of Education and Science, 1985), recognized the strength of feeling against a plural society in which minorities were accepted as equal citizens in that this was seen as 'seeking to undermine an ill-defined and nebulous concept of true Britishness' (p. 7), and noted that attempts by minority groups to claim equal citizenship and also to assert separate cultural, religious or linguistic identities have been met by resentment. There is in Britain, very little discussion as to what a democratic plural society might look like, how the national identity could be redefined and what the values underpinning a modern plural society might be. Instead the crisis of national identity continues to be exemplified externally by a continued reluctance to identity even with other European nations (White, 1994) and a continued resistance to the idea that former imperial subjects and their children be accepted as part of the British nation. Even a winner of a large prize in the British national lottery was, when discovered to be of Asian origin, greeted by racist headlines in the tabloid newspapers (see Sweeney, 1994).

CURRICULUM AND NATIONAL IDENTITY

National identity is bolstered by facts and myths which are recorded in literature, art, science, technology and communication. Transmission of fact and myth via a school curriculum helps shape each generation's view of their national identity and cultural heritage. At one extreme a curriculum can be ethnocentric, xenophobic, monocultural or racist, or it can be open, pluralist, multicultural and antiracist. To understand any nation's curriculum requires a historical understanding of the emphases, omissions and distortions present within a particular curriculum, and of the social groups or controlling elites who have power to influence curriculum decisions. To understand the strength of the exclusive nature of a British national identity there has to be some understanding of the history of British imperialism, colonial expansion and imperial ideologies, and the way in which these ideologies entered the school curriculum. The period 1870–1920, a period in which mass state schooling and a state-influenced curriculum were developing in England, was the high point of Empire and imperialism.

It was during this period of Empire that many aspects of what is now regarded as 'British culture' came to be reflected in the school curriculum, underpinned by a set of values still regarded by many as 'traditional' British values. Some of these values were and are highly questionable in terms of a world-view which was not 'traditional' at all but was created from the 1880s by dominant social and political elites and spread, by education and by imperial propaganda, into popular consciousness (MacKenzie, 1984). This world-view was one in which imperialism, a revived militarism, and unpleasant racial beliefs derived from social Darwinism fused to create a popular consciousness that the English 'race' had a particular superiority vis-à-vis the rest of the world. Historians of English society have dated the period from the 1880s to the 1950s as a time when a 'core ideology' of imperialism emerged, characterized by values of moral superiority, race patriotism and xenophobia (Field, 1982; MacKenzie, 1984).

Theoretical debate about the reflection of cultural values in a curriculum must question who controls and influences the selection of curriculum knowledge, and which social groups or controlling elites have the power to influence curriculum decisions. Lawton described a curriculum as 'essentially a selection from the culture of a society – certain aspects and ways of life, certain kinds of knowledge, attitudes and values, are regarded as so important that their transmission to the next generation is not left to chance' (Lawton, 1975, p. 6) but who makes the 'selection' is of course of the greatest importance. Because the school curriculum is a transmitter of cultural values, curriculum study must focus on the dominant ideas and values which come to be reflected in schools and question the origins of these values.

It is now becoming clearer that the moves made during the 1970s and, 1980s – by teachers, local education authorities, academics and some politicians in government – to influence the curriculum in a more multicultural and global direction were very much resented by powerful right-wing Conservatives and their supporters (see

Hillgate, 1987; Lewis, 1988; Honeyford, 1988; Thatcher, 1993). After the 1988 Education Reform Act and the introduction of a 'national' curriculum, these individuals were able to influence a process of reversing what was only the beginning of a more multicultural curriculum, back into what is fast becoming a 'nationalistic' curriculum (Tomlinson, 1994).

By 1990 an editorial in the Times Educational Supplement suggested that government thinking about minorities had become frankly assimilationist rather than pluralist and that:

> Unspoken anxieties about ethnic differences underlie several different bits of educational policy, all of which are beginning to show a pattern. There seems a definite though unformulated attempt to starve multicultural education of resources and let it wither on the vine. (Times Educational Supplement, 1990)

A MULTICULTURAL CURRICULUM

Moves to disentangle the curriculum from the imperial past began to be made in multiracial schools from the early 1970s. Practitioners in those schools observed that the absence of curriculum policies which took account of the presence of minorities led to the perpetuation of stereotypes, prejudices and misinformation, and the populist view that the presence, cultures and life-styles of minority pupils constituted a problem reinforced a dominant, monocultural curriculum approach. By the late 1970s there was considerable agreement among educationalists that the curriculum needed changing to reflect the multiracial, multicultural society and Britain's changing post-imperial position in the world. There was also some agreement that curriculum change was needed in all schools, not just in multiracial schools. During the 1980s official policy endorsed the development of a curriculum for what official documentation described as an 'ethnically diverse society' (Department of Education and Science, 1985). More teachers began to write about their changed practices and serious attempts were made to define what a curriculum based on multicultural and non-racist approaches would look like (Tomlinson, 1983). The notion of curriculum permeation became popular – practitioners, writers of textbooks, and publishers were thinking more carefully about the incorporation of multicultural and global approaches in science, mathematics, language and literature, the arts, history, geography and social studies, home economics, religious education and other curriculum areas. There was some political leadership in the moves towards a changed curriculum. A 1977 Green Paper, published by the Labour Secretary of State for Education stated quite clearly that

> Our society is a multicultural one and the curriculum should reflect a sympathetic understanding of the different cultures and races that now make up our society...The curriculum appropriate to our imperial past cannot meet the requirements of modern Britain. (Department of Education and Science, 1977, p. 4)

A Committee of Enquiry into the education of ethnic minority children was set up in 1979, and it produced a final report under its second chairman, Lord Swann, in 1985. The Swann Report was perhaps the most consciously multicultural document ever produced in England and represented a high point of political and educational awareness of the need for curriculum change in all schools, to educate all pupils adequately, in an ethnically diverse society (Department of Education and Science, 1985).

However, multicultural curriculum reformers have faced a daunting task. There has been little popular support for teaching all pupils something about the background, cultures and life-experiences of former colonial settlers and their children, and even less for helping white pupils to examine their own attitudes towards minorities. Neither has there been much enthusiasm for re-examining the relationship of Britain to her former Empire, or for re-assessing Britain's place in relation to the rest of the world. There has been instead a growing and determined attack on any such changes in curriculum content or approaches by those educational nationalists who represent multicultural education as subversive of British culture, likely to be associated with left-wing egalitarianism, leading to lowered standards, and having no support from majority or minority parents (Hillgate, 1987, Palmer, 1986, Thatcher, 1993). Changes in a multicultural direction were especially presented as a threat to Conservative Party political values dominant in Britain in the 1980s. At the 1987 Conservative Party conference, the Prime Minister, introducing some of the reforms embodied in the 1988 Education Reform Act, specifically linked left-wing extremism and lowered standards to supposed anti-racist curriculum developments:

In the inner cities where youngsters must have a decent education if they are to have a better future, that opportunity is all too often snatched from them by hard-left education authorities and extremist teachers. Children who need to be able to count and multiply are learning anti-racist mathematics, whatever that may be. (Thatcher, 1987)

Mrs. Thatcher made clear, in her memoirs after leaving office, her opposition to both students and teachers in training being informed about multicultural or anti-racist initiatives (Thatcher, 1993).

Extensive debates on the role of history in the curriculum, bias in historical content and definitions of historical knowledge and skills took place during the 1980s and much criticism of modern history teaching was criticized for concentrating on world history rather than British history, and versions of history which presented colonial history from the point of view of slaves or the colonized were particularly censored (Hastie, 1986). During the 1970s and 1980s, Her Majesty's Inspectors (HMI) consistently noted the need to go beyond a national and nationalistic idea of British history. However, control of subject content in the National Curriculum, imposed on schools in 1988, came to be decided largely by politically appointed working groups which reflected conservative views of traditional British history, or by direct political interference.

A NATIONAL CURRICULUM

Until 1988 central government in the UK did not take a major part in influencing decisions about what to teach in schools. Control of the curriculum was shared between teachers, school governors, local education authorities and examining bodies. The Department of Education and Science influenced the curriculum indirectly through publications giving advice and guidance, and through the activities of Her Majesty's Inspectors. Under the 1988 Education Reform Act, central government took substantial control of the curriculum in all maintained schools. The National Curriculum was intended to:

promote the spiritual, moral, cultural, mental and physical development of pupils at the school, and of society;
prepare such pupils for the opportunities, responsibilities and experiences of adult life. (Education Reform Act, 1988, Section 1.2)

The three core subjects – maths, English, science – and seven foundation subjects – technology, history, geography, art, music, physical education, modern foreign language – plus religious education, were intended to occupy at least 70 per cent of a school timetable; in the remaining time schools were to have discretion to offer other subjects or areas of experience. A task group on Assessment and Testing within the National Curriculum was set up and by December 1987 had produced detailed levels of assessment to test what pupils had 'learned and mastered' at ages seven, eleven, fourteen and sixteen (Department of Education and Science, 1988a). By the time the Education Reform Bill passed into law in July 1988, many practitioners committed to multicultural educational change were considering how to encompass, within a subject framework, the preparation to prepare all pupils for living in an ethnically diverse society. The Act deliberately made no reference to multicultural or non-racist education, although a number of opposition amendments on this were defeated as the legislation passed through Parliament. Lord Pitt of Hampstead, Britain's first black Peer, during a debate in the House of Lords suggested that the first clause of the Act which requires the National Curriculum to prepare pupils for 'the opportunities, responsibilities and experiences of adult life' should continue – 'in a multicultural multiracial society'. However, his amendment was defeated.

Immediate powers to suggest what should be incorporated into the core and foundation subjects lay with the working groups appointed by the Secretary of State. The mathematics group produced proposals in August, 1988, which included an explicitly anti-multicultural statement:

It is sometimes suggested that the multicultural complexion of society demands a 'multicultural' approach to mathematics, with children being introduced to different number systems, foreign currencies and non-European measuring and counting devices. We are concerned that undue emphasis on multicultural mathematics, in these terms, could confuse young children. Whilst it is right to make clear to children that mathematics is a product of diversity, priority must be given to ensuring that they have the knowledge, understandings and skills which they will need for adult life and employment in Britain... we have not therefore included any 'multicultural' aspects in any of our attainment targets. (Department of Education and Science, 1988b, p. 87)

While the idea that children should not learn about other countries' number systems and foreign currencies might seem peculiar, the circumstances surrounding the creation of the National Curriculum for English were even more peculiar. An eminent professor of English language and literature, Brian Cox, was appointed to chair the English working group. His group engaged with debates on standard English, second language speaking, bilingualism and bidialectism:

> We decided that all children must be able to speak and record standard English, but we wanted from the start to dissociate ourselves from the arrogant and ignorant belief that English is superior to all other languages... and a major assumption of the Cox report was that the curriculum for all pupils should include informed discussion of the multicultural nature of British society, whether or not the school is culturally mixed. (Cox, 1993, p. 19)

When the recommendations were submitted to the then Education Minister Kenneth Baker, in May 1989, he frankly disliked it and insisted that it should be printed back to front, starting with Chapter 15, and with the explanatory chapters relegated to an appendix. Cox noted that 'The creation of a national curriculum in English was influenced by several bizarre incidents of this kind' (p. 3). However, the Minister's decisions become less bizarre and more understandable if other moves to suppress multiculturalism and bilingualism in the fledgling National Curriculum are considered.

In August 1988 the Secretary of State for Education wrote to the National Curriculum Council (NCC) requesting that the Council take account of 'the ethnic and cultural diversity of British society and of the importance of the curriculum in promoting equal opportunities for all, regardless of ethnic origin or gender' (Baker 1988). In May 1989 the Council approved the establishment of a Multicultural Task Group and a member of Council who was the head of a large multi-racial school was asked to chair this group. The group was required to prepare for Council, by Easter 1990, guidance on multicultural education in the National Curriculum; suggestions for the incorporation of multicultural issues into the subject-specific non-statutory guidance; and advice on multicultural matters to the Secretary of State's working groups. The group was also to advise on a strategy to deal with multicultural issues in the future. In particular, the group was to examine ways in which the National Curriculum could broaden the horizons of pupils so that they could understand

and respect, learn from and contribute to their multicultural society, and finally, the group was asked to consider the particular curriculum needs of ethnic minority pupils, including bilingual pupils (see Tomlinson, 1993, p. 22).

The group worked to produce a report which they believed would be published as non-statutory guidance to help all schools incorporate a multi-cultural dimension in all National Curriculum subjects and other curriculum areas. The final report, completed by June 1990, set out the aims of effective schools in a multicultural society, offered guidance on planning and developing whole-school policies on multicultural education, some help with planning a multicultural curriculum, including planning for bilingual pupils, and noted the implications for local authorities, governors and parents. In an initial document produced by an NCC officer it was noted that 'the NCC recognises that multicultural education is a controversial area, and the subject of considerable debate, nevertheless it believes that it is a debate which should be central to the thinking of all those throughout the country, with a responsibility for curriculum planning'. The report was intended to be presented to the full Council and the Task Group hoped that it would be published as non-statutory guidance by the autumn of 1990. However, by September 1990 nothing further had been heard of it and two group members wrote asking the Chairman of Council whether it had been presented to the full Council and what the status of the document was. One member wrote that 'nationally such a document is awaited and there is concern that there may be resistance to the publication of a document on multicultural education'. Certainly by the autumn of 1990 local education authorities and schools were beginning to ask what had happened to the report.

What in fact had happened was that over the summer of 1990 Ministers began to have second thoughts about the introduction of any overt references to multiculturalism in the curriculum, and indeed Duncan Graham, the NCC Chairman, who resigned his post in 1991, later wrote that 'it was made starkly clear to NCC by ministers that whatever influence it might have would be rapidly dissipated by entering what was widely seen as a no-go area (multicultural education)' (Graham, 1993, p. 132).

The only publications from the multicultural group were contained in a one-page article in the NCC's own in-house paper and a half-page in a booklet Curriculum Guidance 8: Education for Citizenship (National Curriculum Council, 1990) which noted the implications for Britain of being a plural society. The fate of curriculum guidance designed to persuade young citizens that they live in a multicultural society was perhaps less important than funding for teaching bilingual and second-language speakers, which was progressively cut during the 1980s and 1990s. Controversy about the nature and place of religious education in the National Curriculum has centred on the original requirement in the 1988 Act that such education should be of a 'broadly Christian character', despite the presence of a million Muslims in Britain. Parents have removed their children from schools with minority children, claiming the desire for a 'Christian' education, and evangelical groups and Conservative members of Parliament have led persistent attacks on any religious education syllabus branded as teaching 'a multi-faith mish-mash' (Massey, 1994). The English National Curriculum, even in its second version produced by the Dearing Committee in 1994 (Dearing, 1994), offers little scope for direct teaching about the values and practicalities of a common citizenship for majority and minority students.

EDUCATION AND EQUAL CITIZENSHIP

The need to prepare all young people for a citizenship that transcends class and ethnic divisions and helps them understand the interdependence of individuals, groups and nations, is, however, crucial in the late twentieth century. In Britain, 'how to offer an appropriate and relevant education to young white people, so that they will leave schools able to accept that their equal fellow-citizens, with equal rights and responsibilities, is becoming recognised as a serious question' (Tomlinson, 1990, p. 7). The resistance and antagonism to ethnic minorities in Britain is well documented, particularly as racial attacks and harassment are increasing (Kimber and Cooper, 1991). It is particularly noticeable that people in areas with few minorities are as likely both to deny the reality that Britain is indeed a multicultural, multiethnic society, and to exclude or harass the few minorities that do live in the areas (Gaine, 1988). A study in Norfolk, England, found that 'virtually everyone from ethnic minorities living in rural Norfolk has experienced racial harassment, taunts, discrimination or violence' (Norwich and Norfolk Racial Equality Council, 1984).

While education is undoubtedly *one* vehicle by which knowledge about minorities, intercultural relations, prejudices and ethnic antagonisms can be explicitly offered, the effects may be minimal if non-rational beliefs in white superiority still exist, together with the need to scapegoat minorities for economic and social ills. In historical circumstances in which a majority group recognises itself only through non-rational beliefs in cultural and 'racial' uniqueness and a refusal to acknowledge the valid presence of other groups, it is unlikely that members of the excluded groups will be accepted as equal citizens. If, as is the case in Britain, there is also deep non-rational confusion over questions of origin, 'blood', heritage and tradition, it is unlikely that formal education, even within a more relevant multicultural curriculum, will on its own, have too much effect. However, there was some evidence during the 1980s that curriculum change and teacher awareness were having a limited positive effect on some young people (Department of Education and Science, 1985; Gaine, 1988; Tomlinson, 1990) and it is undoubtedly the case that efforts should be made to counter the influence of curriculum traditionalists and ensure that the National Curriculum encourages multicultural and global understanding.

CONCLUSION

This chapter has discussed one of the major unresolved issues of citizenship in Britain – that of the incorporation of groups perceived as ethnically, racially or culturally different, as equal citizens within the boundaries of a 'British' national identity. There has been little political leadership in redrawing citizenship parameters – politicians and influential figures have been more preoccupied with the exclusion of minorities and a denigration of their cultures, languages and religions, than with their citizenship potentialities and prospects. As Britain moves closer to other European countries via the European Union, it is more important than ever that minorities in Britain are accorded full citizenship rights and recognition that will allow them equal rights as European citizens.

This chapter has documented the crisis of national identity and the rational and irrational beliefs that underpin the reluctance to accept minorities as full and equal citizens. The white British are still attempting to sustain an identity influenced by Victorian beliefs in cultural, political and linguistic superiority. Attempts to change the school curriculum to make it more relevant for a plural, multicultural democratic society have been reversed and a nationalistic National Curriculum is developing which will do little to alter the perceptions of young white people about their minority fellow citizens. Neverthe-less, it is possible to 'reverse the reversals' and use education as one vehicle to create a society in which cultural diversity is respected and minorities have an equal voice in determining the nature and direc-tion of the society in which they live.

NOTES

1. For discussion on the nature of ethnic, and racial groups the reader is referred to Barth (1969), Rex (1986) and Jenkins (1994).
2. Inhabitants of Wales, Scotland and Ireland have continued to maintain an ethnic identity opposed to the English (Hechter, 1975). However, they are generally willing to maintain a common identity in opposition to non-white migrants.

8 Towards European Citizenship

Geoff Hoon

'Will I still be British?' was the pensioner's concerned complaint to her local Euro-MP about the passing of the Maastricht Treaty in 1992. She was only reluctantly reassured that nothing in the Treaty on European Union directly affected her rights as a British citizen. In fact, what the Treaty does, by virtue of Article 8, is to *add* to her rights as a British national by making her a citizen of the European Union. The Treaty on European Union states:

1. Citizenship of the Union is hereby established. Every person holding the nationality of a Member State shall be a citizen of the Union [Article 8(1)].
2. Citizens of the Union shall enjoy the rights conferred by this Treaty and shall be subject to the duties imposed thereby [Article 8(2)] (Treaty on European Union, 1992).

What does such a grand sounding concept as 'Citizenship of the Union' mean in practice? What extra rights will that pensioner, and all other European nationals, enjoy as the result of being a citizen of the European Union? Article 8 continues by setting out four further elements of European citizenship. Article 8a confirms the right to move and reside freely within the territory of the Member States. Article 8b provides for the right to vote and stand as a candidate at municipal and European elections anywhere within the European Union. Article 8c gives an entitlement to protection by the diplomatic or consular authorities of any Member State. Article 8d establishes the right to petition the European Parliament and to apply to the Ombudsman.

This preliminary framework may be supplemented by further rights according to the procedure set out in Article 8e, which allows for the adoption of 'provisions to strengthen or to add to the rights' of European citizenship.

THE RIGHT TO MOVE AND RESIDE FREELY

Even before the Treaty on European Union was agreed, nationals of Member States already enjoyed extensive rights to move, to work and to settle in any other part of the European Union. These rights were set out in the original Treaty of Rome and applied to the economically active and to their dependants. These rights were extended to all European Community nationals by the Single European Act with effect from 30 June 1992. The right to move and to reside is repeated in the Treaty on European Union, 'subject to the limitations and conditions laid down in this Treaty and by the measures adopted to give it effect'.

The main limitation, on this otherwise unqualified right, allows the Member States to refuse the issue or renewal of a residence permit or to expel a person from a Member State on the grounds of public policy, public security or public health. In addition, there are directives dealing with students, pensioners and other 'non-economically active persons'. Where such citizens wish to exercise their rights of free movement, they must be able to show that they will not become a burden on the host State, by having 'sufficient resources' and sickness insurance where relevant. The minimum amount of resources required will be social security payments or their equivalent.

The public policy, public security and public health grounds are likely to be interpreted narrowly under European law. EEC Directive 64/221 provides that no action should be taken against EU nationals amounting to general deterrents or blanket bans. In R. v Bouchereau, the European court held that a criminal conviction can be taken into account only in so far as the conviction provided evidence of 'a genuine and sufficiently serious threat to the requirements of public policy affecting one of the fundamental interests of society'. In practice, this appears to mean that as well as having a relevant previous criminal career, it must be shown that the person involved is likely to re-offend.

THE RIGHT TO STAND FOR ELECTION AND TO VOTE

The Treaty on European Union provides an important extension of the right to stand and vote in local and European elections which has, in the past, been restricted to the nationals of the state where the elections are taking place. Now, as far as local and European elections are concerned, the general proposition has been established that European citizens are free to vote wherever they happen to live within the European Union, irrespective of their nationality. It has been estimated that there are as many as five million European nationals living in European Union Member States other than the one in which they were born. In a sense, Article 8b does no more than give wider effect to the arrangement, long recognized in the United Kingdom, for Irish nationals resident in the United Kingdom to have the right to vote in British elections. However, not all countries will be quite so relaxed about these new rules. Luxembourg, for example, in many respects the very model of European integration, will have its own particular approach. This will try to balance the interests of Luxembourg nationals against the comparatively large number of residents from other Member States, particularly Portuguese citizens, who in some communes are said to make up 54 per cent of the population.

Despite these changes, established for local and European elections, many European national governments seem determined not to extend these rights to national elections. This distinction seems difficult to justify. If an Italian or Greek resident in Britain can vote for a local councillor or a Euro-MP, why not for a Member of Parliament? This reluctance to extend the right of all European citizens to stand for election, and to vote in national elections, does demonstrate the limited commitment on the part of many national governments to the concept of European citizenship.

ENTITLEMENT TO DIPLOMATIC AND CONSULAR PROTECTION

The Treaty on European Union proposes to allow citizens of the European Union to approach diplomatic and consular authorities from any Member State anywhere in the world. This proposal will bring real benefits to the citizens of the smaller European states that have not been able to maintain a comprehensive network of embassies around the world. It will also be welcomed by the Finance Ministries of the larger Member States, particularly if it allows them to share facilities in areas of the world such as central and eastern Europe. There may prove to be some problems in the field of trade competition, as embassies devote increasing amounts of their time to the promotion of their national companies. Whilst it is difficult to see how this could be achieved in common as European Union companies compete for business, the 'Europeanization' of capital may eventually resolve this problem.

THE RIGHT TO PETITION THE EUROPEAN PARLIAMENT AND APPLY TO THE OMBUDSMAN

The right to petition is no more than a restatement of an existing right first introduced into the rules of the European Parliament in 1953. It is now formally set out in Article 138d of the Treaty on European Union. A petition will be considered admissible if it is signed by the petitioner giving name, occupation, nationality and address, and if the subject matter falls within the sphere of activity of the European Union. A special committee of the European Parliament is empowered to deal with petitions and, where appropriate, to investigate, take evidence, draw up a report and request the other institutions to take action on its findings. Over the years, the European Parliament has received a growing number of petitions under this procedure. The majority of petitions are concerned with environmental protection, social security, the recognition of qualifications and taxation.

The right to petition is followed by a complimentary provision in Article 138e, which requires the European Parliament to appoint 'an Ombudsman empowered to receive complaints from any citizen of the Union ... concerning instances of maladministration in the activities of the Community institutions or bodies'. The Council of Ministers and the European Commission have undertaken that almost all of their files will be open to scrutiny by the Ombudsman. The Union's institutions will have to show 'duly substantiated grounds of secrecy' to avoid disclosure. Member States will be able to limit access only to those documents which are 'classed as secret by law or regulation'. How this will be developed in the light of the Council of Ministers' refusal to open up its own internal procedures to public scrutiny remains to be seen.

The Council of Ministers has consistently refused to reveal the position of individual Member States when considering proposals for legislation. The suspicion is that principled objections to particular pieces of legislation are pragmatically 'horse-traded' with other quite different proposals for legislation in order to achieve compromises. It seems unlikely that the minutes of the Council of Ministers, or indeed their preparatory documents, could be 'classed as secret by law or regulation'. Yet in recent proceedings before the European Court of Justice, the Council of Ministers asserted that all such documents must remain confidential. This assertion is likely to be subject to further legal challenge.

EUROPEAN CITIZENSHIP RIGHTS AND IMMIGRATION POLICY

These distinctly limited rights to European citizenship are further constrained by the fact that the definition of who is eligible to citizenship rights is left firmly in the hands of the Member States. There is something of a paradox in the European Union asserting the rights of European citizens whilst leaving it to the Member States to determine eligibility to that status. The Member States will continue to determine who is one of their own nationals and, by virtue of Article 8(1) therefore, who is a European citizen. This is because the debate over entitlement to nationality raises the still controversial question of immigration into the European Union, of how European citizenship is to be obtained, and what rights that will give in the wider Union. Given the obvious pressures on the European Union to take immigrants from a variety of origins, it is hardly surprising that efforts have been made to develop a common European immigration policy. An *ad hoc* Group on Immigration was set up by the Member States in 1986. It operates on an intergovernmental basis and reports to a meeting of Ministers responsible for immigration, the Trevi Group, at the end of each six-monthly presidency of the Council.

The development of immigration policy has had to respond to significant changes in the nature of immigration into western Europe. Immigration that was previously encouraged, to supplement the western European workforce in the 1950s and 1960s, has been largely transformed into settlement immigration as people look to improve their economic prospects on a more permanent basis.

The current picture of immigration into western Europe seems to depend on historical as well as geographical factors. Those factors affect the attitude of existing citizens towards the granting of citizenship to the incomers. For example, immigration into northern European countries from former colonies, mainly into the United Kingdom, Germany, Belgium, the Netherlands and France, is now to a large extent the consequence of the reunification of families. It should continue on humanitarian grounds and, indeed, it is protected by provisions in Article 8 of the European Convention on Human Rights which safeguards a citizen's 'right to respect for his private and family life'. There ought to be few political problems as the numbers involved are comparatively small. Despite this, some countries can still get excited about the problem, and the strict operation of the

United Kingdom's 'primary purpose' rule perhaps best demonstrates how attitudes can affect legislation and its enforcement.

Migration from north Africa has continued; mainly into the southern European countries such as Spain, Portugal, France and Italy. These countries receive significant numbers of immigrants from the other side of the Mediterranean, attracted by the prospect of jobs and higher wages, particularly in the relatively deregulated European tourist economies. Most of these immigrants tend to be single men who have left their families behind temporarily. Understandably, many of them will expect, after a reasonable period of regular employment, to be able to bring their dependants to settle permanently in Europe. They will then expect to enjoy the full rights of European citizenship. The question arises as to whether such rights should be extended to persons whose initial period of residence might not have been legal. And another question arises with respect to the willingness of other countries of the European Union to extend the benefits of citizenship to all residents of other Member States. The growth of far-right political groups and parties in France and Italy appears to be a direct consequence of the exploitation of fears aroused by this recent immigration.

In the late 1980s, with the collapse of communism, there was a growing wave of immigration from countries in central and eastern Europe, particularly from Poland, what was then Czechoslovakia and Romania. It was estimated that in 1989 more than 1.3 million people emigrated from eastern to western Europe. There is also evidence of immigration from the areas of the former Soviet Union. The future flow of immigration will depend entirely on economic and political factors. If the efforts to promote democracy, economic growth and stability prove successful, then this will reduce, if not eliminate, the pressure to move. However, if any of the new states fail economically or politically, there will be a further and significant move westwards. The response of the European Union will depend on its own economic wellbeing at the time.

Immigration from already advanced industrialized countries such as the United States, Canada, Japan, and what is left of the original EFTA (European Foreign Trade Agreement) countries rarely, if ever, arouses political controversy. In 1987 this involved 1.8 million persons; but such people are more likely to want to maintain their citizenship of origin. Nevertheless, there are obviously questions involving the rights of their dependants, as well as reciprocal rights for European Union citizens going in the other direction. And the question arises as to why, in principle, should people from some advanced industrialized countries be treated any differently from poor immigrants from northern Africa.

The pressures from different sources of immigration, combined with the efforts to create a Single European Market, has intensified the debate about a common immigration policy for the European Union. This has to be considered against a background of the very different rules of residence and citizenship operating in the different Member States. Those rules have developed almost entirely haphazardly, partly in response to different national historical attitudes towards former colonies, but also as a more recent reaction to the political pressures that have resulted from previous immigration. For example, Portugal grants full Portuguese citizenship to citizens of Macau, which gives the Macau Chinese all of the rights enjoyed by any other citizen of the European Union. Contrast their position with those Hong Kong Chinese unable to claim rights as a result of the new definition of British citizenship, and who are thereby excluded from EU citizenship. France has defined people from Guadeloupe and Martinique as EU citizens, but not people from its other overseas territories.

In fact, a citizen of Macau will be legally much better off than those legal non-British residents of the United Kingdom who, for whatever reason, have chosen to retain their original nationality. Without current British citizenship they will not automatically be entitled to take advantage of the European Union rules on free movement. In the European Union as a whole, it has been estimated that there are as many as eight million legal residents who are not EU nationals.

The need for a common European approach arises, to a large extent, out of efforts to complete the Single European Market. As Jacques Delors has said, unless 'the philosophies and practices which characterize the immigration policies of the Member States move closer together, the realization of free movement of persons within the large single market will be put to a difficult test'. In this area it is clear that actions by one Member State have profound consequences for the others. In 1991, the European Commission issued two 'Communications on Immigration' and, although the emphasis in the documents is on controlling the sources of immigration, they both acknowledge the need for the strengthening of 'integration policies for legal immigrants'. Amongst these is the adoption of common criteria for re-uniting families. The European Commission recognizes that practices in this field vary widely across the Member States and that, initially, an inventory must be drawn up in order to encourage a greater consistency of approach.

In a similar drive for consistency, a common framework for temporary employment contracts made with non-EU nationals is to be established, based on current practices in Member States. On this matter, it is the European Commission's final recommendation that is crucial; – i.e. equality of treatment of legally resident immigrants is a fundamental objective. The implementation of such a policy means that schooling, vocational training, employment and housing should be non-discriminatory. There has been a determined effort, at the European level, to make equality of treatment a practical reality. The difficulty has been to persuade national governments that they should abandon some national traditions, and perhaps prejudices, for the greater good of a Single European Market. This debate demonstrates the dilemma that is at the heart of European policy-making; particularly policy-making in relation to something as apparently abstract as the rights of the European citizen.

The debate is central to the development of the European Union and cuts across every political issue. It turns upon fundamental questions of whether the European Union is seen as an evolving entity in its own right, with its own rolling programme of institutional and political development, or no more than the collective expression of the Member States agreeing to take common action for limited and well-defined purposes. The idea of granting a common European citizenship is seen by some as a step on the road towards a United States of Europe, where constitutional questions are determined by a centralized bureaucracy in Brussels. Others regard 'Europeanization' as no more than the logical consequence of the (partial) creation of a Single European Market where goods and, of course, people are free to travel across national borders within the external frontiers of the European Union, but where all other questions are left to national governments to determine. Whilst some politicians and citizens are enthusiastic, others are concerned that legal rights extended to European citizens amount to more than those extended to citizens by the individual constitutions and lawmakers of the Member States. In a strict legal sense, of course, European citizens already enjoy certain rights by virtue of a European Constitution, now enshrined in the Treaty on European Union.

The controversy over Britain's 'opt-out' from the Social Chapter highlights some of the difficulties of emphasis. Fourteen member states are prepared to accept the Social Chapter as both a source and a means of implementing a wide range of social rights for their citizens. The United Kingdom, under a Conservative Government, has not been willing to accept such an approach, arguing that these are matters best left to national governments and national legislation. A Labour government would see things differently and would be keen to sign up to the Social Chapter.

A similar debate took place in the negotiations on immigration policy in the lead up to the Maastricht Treaty. The Member States were divided. On one side were those countries that would have allowed the European Union competence, albeit acting unanimously, to adopt measures that would achieve EU policy objectives on such questions as asylum, visas and immigration policy. Those opposed were the Member States that argued that such questions could only be dealt with on an intergovernmental basis, outside the law-making powers of the European Union. The final outcome was inevitably a compromise. Although Article 100c of the Treaty allows the European Union to establish both a common list for those nationals that will be required to produce a visa to cross European Union boundaries, as well as a uniform format for visas, all other questions relating to immigration were left to further intergovernmental negotiation. It is difficult to see how, in the foreseeable future, such negotiations could include allowing the European Union to determine who should be able to take advantage of its citizenship.

TO BE CONCLUDED

The official start of discussions on a further revision of the Treaty on European Union is scheduled for 1996, but it is highly unlikely that this will involve the fundamental constitutional questions raised above. Instead, it is probable that the precise rights set out in Article 8 will, over time, be added to in a way that will provide for a more comprehensive definition of European citizenship. In the longer term, there is the question of whether citizens of the European Union will come to see themselves both as Europeans as well as British or German or French. Some citizens are already willing and able·to accept the idea of multiple identity (see Eurobarometer No 38, 1992; Fountaine 1994). Indeed, some citizens are keen to celebrate their multiple identities. For the moment we can only speculate that whilst some will accept the idea enthusiastically, others might not. Much depends on the content and on the form of influence on citizens – that is to say, on the competing influences provided through education, the media, the political parties and by politicians themselves.

9 Political Citizenship, Activism and Socialist Beliefs

Bryn Jones

It has become fashionable to associate the rise of new forms of political activism with a renaissance of active citizenship, in 'new social movements', and a decline of bureaucratic, corporatist-style, politics (Crook et al., 1992, pp. 147–154). Prompted, perhaps, by 'Red–Green' coalitions in continental Europe, some analysts foresee strategic alliances between traditional left-wing politics and the 'green/peace' movements (Parry et al., 1992, p. 426). However, this focus on the grass-roots activism of new social movements tends to neglect the alternative possibility of a corresponding decline of lay political activism between the mass political parties and the mainstream of the representative democracy – a decline which might, if widespread, have serious implications for the efficacy and mass legitimacy of the broader democratic system.

Since the establishment of universal suffrage, socialist and related parties of the political Left have often led the way in harnessing such mass forms of political activism. Often, in combination with trade unions, they have acted as channels for the promotion of talented individuals into local and national government posts, provided the indispensible armies of volunteers for election campaigns, and served – in a variety of ways – to keep political leaderships aware of changing popular concerns and interests. However, this mass political involvement was always subject to internal organizational tensions over the role of the political activist, and in recent years external social developments have increasingly threatened to undermine it.

This chapter will review the arguments for the centrality of active party members and examine evidence that this contribution to political citizenship is in decline. To simplify the discussion, the term 'active socialists' will be used to refer to members, and ex-members, of the British Labour Party, who have participated, even in minor ways, in its internal and external activities. As the context should make clear, the term 'activists' will be used in the more conventional British sense to refer to individuals who take on regular party duties, normally of a representative nature.

The analysis begins with an overview of relevant theories of political activism, leading on to a brief historical sketch of Labour Party politics in the last few decades. After a further, specific look at the changing link between political culture and political activism, I will argue that the political citizenship of active socialists has hitherto been sustained by political beliefs. However, these beliefs are becoming increasingly remote from the policies, practice and leadership of the contemporary Labour Party. New evidence on members and ex-members from a typically hard-pressed constituency Labour Party illustrates the significance and likely extent of disenchantment with the ideological retrenchment of national leaders. It suggests a weakening of the role of socialist parties, such as Labour, as channels between popular dissatisfactions with market capitalism and the processes of citizenship which have helped to stabilize and moderate that socio-economic system.

CITIZENSHIP AND SOCIALIST ACTIVISM

Despite their early goals of securing power within, or from the national state organs, left-wing and socialist parties such as the Labour Party typically became participants in a range of local and functional civic institutions. Unlike the national representatives, most of this local participation was undertaken on a voluntary or semi-professional basis. In addition, the administration of the party's local electoral machine required an active and mostly unpaid commitment on the part of the rank and file membership. To the extent that the democratic system became synonomous with competition between party programmes, policies and representatives, political citizenship depended on active involvement inside local party organisations.

> The local Parties are... the great training schools of service ... in them, day by day, there is given that devoted, unpaid, freely-rendered work by great numbers of men and women, often unheard of outside their own area. (Hamilton, 1939, pp. 62–63)

The next section assesses whether this voluntaristic commitment, in the specific case of active socialists in local Party organisations, is in decline. So what, firstly, were the preconditions for its development?

One precondition was the large numbers of industrial wage workers who saw in trade unionism and class-based socialist policies the means to ameliorate or transform economic exploitation and deprivation. A second factor was the growing network of local government activities which needed elected representatives and electoral mobilization to define and execute them. A third precondition was the spread of a common political culture which linked the doctrines of socialism – social equality, common ownership, democratic accountability and so on – to the ethos of commitment, involvement and personal participation. Ironically, in some respects, such anti-establishment socialist codes of political conduct sustained and legitimated the existing political system's need for active citizenship.

Particularly in Britain, local Labour Party organizations developed an omnibus function which made them crucial to the national leadership's conduct of Party affairs. Because of the system of single-member parliamentary constituencies local parties dominated the selection, campaigning and promotion of parliamentary candidates. Full-time election agents were employed in many, especially the electorally successful, local parties. However, the specific duties of these agents were controlled not by the national Party bureaucracy but by the local volunteers staffing the constituency party's executive and general management committees. These same local volunteers would also be responsible for all aspects of the Party's local election campaigns. Indeed Labour local government councillors have frequently also held administrative offices in their ward or constituency party organisations.

Since Michels formulated his 'iron law of oligarchy' at the turn of the century (Michels, 1962), it has been a commonplace of political sociology that mass party organisation entails inherent tensions between the rank-and-file and the leadership. In the British case the Labour Party's dependence on volunteer activists to run virtually all local aspects of its activites gave this tension a special twist. Like other European left parties – and consistent with its trade union origins – the organizational ethos of the British Labour Party has been one of democratic centralism. Elected representatives are viewed as delegates but essential authority is given to each, successively, higher tier of the party machine. However, the *de facto* delegation of the administration of electoral campaigning to branch parties, plus a long-standing current of 'municipal socialism' (Bassett, 1984, pp. 82–88, pp. 100–104), has tended to foster a distinct identity amongst local activists. The potency of this identity is periodically demonstrated in matters of procedure and policy such as the running of Party conferences.

In theory the Labour Party constitution enshrines decisions at the annual conference as the guiding principles of national Party policy. In practice the flood of often radical resolutions from the constituency party activists is controlled and dammed – or 'damned' – by leadership powers. The conduct of the conference is controlled by the leadership's dominance of its National Executive Committee which oversees the conduct of the Conference and ratifies the Parliamentary leadership's interpretation and redefinitions of policy. At the Conference itself the numbers of votes allocated to the constituency parties are dwarfed by those of the large trade union delegations, whose leaders have normally preferred elite control, in concert with the Parliamentary leaders, to support for rank-and-file radicalism. Significantly, the Party's deepest recent period of crisis, from 1975 to 1983, involved a deviation from this alignment; when sections of the Parliamentary and union leadership sided with the radical Left element amongst the constituency parties.

This brief picture of socialist activism in the Labour Party is necessary because most of the systematic analysis of the phenomenon is subsumed within the study of party organizations. The significance of local activists is neglected either because the party is taken as a 'unitary actor' or because the identification of the principal power in the leadership or bureaucracy focuses attention at these levels (Daalder, 1983, pp. 21–23). Perforce, the wider significance and status of the activists has to be situated within the debates about their context – the mass party.

Duverger's characterisation of the mass party provides a useful 'ideal type', in both the positive and negative aspects of that term, for the role of the activists and specific cases such as the Labour Party. Mass parties, in Duverger's view exemplified: high participation, permanent and capillary organisation, systematic social programmes, coherent ideology, and subjugation of the parliamentary party to the extra-parliamentary party and to the programme (Duverger, 1954, and the précis in Bartolini 1983b, p. 220). As the preceding sketch makes clear, the Labour Party has not achieved the last of these properties. Moreover, as the next section shows, it has also failed the coherent ideology criterion. Duverger's characterization is, therefore, more useful as a guide to the model form a mass party ought to take if it were to function effectively.

This point is made more relevant by political scientists' recent diagnosis of the decline of the mass party and the styles of political activism associated with it. It has been conjectured that the ideologically and class-based parties have declined as more pragmatic, issue-based, types of political activity capture the interests of an increasingly segmented and instrumental electorate. A related interpretation is that mass parties have metamorphosed into 'catch-all' parties trying to win votes across the social spectrum on issues beyound their principal class-ideological constituency. In much of continental Europe this trend has been also associated with the provision of public funding which has diminished, in part, the previous reliance on mass membership (Bartolini 1983a, pp. 208–209). In Britain there is no public funding of parties, so the Labour Party continues to be dependent on its membership – increasingly so as it tries to reduce its historic reliance on direct and indirect trade union funding. As the following analysis also indicates, many of Labour's recent and continuing difficulties are linked to a perceived need to achieve Duverger's condition of coherent ideology as a social glue between the membership on the one hand and the Party bureaucracy and leadership on the other.

POLITICAL CULTURE AND PARTY ACTIVISM

In Parliamentary and in local government elections Labour Party candidates are often locally-known activists. This does not mean that they are necessarily members of the local communities covered by the electoral boundaries. It is an exaggeration, therefore, to say that they are motivated by the immediate concerns and experiences of those communities that they try to represent (Forrester, 1976, pp. 100). For these activists/representatives the relevant community and pattern of beliefs are thus more likely to be the political community of councillors and other Party activists (Hampton, 1970, p. 49).

Political scientists have proposed three main reasons, 'incentives', for Party activism. These are, firstly, immediate personal material gains: money, gifts, favours. The second reasons are intangible rewards which come from collective participation: personal prestige, or enjoyment of the participation amongst the political reference group. The third is a 'purposive' or abstract reason: long term, universalistic gains which, if they are material, will accrue to a much wider section of the population (Ware, 1985, p. 71). Socialist beliefs in full employment, the welfare state, or collective ownership of the means of production clearly fall into this category. For most individuals, active Labour Party membership provides little direct opportunity for patronage benefits of the first category. The most plausible reasons for active involvement will either be the personal – abstract benefits of collective involvement and status, or the concern for 'purposive' goals which can bring little or no direct personal benefits. The importance of abstract – collective, purposive motivations is re-inforced by Inglehart's observation on the recent growth of alternative social movements – the peace, environmental and women's campaigns:

> ... people do not act unless they want to attain some goal, the existence of problems and organisations would have no effect unless some value system or ideology motivated people to act. (Inglehart, 1990, p. 42)

At the very least, therefore, we can say that some sort of universalistic principle is a necessary, if not a sufficient condition for motivating active membership within socialist Parties such as the British Labour Party. Yet, critiques of Labour Party values have been able to make much of the Party's inability to fashion these into a coherent ideology which mobilizes its potential supporters, inside and outside the movement, and challenges the assumptions of the predominantly conservative national value system (Forrester, 1976, p. 51; Nairn, 1965, p. 175). The evidence suggests that unequivocal socialist ideologies are indeed rare in the Labour Party, but what counter-ideology there is tends to be more common amongst activists. Forrester's 1973 study of Brighton's Kemptown consituency Party found that class struggle sentiments were more pronounced amongst activists than amongst the non-active membership. 'Creating social equality' and 'public ownership of production' (*sic*) were the first and second most popular values of the activists but were only sixth and seventh amongst the rest of the members participating in the survey.

Later in the 1970s, of course, more radical socialist ideas came to dominate constituency parties in a way that approximated a distinct and coherent anti-Establishment ideology. A development that is discussed below in the next section.

Drucker's distinction between doctrine as a system of abstract ideas and the practical ethos of organizational behaviour provides a more subtle characterization of Labour's political culture. In the post-war period, argues Drucker, Labour's doctrine was composed of beliefs in public ownership, planning and various concepts of equality. Its ethos, on the other hand, consisted of social norms of unity, loyalty, life-style and thrift (Drucker, 1979). Drucker's list is hardly systematic. It awaits refinement by a thorough sociological study. More importantly, the ethos – ideology distinction needs exploring to determine how the two types of belief can interact, in both complementary and contradictory ways.

However, if motivations to party activism can be divided into the personal-participation rewards and purposive-generalized goals referred to above, then these correspond closely to Drucker's ethos and doctrine aspects of ideology. By participating in an organizational ethos expressing norms such as loyalty, collective endeavour and a committed life-style, active members could gain an element of self-esteem and sense of psychological reward. Alternatively, or in combination with the personal–participative incentives, other activists would be 'rewarded' by pursuing universalistic–collective goals defined by egalitarian, collectivist, rational planning (etc.) principles. The homogeneity and coherence within and between the personal–participative ethos and the purposive–ideological doctrine should not be exagerated. However, a case could be plausibly made that for much of the post-war period this link helped to sustain the commitment and validity of party activism amongst the branch constituency parties.

THE RISE AND FALL OF IDEOLOGICAL UNITY

The preceding thesis is supported by the turbulence and fragmentation of local activism which occurred when both doctrine and ethos erupted into Labour's governing circles from the 1970s onwards. After its electoral defeat by the Conservatives in 1979 the Party's political stance shifted to the left. Public ownership, state intervention in the economy, nuclear disarmament and increased welfare provision became prominent Party policies, which were associated with an alliance between left-wing MPs, some trade union leaders and coalitions of activists in the constituency parties. This leftward shift was accompanied by an increase in grass-roots influence by Trotskyist organisations, especially the Militant Tendency. Right-wing opinion in the Parliamentary Party and leadership was weakened when ex-Cabinet ministers and several MPs decamped to form the centrist

Social Democratic Party. Although this split probably had little effect on the mass membership, it may have served to strengthen the left political sentiments and identity at local level.

The catastrophic election defeat of 1983 ended the high tide of this combination of Leftism and constituency activism. Under the leadership of Neil Kinnock, and subsequently the late John Smith, centrist and right-wing opinion re-grouped and began a series of reforms to the Party organization and policies. Trotskyist activists were expelled and their influence curtailed. The influence of 'activist democracy' was reduced by reasserting National Executive powers over the selection of certain Parliamentary candidates, by requiring membership ballots in leadership elections, and by reducing the influence of the Annual Conference of all delegates, in the formation of policies. Along this route, commitments to nuclear disarmament, nationalization and higher public spending were dropped or minimized by the leadership.

It is difficult to assess the impact on ordinary Party members of this accelerating swing away from the doctrines and ethos that had intensified in the late 1970s and early 1980s. Presumably many activists as well as ordinary members were chastened by voters' preference for Thatcherite rather than 'socialist' reforms. Although this author's experience is that anecdotal evidence of individual disenchantment is easy to uncover, there have been also been cases of formerly prominent leftist activists adopting markedly more moderate and centrist stances, not dissimilar to the rightward shift of Neil Kinnock himself. Moreover, the national evidence is that most Party members have not so far strongly opposed greater leadership control of the Party, nor the procedural reforms that are supposed to have weakened the influence of local organizations (Seyd and Whiteley, 1992, p. 240–244).

However, this evidence was collected before the Party's fourth successive General Election defeat in 1992, the replacement of the formerly leftist Kinnock as Party leader by the explictly centrist Smith, and then in 1994 by Tony Blair – who has made ideological moderation of the Party a centrepiece of his electoral strategy. From the point of view of Party members, especially active socialists, one might expect disillusionment with the Party's continuous dismantling of traditional procedures and ethos, and socialist doctrines and policies. Not only did the leadership push through these changes over a ten-year period but they did not result in the promised return to electoral success and a Labour government.

Until recently, leadership campaigns to recruit large numbers of new members have not had great success. It therefore seems likely that a majority of Party members might retain a basic attachment to the older ethos and ideological principles that preceded the 'modernization' programmes of the last ten years. As Seyd and Whiteley comment, while the Party as a whole 'remains unclear about its underlying beliefs', the leadership's attempts to promote a Statement of Democratic Socialist Aims and Values in the late 1980s had little impact – 'the membership does have principled commitments'. The latter authors found majority support for the 'socialist touchstones' of: 'public ownership', 'the legitimacy of trade unions', reduced and non-nuclear defence spending, and 'high public expenditure' (Seyd and Whiteley, 1992, p. 44–45). However, it could be questioned whether these four aims constitute underlying ideological / philosophical beliefs, or the guiding principles for particular policy areas. The more recent attempt to recast the Party's basic aims and values, and thus also the associated commitment to public ownership, by Tony Blair and his colleagues, might therefore offer a more decisive test of the nature and strength of the beliefs of Party members and activists.

SOUTHTOWN – A MICROCOSM OF ACTIVIST DECLINE

Labour has been much exercised in recent years by the decline of its share of the vote amongst southern electors. Especially in the consumer boom of the 1980s, the affluent, house-owning, under-unionized, service-sector workers and voters of the South were seen as the paradigmatic electorate of the 'new times' which had been captured by the market-driven consumerism of Thatcherism. This characterization was strengthened by the electoral geography of the 1980s. Labour continued to hold most of its vote in the large cities and industrial areas of the North, Scotland and Wales; but after the 1987 general election it was left with no seats outside and south of London and Bristol. In a series of pamphlets the Labour MP Giles Radice has argued for the indispensibility of this southern region for a Labour victory, and for the continuing disenchantment of lower- and middle-class voters with Labour's image and programmes (cf. Radice and Pollard, 1993).

However, this lack of rapport is not solely explicable in terms of a direct relationship between voters and the national Party and its leaders. Seyd and Whiteley argue that more and more active members in the local parties can enhance Labour's share of the vote in those localities by several percentage points; at least enough to have swung key marginal constituencies to Labour in the 1987 election (Seyd and Whiteley, 1992, p. 195–198). Local parties, activism and local government successes can also influence perceptions of potential Labour voters.

Although London and south-east England have high proportions of the total Party membership, these may reflect only high population density in those areas; they do not not translate necessarily into Labour activism, nor sucesses in local government elections. Indeed, for much of the 1980s and early 1990s Labour failed to hold or gain control of councils throughout the southern and south-western counties. In many cases it was the Liberals and SDP, and their successor party the Liberal Democrats, which were the most successful competitors for the Tories, capturing a number of county and borough councils. For many southern Party members these circumstances indicate a depressed and isolated condition. From 'above' they seem to have been increasingly distanced, both ideologically and organisationally, from the Party leadership, while, from below, shifts in electoral opinion and attenuation of local government influence have increased members' and activists' marginal status.

Southtown conforms closely to this characterization. Its electorate of 60,000 has fallen increasingly away from the heights of Labour support in the 1960s; when there was a Labour-controlled council and the Party came within a few hundred votes of taking the Parliamentary seat from the Conservatives. In the intervening years manufacturing employment contracted, service sector jobs increased and the proportions of professional and managerial jobs grew steadily. The Liberal Democrats and their predecessors gradually usurped Labour as the main challengers to the Conservatives in local and Parliamentary elections, taking control of the council in 1994.

In late 1994, in cooperation with the local Labour Party officers, I undertook a sample postal survey of Party members and ex-members. The aim was to assess the importance of political beliefs for continuing membership and local activism. The detailed findings from this survey would take us beyond the remit of the present article. However, the reasons for leaving the Party, the decline of activism, and the extent of commitment to socialist ideals all shed additional light on the outlook and plight of members and activists represented in broader national terms by the Seyd and Whiteley study.

LEAVING AND LOWERING INVOLVEMENT

Seyd and Whiteley reported a general decrease in activity amongst the national membership. However, because theirs was a survey of current members it cannot compare current members with those who have left the Party. The Southtown study was explicitly designed to examine the differences in views between those who have quit the Party, those who have remained members but have lowered their involvement and activism, and Party members who remain, or have become, active. Thus one likely pattern, in view of the preceding account of national de-radicalization, organizational change and electoral decline might be that older activists and members, with more left-wing views, have become disillusioned and either left the Party or decided to be less active. Alternatively, it might be hypothesized that modernization, moderation and recruitment drives by the Party leadership have attracted more moderate new members and motivated less leftist individuals to be more active. The data partly support the first of these two views, but not the second; at least in constituency parties which resemble Southtown.

Rather than compress their views into predefined options, members and ex-members were asked to describe what they thought was Labour's most important social or economic goal. These responses were then classified into ten types of aim:

1. Increased provision of welfare and public services, such as health and education;
2. Action to regenerate the economy, or social aspects of this, such as curbing unemployment, income redistribution etc;
3. Strictly political or constitutional aims, related to the exercise of power or government;
4. Cultural or ideological aims, such as changing moral or political values;
5. Short-term electoral objectives, such as campaign strategies;
6. Radical changes in social structure, e.g. redistribution of property, dismantling class divisions, etc;
7. Combinations of economic and social welfare policies, otherwise separable under 1 and 2 above;
8. Organizational changes to the Labour Party itself;
9. Environmental and 'peace' objectives, such as nuclear disarmament, or scrapping nuclear power stations;
10. Multiple aims, covering three or more of the above categories.

Thirty-one per cent of the sample had left the Party within the last five years.[1] But there was little difference between these 'leavers' and those who remained as members. For both groups the most important goals for Labour were defined as welfare and public services (goal 1), followed by economic intervention (goal 2), or goal 6 – measures which combined economic and welfare aspects. As Table 9.1 shows, very small minorities thought that 'green', 'peace', or internal Party or electoral aims should take priority. Indeed there was little difference between such electoral and constitutional enthusiasts and the numbers favouring radical social transformation as the goal. It can safely be said, therefore, that a clear majority of both current and ex-members favour traditional post-war Labour priorities of social amelioration through welfare provision, enhanced public services and economic regeneration. The description of the economic improvement goal was also, invariably, in terms of state intervention, or improvements that would benefit disadvantaged groups such as the unemployed, rather than better management of the economy as a whole.

Table 1 also shows that there was also little difference between activists and non-activists in their preferred priorities for Labour. Amongst those who considered themselves active members a total

Table 9.1 Most preferred Labour Party goals amongst non-active and active members and ex-members

Active now or in past	Welfare	Economic action	Welfare and economy	Social structure	Election	Constitution
	%	%	%	%	%	%
Yes	21	21	26	9	8	1
No	24	14	22	12	16	8
All	22	19	25	10	10	3

of 68 per cent rated welfare, economic improvement, or a combination of these, as the most important goals. Amongst those who were not not active, electoral aims ranked slightly higher; but those favouring this priority were still outnumbered by those who rated welfare, then welfare with economic improvements, as most important.

However, the most significant finding related to the importance attached to common ownership. At the end of the questionnaire

respondents were asked whether 'collective ownership and democratic control of key social and economic resources (not necessarily
nationalized industries)' should be 'a central Labour goal'. The question was phrased in this way in order to recall the sentiments of
Clause 4, paragraph 4 of Labour's 1918 constitution, while avoiding
conflation solely with the policy of nationalization. Table 9.2 shows
that, overall, almost 78 per cent of current and ex-members agreed
that common ownership and democratic control should be a central
goal for Labour. The differences between those who were currently,
or had previously been active, and non-active members was negli-
gible: 78 per cent and 76 per cent respectively. Even more interesting
were the views of common ownership by members and ex-members.
Ex-members were, overall, slightly less supportive of this principle.
While a massive 84 per cent of current members thought common
ownership should be central, a clear but lower majority, (64 per
cent) of ex-members thought so.

Table 9.2 Support for common ownership (not necessarily nationalization) amongst active members, members and ex-members

Support common/ ship?	Was active %	Never active %	Left party %	All %
Yes	78	76	67	78
No	16	12	18	13
Don't know	9	12	12	9

May not sum to 100 because of rounding

Overall these figures suggest that, in Southtown at least, the Party
members with more more radical left-wing views have not left the
Party or stopped being active solely on ideological grounds. There is
little difference in preferred priorities between active and inactive
members, nor between members and leavers. Even members and ex-
members share similar beliefs in the priority of some mixture of
welfare state, economic interventionism, and social ends for economic policy. On these measures of ideological perspective there is
little difference between activists and non-activists – a finding which
departs from Seyd and Whiteley's assessment of a more radical, left-
wing ideological stance amongst activists.[2]
Moreover, on the political–ideological touchstone of common
ownership, the nub of recent debates on the reorientation of the

Party's goals, supporters of this principle are more likely to have stayed in the Party than leave it. A new Party constitution which eliminates common ownership is thus more likely to offend current members than it is to confirm the worst suspicions of ex-members; even though a majority of the latter also suppport the kind of sentiments expressed in the old Party constitution. If, however, leavers and non-active members are not more left-wing in their political beliefs than members and active members, why did they leave or become less active?

DETATCHMENT FROM THE PARTY: THE ROLE OF EXTERNAL FACTORS

Two broad classes of political motive might reduce activity or lead to departure from the Party. One is the rival attraction of other social and political activities. If exclusion from power and de-radicalization have made the Labour Party a less effective channel of political action and protest, members might have become more involved in other, external movements or activities. Theories of the rise of 'New Social Movements' would lead us to expect some such transfer of allegiances. One major study of citizen participation has claimed that 'old' left-wing activism may overlap with new social movement politics (Parry, Moyser and Day, 1992, p. 224). This possibility is especially plausible for an area like Southtown, in which the professional middle class, various environmental protests and other socio-political forums, and Green Party activism have all grown in recent years.

The second type of political motive is a more general disenchantment with the rightward drift of Party policy and rhetoric in the late 1980s and early 1990s. For generations of members who joined or became active during the rise of leftist influence and policies in the late 1960s and 1970s, this seemingly decisive shift to the right might have had a demoralizing effect. Why stay within, or be active in, a Party whose general interest in the the socialization programmes of the 1945 government, let alone the goals of 1970s Bennite socialism, seems to have evaporated? This second influence seems especially plausible in the light of the dominant political priorities amongst Southtown's Labourites described above. Few of these referred to the Party's more recent aims of promoting constitutional change, or targeting of equal opportunities for women or other socially-marginal groups.

Once again, however, the survey responses do not correspond unambiguously with either the rival pull of new social movements, nor with the internal 'push' of ideological disenchantment, as reasons for inactivity or leaving. Distaste for the stances taken by the national Party is partly confirmed in Table 9.3. 'Policy or leaders of the national Party' was 'definitely' or 'partly' an important reason for leaving for 47 per cent of the responses. However, this figure was exceeded by the 70 per cent of citations of 'financial reasons' as definitely or partly important; and the 70 per cent of references to the importance of 'too many other commitments'.[3]

Activities in 'new social movements' did not figure prominently in these 'other commitments'. Both leavers and current members were able to say whether they were now less involved with Labour and more with other social or polical movements or organisations; e.g. the women's movement, trade unions, environmental campaigns. Only 15 per cent of current members and 19 per cent of ex-members were active in other social or political organizations. Amongst those less active members that did report activity elsewhere, the most common involvement – of over half the members – was trade union or other labour movement activity. Although environmental causes were the next most popular activity, these involved less than a quarter of the 'otherwise engaged'. Amongst ex-members the dominant activities were again trade unions, and voluntary bodies dealing with various kinds of local welfare.

The primary reasons for reduced activism are set out in Table 9.4. This pattern was similar to the reasons for leaving the Party. 'Job and/or financial reasons' were 'definitely' or 'partly' influential in 76% of the responses. Some respondents, who reported being less active, did not state fully the relative importance of the reasons for inactivity. Yet a large majority of members and a slightly smaller majority of ex-members thought that the job/financial factor was definitely or partly relevant.

Amongst those who assessed 'Party policy/activities,' a smaller majority of members thought that this was to some extent relevant. Moreover, of those who elaborated on the 'other' reasons for their reduced activism, some aspect of local or national Party affairs was frequently cited. By a small majority the ex-members dealing fully with this point said that the Party itself was an irrelevant reason for lowering their involvement – presumably prior to their giving up membership. In contrast, 'other social or political commitments' were deemed definitely or partly influential by noticeably smaller

Table 9.3 Importance of various reasons for leaving the party

Factor influential in leaving Party?	Finances	%	Not asked	%	Other commitment	%	National Party	%	Local Party	%	Changed views	%
Definitely	13	23.2	8	17.4	8	17.8	5	12.5	10	23.8	0	0
Partly	16	28.6	10	21.7	23	51.1	14	35	16	38.1	15	40.5
Not relevant	27	48.2	28	60.8	14	31.1	21	52.5	16	38.1	22	59.5
	N = 56		N = 46		N = 45		N = 40		N = 42		N = 37	

Table 9.4 Importance of reasons for reduced activity

Important	Personal Number	%	Party Number	%	Other commitm't Number	%	Financial Number	%	Own reasons Number	%
Definitely	38	35.9	19	22.3	7	10.4	37	37.3	29	70.7
Partly	42	39.6	26	30.6	14	20.9	38	38.4	12	29.3
Not at all	26	24.5	40	47.1	46	68.7	24	24.2	0	0
	N = 106		N = 85		N = 67		N = 99		N = 41	
	*= 79		*= 100		*=118		*= 86		*= 144	

Note: *= Number not responding at all to this factor

numbers of both members and ex-members. Only 22 per cent of all respondents said that they were less involved with Labour and more with other social or political movements or organizations. Moreover, amongst those who said that they had reduced their level of activity in the Party, only 12 per cent said such 'external' activities were 'definitely' a reason. Of these, less than half, 40 per cent, of members, and only 20.5 per cent of ex-members thought that it was an influence.[4]

In sum, reduced activism and departure from Southtown Labour Party can be largely attributed to either internal political factors or external personal – economic influences. The most cited reasons for leaving or declining involvement in the Party were either financial and job-related or, for the leavers, 'too many other commitments'. The small numbers of both leavers and members involved in other social and political organizations strongly suggests that 'other commitments' are more likely to be related to domestic, family, or informal social responsibilities. Widespread pressures on employment, incomes and general economic security since 1989, coupled with increases in working hours, are likely to form a large part of these job-related and financial preoccupations. Similarly, there is no reason why Labour Party members should be sheltered from the increasing demands of caring for children or elderly relatives, as institutional services have been dismantled or reduced. These trends, plus other shifts towards more employment for married, co-habiting and single mothers, must also have had an impact on the 'time-budgets' of members' households (Lee and Piachaud, 1992, p. 76–78; Gershuny, 1989, Figure 1, Horrel et al., 1994, p. 119–120, 128).

However, the Party policies, activities and leadership at national level did constitute the second most important reason for reduced activity and leaving. The questionnaire did not allow a more specific identification of the precise Party-political policies or stances which had discouraged members from activism. However a few such respondents added spontaneous comments suggesting that either political incompetence or the rightward shift in their leaders' policies and ideology fuelled their dissatisfactions. The significance of these hints is supported by the preponderance of members and ex-members believing in welfare and economic policies of a broadly egalitarian and re-distributive nature, and their predominant support for common ownership. Compared to these beliefs and expectations, the caution and moderation of the Labour leadership's programmes is highly likely to be discouraging.

CONCLUSION

Party activists have been the core of the volunteers who have staffed the electoral and local political systems of post-war British society. The decline of activism, allegedly an international phenomenon, therefore weakens the functioning of political citizenship. The case of the British Labour Party illustrates both the importance and elusiveness of Duverger's prerequisite of ideological coherence for the functioning of the mass party. The fit between official Party doctrine and local organizational ethos seem to have come under increasing strain since their partial, but ultimately unworkable, union in the rise of the extra-Parliamentary Left in the 1970s and early 80s.

Southtown, in many respects a typical case of both Labour's organizational and electoral decline in the South of England, illustrates some probable causes of the decline of activism. Here the Labour Party's failures in national elections have been exacerbated by lack of success in local elections. Whilst this must have some effect on the morale of members and their commitment to the Party, relatively few respondents to the survey volunteered this as a reason for leaving the Party or for reducing their activity within it.

A variety of personal, family and financial concerns and commitments were the most common reasons for leaving the Party. These types of factor also predominated as reasons for reducing levels of activity within the Party. However, the numbers who attributed their detachment to the activities, policies, or leaders of the Party were only slightly smaller. There is insufficient evidence to claim a direct causal relationship between members' political beliefs and their antipathy to Labour leaders' modernization and moderation programmes. However, the large majorities favouring both traditional Labour welfare and economic interventionist goals and support for common ownership, suggest strongly that such beliefs are a key factor reducing faith in the national Party's efficacy.

As for the the broader issues about the contribution of socialist political involvement to processes of political citizenship, the findings from Southtown are even more critical. Activism within the Party does spill over into participation in the wider democratic process – providing channels for candidature of civic offices, mobilizing ordinary voters in elections, providing organizational support for local councillors and the electoral process itself. Increasing detachment from Labour can only weaken the Party's political contribution to democracy, especially as more centrist parties appear to have fewer ties with the lower social classes. Moreover, there is little evidence from Southtown that 'new social movements' – women's, environmental, peace, movements etc. – constitute alternative causes, or vehicles of political activism, for disaffected socialists. They seem to adhere to their traditional beliefs when they leave or become inactive in the Labour Party. Under the twin impact of ideological isolation and the personal economic pressures of an increasingly individualized society, they are lost to the wider political arena and democratic processes.

Other evidence has shown that pressures of reduced earnings and more female employment are restricting the 'time-budgets' of family households. Often these will be the women and men whose personal circumstances should provide strong motives for participation in the kind of social reforms and economic rights associated traditionally with the labour movement. However, the pressures of expanding work and family commitments seem, on the Southtown and other evidence, to be diminishing the 'free' time and finances such groups have for political participation. Therefore strong ideological motivators would seem to be even more important to stimulate individuals to devote their precious free time to political actions which confer no material compensation.

In this respect the Southtown data tend to confirm Inglehart's claim that 'people do not act unless they want to attain some goal', one defined through a common ideology. The Southtown findings corroborate Seyd and Whiteley's evidence for Drucker's thesis on the interlocking strength of ethos and doctrine amongst Party rank and file. Many Labour Party members share a common belief in collective and redistributive solutions to practical social and economic problems. These views, embedded in the ethos of Party membership, are expressed in the belief in common ownership and democratic control of economic and social resources. This belief may have a utopian tenor but it also seems contiguous, in members' minds, with their other views on more practical and immediate issues, such as poverty and employment.

The two trends noted at the beginning of this paper, towards ideological moderation and pragmatism within the Labour Party, and the rise of a 'new politics' of social movements outside it, do not seem likely to regenerate political activism amongst its traditional membership. The 'New Labour' project of the Blair leadership has begun to replace the framework of beliefs in economic and social interventionism with an ethical socialism expressed in abstract values. Judged by the depth of feeling for traditional socialist beliefs in Southtown, there must be considerable uncertainty as to whether this leadership strategy will fuel renewed commitment or, instead, weaken still further active involvement in the Party. In view of the absence of any metamorphosis into alternative political action, even into activism in the less political aspects of the new social movements, the long-term deficit for political citizenship may be even more severe.

NOTES

1. The ex-members were not part of the same random sample as current members. The latter sample was taken from current membership lists. The ex-members' names came from a separate record of 'lapsed members'. The principal research instrument was a postal questionnaire, which was returned by a total of 196 members and ex-members constituting 38 per cent of lapsed members, 25 per cent of current members, and a response rate of 56 per cent. Further discussion of aspects of this survey is due to appear in the journal *Sociology*.

2. Size of national sample and designation of ideological profiles may partly explain the contrast with the closer correlation of activism and left-wing ideological views detected by Seyd and Whiteley. With a large national sample of 8,075 covering 450 constituencies, representation for different types of constituency would clearly be difficult. Seyd and Whiteley opted for a more realistic stratification of sample by region (Seyd and Whiteley, 1992, p. 221). Thus these average figures are not necessarily representative of the distribution of views amongst Party members in any particular constituency. The classification of ideological perspective used in that national survey also differ from those used for Southtown. In the former the basis was self-designation of respondents on a left–right scale of political views relative to other Party members and the general public (Seyd and Whiteley, 1991, pp. 81–82, pp. 99–102). For Southtown ideological position was interpreted through the respondents' own definitions of Labour's priorities, plus their evaluation of the principle of common ownership. While this crude device does not allow the construction of sophisticated scales of ideological values, it might be questioned whether political and social beliefs are in principle translatable into such unidimensional quantities.

3. Almost 50 per cent of ex-members cited their own 'other' reasons for leaving. The most common reference was some form of disappointment with the Party; either electoral, organizational, or procedural. The next most common type of 'other' reason was personal/familial: health, childcare, geographical mobility.

4. This finding problematizes the inference made in Seyd and Whiteley's national survey, where they reported high levels of membership in outside

organizations, such as 'green' and peace groups, and deduced that Party members are also 'involved in many kinds of political campaigns' (Seyd and Whiteley, 1992, p. 93). On the Southtown evidence it seems that membership of external socio-political organizations does not translate into activism within them.

10 Citizenship, Welfare Rights and Local Government

Ruth Lister

The key task of an 'enabling and empowering' local authority in providing effective community governance is 'to build citizenship'. This statement by John Stewart (1993) provides the starting point for this chapter which takes that theme further, with a particular emphasis on social or welfare rights which cannot be ignored in any discussion of citizenship.

This chapter will address three main questions. First, what do we mean by citizenship? How is the concept being used in political debate? Second, what is the meaning of citizenship for disadvantaged groups? If we divide citizenship into its civil or legal, political and social components, we can see the ways in which poverty and other forms of social division are corrosive of people's citizenship rights and undermine their ability to fulfil their citizenship obligations (see also Lister, 1990). Finally, what are the implications for local government? What *can* a local authority do to 'build citizenship'? I do not claim to have all the answers but I hope, at least, that in posing the questions in this way I can contribute to how we think about the role of local government in promoting citizenship.

CITIZENSHIP: A CONTESTED CONCEPT

The language of citizenship made something of a comeback in the late 1980s. It is a concept with generally positive connotations, unless, of course, you are the victim of increasingly restrictive citizenship laws. But it is being used in very different ways at different points in the political spectrum, for it is an 'essentially contested concept' (Gallie, 1955–6).

On the right, the emphasis has been on:

- the obligations of citizenship, in particular the obligation of poor citizens to work and of absent parents to provide adequate financial support for their children, in both cases with implications for people's rights as citizens. The aim has been to undermine

the post-war notion of citizenship as carrying rights and the expectations of the State founded on such a conception;
- *active citizenship*, an idea promoted in particular by Douglas Hurd to soften the harsher edges of Thatcherite individualism. It represents a more traditional, paternalistic form of Conservatism which seeks to mitigate growing inequalities by means of charitable giving and good works;
- the citizen as *consumer or customer* as exemplified by the Citizen's Charter. As John Stewart (1993) argued, this narrow approach cannot capture the essence of the relationship between government and the public.

For some on the centre left, the rediscovery of the language of citizenship has represented a reaction against the arid tenets of market liberalism without a return to full-scale collectivism. Citizenship has been seen as a way of reconciling the individual and the social.

Some have placed all the emphasis on rights; others have sought a balance between rights and obligations, with a growing emphasis on the latter as the 'discourse of obligations' increasingly overtakes that of rights (Roche, 1992). Some, such as Charter 88, have focused almost exclusively on civil and political rights of citizenship, while others have argued that such rights can only be meaningful for the disadvantaged if underpinned by social rights (see e.g. Lister, 1993b).

Some of the more radical writings on citizenship have sought a way of reconciling what is essentially a universalist concept with a recognition of the importance of difference and diversity, so that citizenship has, for example, something to offer women as well as men; black people as well as white people; disabled people as well as non-disabled people; gay men and lesbians as well as heterosexuals. They have also emphasized what might be called active citizenship, but of a very different kind to that promoted by the right. This is the active citizenship that disadvantaged people do for themselves rather than having it done for them; an active citizenship which creates them as subjects rather than as objects. This formulation, with its emphasis on active participation, comes closer to the classic republican notion of citizenship as engagement in the public sphere of the *polis* (Lister, 1995).

The use of words, and the meanings they convey, is important, and not to be dismissed as mere 'political correctness', as Lewis Carroll illustrated beautifully in the exchange between Alice and Humpty Dumpty:

> 'When *I* use a word,' Humpty Dumpty said in a rather scornful tone, 'it means just what I choose it to mean – neither more nor less.'
> 'The question is,' said Alice, 'whether you *can* make words mean different things.'
> 'The question is,' said Humpty Dumpty, 'which is to be master – that's all.' (Carroll, 1947)

The concept of citizenship remains a contested one; which meaning is 'to be master' (we will forgive Carroll his sexist language) has potentially profound implications for disadvantaged groups.

The idea of citizenship is an ancient one. Its use in the post-war era has been very influenced by T. H. Marshall's classic *Citizenship and Social Class* (1950) in which he defined citizenship primarily in terms of equality of status and the rights and duties stemming from full participatory membership of a society. He also held citizenship out as an ideal towards which we can aspire.

Marshall identified three dimensions of citizenship: the civil or legal, the political and the social. I will look at each of these in turn from the perspective of those for whom genuine citizenship may still appear more as an ideal than a reality.

EXCLUSION FROM CITIZENSHIP

In separating out the three elements of citizenship, it is important not to lose sight of their interdependence. In particular, a central theme of this chapter is that the effective exercise of civil and political rights is partly dependent on an effective floor of welfare or social rights. An understanding of citizenship rights and obligations cannot be divorced from their wider social and economic context and the inequalities of power, resources and status that permeate it. The increase in social and economic inequalities over the past fifteen years means that the ideal of genuine citizenship is moving further away rather than closer.

The civil or legal

Marshall defined the civil element of citizenship as 'the rights necessary for individual freedom ... and the right to justice', the latter representing 'the right to defend and assert all one's rights on terms of equality with others and by due process of law'.

Although the 'right to justice' has, in theory, been achieved in the United Kingdom, in practice many citizens living in poverty or on a modest income are not able to assert this right on equal terms with better-off members of the community. The Legal Aid scheme was introduced as a means of redressing this inequality of access to the law. It has been supplemented by the development of a network of law centres, advice centres and welfare rights services. Yet large numbers of people on low incomes still do not have access to the kind of advice and assistance they need to make a reality of their legal and welfare rights – and the situation is growing worse, not better.

During the 1980s, between ten and thirteen million dropped out of the legal aid net. It has been estimated that legal aid and advice cuts implemented in the early 1990s could affect as many as a further fourteen million, either by denying them legal aid altogether or by forcing them to pay a much higher contribution. The law and advice centre networks are working under increasing pressure in the face of cutbacks, at a time when demand for their services has been growing.

Welfare rights is one visible point of intersection between legal and social rights. Local authorities have played an important role in the promotion of welfare rights services, both directly through the development of the authorities' own services and indirectly through the funding of voluntary agencies such as Citizens Advice Bureaux whose caseloads have become increasingly dominated by such work. Many bureaux are buckling under the strain.

Welfare rights work does not have to be the preserve of people called welfare rights or advice workers. There are many professional groups working in the community who could usefully bring an awareness of welfare rights to their work: social workers and probation officers are perhaps the most obvious group, but there are also others such as doctors and health visitors. Some do but unfortunately many do not.

The advent of the community care legislation has meant that welfare rights work has come more into the mainstream as part of the financial assessment social service departments need to carry out in deciding on the best care package. Unfortunately, in this case the motivation may sometimes be more to assess the potential for charging than to maximize the wellbeing of the individual. Social work with families, on the other hand, has become increasingly dominated by statutory crisis work, with little time and resources for the kind of preventive social work in which welfare rights can play an important part. Interestingly, a report by CCETSW, the social work training council, made the case for welfare rights as part of social work with reference to the citizenship claims of users of social services (Curriculum Development Group, 1989).

The differential status of citizens in the face of the law can also be seen in the different attitudes towards and the treatment of those who fiddle their tax and those who fiddle their social security. Dee Cook (1993), who has done a considerable amount of research into this question, has argued that 'these differential responses give rise to a fundamental social injustice which renders hollow any claims of equality before the law and of equal citizenship'.

The political

The different treatment of tax and social security fiddlers partly reflects the relative power of the two groups and the different roles they play in the politics of the welfare state. This brings me to the political element of citizenship, defined by Marshall as 'the right to participate in the exercise of political power'.

Traditionally, this right is understood in terms of participation in the formal political system (which is important), and I will start with that. But that is not the only form of political participation: we need also to take account of more informal forms of politics.

As with legal rights, the exercise of political citizenship rights is in part both a function of social and economic rights and can influence the nature and quality of those rights. Thus, the kind of demands associated, for example, with Charter 88, for a set of civil and political rights to turn subjects into citizens, is important. But it is not *sufficient* to ensure genuine political citizenship.

Most of the classical theorists of citizenship argued that significant inequalities of economic resources were incompatible with political citizenship (though, in some cases, this was by defining women and slaves as beyond the pale of citizenship). We live in a deeply unequal society and it is no coincidence that people from poor backgrounds, members of minority ethnic communities, women and disabled people are underrepresented in the formal structures of political power.

Being poor can take up a considerable amount of time and energy and it is, in particular, poor *women's* time and energy which is spent in the daily balancing act of making ends meet and in negotiating with the institutions of the welfare state. Political meetings are often off-putting and may be difficult to get to – either because they are at the wrong time (and in some areas women, in particular, are afraid to go out after dark) or transport is difficult, or they are inaccessible to disabled people.

Indeed, the most basic right of political citizenship – the vote – can effectively be denied to disabled people. A study by the Spastics Society (Enticott et al., 1992) at the time of the 1992 General Election found widespread evidence of disabled people who did not vote because of the difficulty of getting (in) to polling stations and because they felt that a postal or proxy vote was discriminatory.

Other groups have effectively been disenfranchised also: those who chose not to register in the hope that they would thereby evade the poll tax; the growing number of homeless, few of whom will be on the electoral register. The danger is that such groups will remain outside the electoral system and will thereby aggravate an existing problem of relatively low levels of electoral registration in inner city areas, particularly among minority ethnic communities. According to the Office of Population Censuses and Surveys, up to 3.4 million eligible voters were missing from the 1991 electoral register in England and Wales. In London, one in five failed to register and black and other ethnic minority voters were significantly less likely to have registered than whites.

Trends such as these contribute to the further political marginalization of the poor, so that increasingly national politics is directed towards attracting the votes of the relatively comfortable majority. This is a process which has gone much further in the United States. In a public lecture in Britain, J. K. Galbraith (1994) warned of the dangers. 'Democracy', he argued, 'can be an imperfect thing. So it is when the most needful and most vulnerable of people do not participate in the political process, do not have voice and influence.' Such exclusion can lead to social tensions and conflict.

Political marginalization and powerlessness reinforce each other. However, it would be wrong to conclude from this that people living in deprived communities are all passive and apathetic. Some are, not surprisingly, given what they have to put up with; but others are not and are able to provide us with some heartening examples of what active citizenship can really be about. They may not be involved in formal politics, as envisaged in the classical republican notion of citizenship, but they are engaged in political, with a small 'p', action.

In one of its first reports, the Commission on Social Justice (1993) commented that

... in visits around the country, the Commission has seen how much is being achieved by community and voluntary organizations, sometimes in partnership with the local authority, sometimes independently of it....they are a key route to community regeneration... we have seen areas blighted by economic waste ... blessed with strong and vibrant communities, often led by women. (pp. 28–29)

Similarly, as a member of the independent Opsahl Commission into the future of Northern Ireland, I found the creativity and resilience of women's groups working against all the odds to improve life in their communities, especially for the young people, truly inspiring.

Two other examples I take from my time in Bradford. The first example is of a community development initiative on a severely deprived and run-down council estate. Following a major community consultation, carried out by local people themselves following training, an impressive report, setting out the views of local residents and an integrated regeneration and economic strategy for the estate, was published (Buttershaw Community, 1992.)

The second example concerns a campaign against water metering initiated by a group of working-class women from an estate where meters had been introduced, leading to soaring water bills for many of them. The campaign has been successful both in helping to get the issue of water metering on the national political agenda and also in transforming the way the women involved think about themselves.

In all these examples, it has been women who have taken the lead, despite, or perhaps because, of their exclusion from the formal political process. This phenomenon has been described as 'accidental activism',

activism born of the immediate experience of social injustice, rather than as a consequence of a pre-existing ideological belief. Through such accidental activism, women who previously did not see themselves as in any way 'political' are becoming advocates and agents for social change (Hyatt, 1991).

Similarly, one of the women from North Belfast who gave evidence to the Opsahl Commission said,

We are involved with politics with a little 'p' on the ground, but we get no recognition for it from politicians who are involved in politics with a big 'p'. There needs to be recognition for those engaged in politics with a little 'p'. (Pollak, 1993, p. 12)

The American writer, Robert D. Putnam (1993), has written of the importance of a strong network of grass-roots organizations as providing 'the capillaries of community life', vital to the economic and social health of local communities. 'If we are to make our political system more responsive, especially to those who lack connections at the top, we must' he argues, 'nourish grass-roots organization'.

In Britain, Suzie Croft and Peter Beresford (1989) of the Open Services Project have emphasized the importance to citizenship of including disadvantaged groups in the political process; 'of gaining a say' and in the definition and conceptualization of their own social needs. The disabled people's movement provides an example of the struggle to achieve this position. Disability studies and politics have been informed by the language of citizenship. For example, Mike Oliver (1993, p. 6) states:

> To be disabled in Great Britain is to be denied the fundamental rights of citizenship to such an extent that most disabled people are denied their basic human rights. Further, many of our key social institutions such as the political process, the provision of welfare and the education system contribute to, rather than alleviate, these denials.

The social

This brings me to the third (social) element of citizenship, defined by Marshall as 'the whole range from the right to a modicum of economic welfare and security to the right to share to the full in the social heritage and to live the life of a civilized being, according to the standard prevailing in the society'. This involves, Marshall argued, ' a universal right to real income which is not proportionate to the market value of the claimant'. As such, social citizenship rights have the potential to challenge the inequalities generated by the market.

There has been something of a political and academic debate as to whether social rights can have the same status as civil and political rights, which I will not pursue here (see Plant and Barry, 1990; Coote, 1992.). There is some evidence that the man and woman in the street do believe in a notion of social rights of citizenship. Commenting on research which asked people directly what were the most important rights of citizenship, the Speaker's Commission on Citizenship (1990, p. 6) observed that 'the majority of British citizens had no hesitation in according primacy to social rights – to a minimum standard of living, to medical care, to a job and to education'.

It is a measure of the inadequacy of existing social citizenship rights that so many are still denied access to full citizenship by poverty. Poverty spells deprivation; lack of choice; poor health, housing and educational opportunities; insecurity; social isolation. In short, it spells exclusion from the life-styles and life-chances taken for granted by the wider community; exclusion from full participation in the wider community.

It is not only people's rights as citizens that are undermined by poverty; so too is their ability to fulfil their obligations. This is felt particularly keenly in relation to the fulfilment of parental obligations, highlighted as one of the responsibilities of citizenship by John Major in his foreword to the Citizen's Charter. A recurrent theme in studies of poor families and reports from charities working on the ground is how parents worry that lack of money is preventing them from fulfilling their role as parents adequately and about the consequences of that for their children.

There are other dimensions of inequality which in many cases intersect with and aggravate that of poverty in corroding citizenship rights. I have mentioned the conceptualization of the impact of a disabling society as denying full citizenship to disabled people. Women and members of black and minority ethnic communities are other examples of groups whose citizenship status is at best often second class and who are particularly vulnerable to poverty.

The treatment of poor black people in this country has to be understood in the context of a succession of immigration and nationality laws which have defined legal citizenship in ways which have served to exclude many black people. There are fears that the situation could worsen as Fortress Europe erects barriers against migrants and asylum-seekers.

Links between welfare and immigration laws place limits on social rights of citizenship which can inhibit claims from those not technically effected who fear that their immigration status might be jeopardized.

The second-class treatment of some minority ethnic citizens under the social security system is then compounded by the system's ethnocentrism and by the racist attitudes displayed by some officials. Evidence from the National Association of Citizens Advice Bureaux (1991) and others, documenting the treatment of minority ethnic claimants, has at least prompted the Benefits Agency to address this issue.

Although the official statistics on low income are not broken down according to ethnic status, it is clear from the over-representation of black people amongst the ranks of the unemployed and the low paid that they are particularly vulnerable to poverty (see Amin with Oppenheim, 1992).

Continued racial discrimination and racial attacks and harassment are incompatible with genuine citizenship, both in terms of denying economic opportunities and of creating a climate of fear which can then limit access to public institutions and public spaces.

Violence and the fear of violence are also factors in the curtailment of women's citizenship rights, especially in the case of poorer women who cannot afford private forms of transport and who may live in areas which feel dangerous after dark. A crime survey in Islington suggested that many women are living 'under a state of virtual curfew'.

Moreover, violence does not stop at the front door and to understand women's relationship to citizenship we have to look at their position in the so-called 'private' sphere of the family and at how this relates to their participation in the public sphere of the economy and politics (see Lister, 1993a).

Women's position in both the family and the labour market helps to explain their greater vulnerability to poverty. Although this is changing rapidly, with women's increased economic participation, by and large the jobs which women are moving into are part-time, low-paid and insecure. Research suggests that the wages from such jobs are not generally sufficient to provide women with genuine financial independence and economic power (see Lister, 1992).

Women's poverty is closely related, either directly or indirectly, to their financial dependence upon men. Even women who are financially independent, such as many black women heads of household or lesbian women, may be affected by the ideology of women's financial dependence which still permeates their treatment in the labour market.

The social security system does not guarantee women without paid work an income in their own right. Although direct sex discrimination is more or less eliminated, women still face a number of disadvantages under the social security system. In particular, the contributory insurance principle, which is often held up as the epitome of social citizenship, excludes many women completely because they cannot conform with the male employment patterns upon which the scheme is predicated.

That said, a growing number of women have been building up an entitlement to benefit under the scheme. However, that entitlement has again been eroded by changes over the past few years which have tightened up some of the contribution conditions and cut back on some of the contributory benefits. The most recent example of this is the proposal to replace unemployment benefit paid for twelve months by a job-seekers' allowance, only six months of which will be paid on a non-means-tested basis. This will mean many women living with men will cease to be entitled to benefit because their partner is either working or claiming on behalf of the family. It is officially estimated that nearly three-fifths of women affected will not qualify for income support compared with under a third of men affected.

This is one example of how greater reliance on means-testing disadvantages women by reducing their access to an independent income. Moreover, because means-tested benefits take the couple rather than the individual as the unit of assessment (and it would be difficult to envisage a means-tested benefit which did not do so), they cannot 'target' or 'focus' (the latest euphemism for means-testing) resources on individuals in need within families where resources are not shared fairly. There is a growing body of research which shows that income is not always shared fairly to the detriment of women and children.

One of the aims of the post-war social security system was to reduce reliance on means-testing, which was seen as divisive and as creating second-class citizenship for the poor. The aim was never achieved and over the past decade social security policy has deliberately placed greater emphasis on means-tested benefits to the detriment of benefits such as child benefit and unemployment benefit.

Within the means-tested scheme for those out of work, rights have been eroded and greater use is made again of discretion. The main examples of this are the introduction of the social fund and the withdrawal of the right to income support from 16–17 year olds. One consequence has been an increased reliance on charities for help with basic needs, an example of the effective privatization of citizenship.

Privatization has been the other main trend in social security policy, particularly in the sphere of pensions where private provision is being encouraged as rights under the State Earnings Related Pensions Scheme are cut back. The implications for the citizenship rights of older people who have been disadvantaged in the labour market during working life are serious.

These developments in social security policy are likely to be taken further as the current major review of social security policy unfolds. At the same time, proposals to amend homelessness law threaten homeless families' rights to rehousing. What had come to be accepted as a basic right of social citizenship is in danger of being lost with very serious implications for the security and well-being of many disadvantaged families.

The steady move away from a welfare policy informed by notions of social citizenship rights takes place in the context of growing poverty and inequality which, as I have already suggested, is itself a threat to citizenship and social cohesion.

The latest official figures show that in 1992–93, 14.1 million people, a quarter of the population, were living on incomes below half the national average – the nearest we have to an official poverty line. In contrast, the figure in 1979 was five million, just under a tenth of the population.

The increase in poverty has been matched by the opening up of a chasm between the living standards of the poorest and the rest of society. Over the same time period, the real income (after housing costs) of the bottom tenth of the population fell by 18 per cent. Average living standards rose by 37 per cent; those of the top 10 tenth by 61 per cent.

This is partly the product of labour market trends. But it also reflects tax-benefit policies which, in this country, have aggravated rather than mitigated these trends. In doing so, they exemplify J. K. Galbraith's dismissal of the 'trickle down' theory which has been widely used to justify regressive economic and fiscal policies on the grounds that the fruits of the consequent wealth creation would trickle down to the poor: if you feed enough oats to the horses, some of them will eventually trickle down to the sparrows, but it is a theory which has rather greater support amongst the horses than the sparrows.

As the living standards of the poor fall further and further behind those of the rest of the community, it has become increasingly fashionable to describe them as an 'underclass'. People like Frank Field (1989) and Sir Ralf Dahrendorf (1987) have used the term in the context of loss of citizenship. Others such as Charles Murray (1989, 1994), an American writer who has had great influence on the British right, have popularized the notion of the 'underclass' to describe those whose poverty is, it is argued, the product of their own behaviour – e.g. work avoidance or having illegitimate children. This behaviour, the theory goes, is then reinforced by the social security system which itself encourages and perpetuates dependency.

The 'underclass' label tends to be used freely by the media as if it were synonymous with poor people generally. Indeed, it is just the kind of word that Humpty Dumpty was talking about: people use it to mean what they want it to mean. The powerful use it to devalue and stigmatize the powerless. Yet, when it comes to measuring the extent of this 'underclass', Murray (1989) himself concedes that it is a waste of time trying to count it as 'it all depends on how one defines its membership'. A review of the available U.S. evidence by William R. Prosser (an official in the Bush Administration writing in a personal capacity) concluded that 'we still do not have agreement on what we mean by the underclass, much less what factors are associated with its growth' (Prosser, 1991, p. 17).

The language of the 'underclass' is not only imprecise; it is also very disturbing. It is the language of disease and contamination. Murray, for example, described himself, in the *Sunday Times*, as a 'visitor from a plague area come to see whether the disease is spreading'.

Language such as this encourages a pathological image of people in poverty as a group different from the rest of us. This is not borne out by research in this country. The danger is that the more poor people are described in such value-laden language, the easier it becomes for the rest of society to write them off as beyond the bonds of common citizenship. The end result is more likely to be defensive or punitive policies designed to contain the dangerous 'underclass' and to protect the affluent rather than policies designed to heal the growing divisions in our society through the weaving of an effective web of citizenship rights.

CONCLUSION: THE IMPLICATIONS FOR LOCAL GOVERNMENT

In conclusion, I would like briefly to consider some of the possible implications of this chapter for local government. Ultimately, of course, the power to underwrite the citizenship rights of all members of society lies primarily with central government. Nevertheless local government has an important role to play in enhancing the citizenship of local residents.

This point was made forcefully in a paper by David Donnison (1994) for the Commission on Social Justice. The paper made the case for 'social justice from the bottom up', promoted by strong and active civic leadership:

> Civic leaders' first and most important aim should be to enable their fellow citizens to develop their talents as fully as possible, and to make a decent living if they are capable of doing so – and to gain their welfare rights if they are not (p. 31).

> Local action is needed to give excluded people a voice which cannot be disregarded, to ensure that women and ethnic minorities get a fairer deal, to focus the resources of mainstream services more effectively on poor people and the neighbourhoods in which they live, to stabilize disintegrating communities, and to respond more effectively to people suffering special hardships (p. 28).

John Stewart (1993) emphasized the value of local government in promoting active political citizenship beyond the limits of participation in local elections. He argued that 'there is an important role for local government in providing resources, space, and support for citizenship'. To add a postscript, echoing Donnison: local government needs to ensure that the citizenship of less powerful groups is promoted so that their voices are not silenced or drowned out by those of the more powerful.

In many ways, local government is better placed to do this than central government because it is closer to the people. Through community development initiatives, often in partnership with community groups and the voluntary sector, it can help people find the confidence and enhance the skills they need to be active citizens.

In a report about participation in social services, the Open Services Project argues that the schemes they studied suggest that the crucial components of effective involvement are support and access. Without adequate support and suitable structures and opportunities for involvement 'people may either lack the confidence, expectations or abilities to get involved, or be discouraged by the difficulties entailed. Without them, participatory initiatives are likely to *reinforce* rather than overcome existing race, class, gender and other inequalities' (Croft and Beresford, 1990, p. 14).

Stewart spoke of local authority community strategies 'built on listening and learning, and the involvement of citizens'. This needs to include both individual citizens and those who have come together to engage in the kind of informal politics with a small 'p' mentioned earlier.

Underlying these arguments is the fundamental one of the need for greater accountability. In the words of the Commission on Social Justice (1994, p. 352) 'only if accountability can be strengthened will people gain rights, not merely as customers but as citizens'. As elected authorities have increasingly lost power to unelected quangos, accountability has been diminished. It needs to be rebuilt and refashioned (see Commission on Social Justice, 1994).

Local authorities, nevertheless, can still make an important contribution to the quality of social citizenship enjoyed by local residents. One of the more positive developments in recent years has been the growing number of authorities committed to anti-poverty strategies of various kinds, despite the ever-tighter constraints within which they are operating. The integration of economic and social development; service and benefit delivery policies which are sensitive to the needs of disadvantaged groups; the promotion of advice and advocacy services – all these are valuable strands in the web of social citizenship at local level.

Similarly, in the field of education, which constitutes a basic building block of citizenship, local authorities have a vital role to play despite the erosion of their power and influence in recent years. In particular, there is growing recognition of the value of pre-school education and of an integrated education and child care strategy for the under-fives (see most recently the report from the Commission on Social Justice, 1994). Investment in early childhood is an investment in the citizens of the future.

Local authorities can also use their knowledge and experience to help raise public consciousness about the divisions in our society and to draw to the attention of central government the social and economic costs of such divisions.

A decade ago the *Faith in the City* (1985) report declared that

> the critical issue to be faced is whether there is any serious political will to set in motion a process which will enable those who are at present in poverty and powerless to rejoin the life of the nation.

A decade later that challenge is more urgent than ever. A society which banishes a growing number of its members from full citizenship puts itself at risk. Local authorities can, at least, try to ensure that those who are in poverty and powerless are full citizens of their local communities even if they are not yet full citizens of the nation.

11 Citizenship and Disabled People: A Cause for Concern

Len Barton

The title of the chapter indicates serious concerns over the position and experiences of disabled people in relation to the question of citizenship. Given the complexity of the issues involved, combined with the limitation of space, it is necessary to control the number of factors to be explored. Many of the contributors to this book have discussed some of the key assumptions and historical antecedents associated with notions of 'democracy' and 'citizenship' and thus I do not propose to give much attention to these matters. Such material provides the theoretical context against which this discussion will be developed.

It is my intention to give more space to considering the question of disability, and in particular, to give prominence to the voices of disabled people. These will express their concerns, priorities and struggles for rights, choices and participation in an essentially disabling and offensive material and social world.

DISABILITY, DEPENDENCY AND CONTROL

The issue of disability is connected to questions of status. Thus, how disability is defined, by whom, and for what purposes, are all important questions needing to be carefully explored. They are important, for example, in helping to ascertain the extent to which official definitions and decision making take the voices of disabled people seriously and thereby legitimize positive or negative images through particular policies and provisions. With regard to the latter, they may give us some purchase on the reasons why disabled people do not experience the benefits of real citizenship (Finkelstein, 1993; Oliver, 1993).

In order to achieve an adequate understanding of the status of disabled people it is essential to consider the key historical antecedents which have helped to shape current definitions of both an official and commonsense level of understanding. This includes asking questions about specific policy provisions such as:

What view of disability do they perpetuate?
Whose interests do they serve?
On what basis are they justified?
What are the outcomes for those they claim to support?

Approaching the question of citizenship in relation to disabled people necessitates engaging with the issue of power. This involves degrees of freedom, choice and participation. These are expressed within asymmetrical sets of social relationships which influence how we relate to, and may effect one another. Thus as Bauman (1990) maintains:

> To have power is to be able to act more freely; but having no power, or less power than others have, means having one's own freedom of choice limited by the decisions made by others (p. 113).

Disability is a significant means of social differentiation. To be disabled means to be discriminated against and involves experiencing varying degrees of stereotyping, social isolation and restriction (Oliver, 1990; 1995). This perspective is a key aspect of a social model of disability, one which seeks to identify the ways in which society disables people. The task then is to remove those disabling material, economic, ideological, attitudinal barriers that cumulatively prevent disabled people from experiencing the entitlements of citizenship. This includes challenging the mythology of the rhetoric of democracy in the light of the position and experiences of marginalized and oppressed groups (Abberley, 1987).

A significant feature of the oppression of disabled people is the extent to which their voice has been excluded from developments and decisions affecting their lives. An historical perspective is important in helping us understand this because the conditions and factors which have influenced the status of disabled people have changed over time. Historically, a medical model of disability has powerfully influenced policy and practice. In this approach an emphasis is placed on an individual's loss, inabilities, inferior condition or syndrome. From this approach strong custodial measures have been viewed as the most appropriate response for those individuals who were defined, as a menace needing total institutional provision, or a burden needing sterilising and even exterminating and as vulnerable thus in need of protection (Scull, 1982; Wolfensberger, 1993; Tomlinson, 1982; Ryan & Thomas, 1980).

Official definitions often enshrined in legislation are an important indicator of the marginalization of oppressed groups. Various labels have been used to define them, including: 'deformed', 'invalid', 'spastic', 'cripple', 'mad', 'idiot', 'lunatic' and 'subnormal'. Historically, they have been essentially powerless and the 'objects' of decisions made by significant others claiming to act on societies and/or their behalf.

A very significant factor of the history of disabled people has involved them being the recipients of policies and practices legitimating models supporting custody-control, personal-tragedy conceptions of the individual as well as being objects of charity. They have been systematically devalued through institutional discrimination and the impact of the media through the representation of disabling stereotypes and patronizing images has negatively influenced how we both define disability and our expectations of disabled people (Barnes, 1991). If such disabling barriers are to be overcome then there is absolutely no room for complacency and an urgent need to recognize the seriousness of the struggle which this entails.

In a brief but important introduction to a booklet promoting a series of films examining images of disability in the cinema, at the Watershed Media Centre in Bristol, Darke (1995), a disabled writer and the Season Film Adviser, raises several crucial issues. These include cultural misrepresentations of disability, the ways in which disability and impairment are used interchangeably and the neutralizing of political factors through the emphasis on entertainment. He contends that:

> As entertainment works by creating a simplified world where problems are individualized (and, as such, only solvable by the individuals affected), social problems, and groups, are marginalized and deemed to be responsible for their own suffering and salvation; and society is absolved of any responsibility whilst being left unaffected. The simplest method by which the problem of disability is solved, as cinema and society see it, is for it to solve itself by either medical or miracle methods (the cure) or for it to simply disappear (i.e. death). Either way the audience is entertained and the problem is solved in front of their very eyes, and disability, to the non-disabled, remains as a tragic state of being. The status quo

remains intact and the marginalized blamed for their own situation (p. 4).

This individualized, deficit view of disability, along with the discriminatory policies and practices supporting it, needs to be critically engaged with and removed. A crucial aspect of this change process will be the introduction of an alternative social model of disability. It is this which organizations of disabled people are increasingly committed to.

Disabled people's history needs to be viewed as one of an increasing struggle to establish and maintain positive self-identities. This includes an unwillingness to acquiesce to a subordinate role or stigmatized identity. It is about developing self-respect, self-confidence and solidarity with other disabled people. This is part of their struggle for rights, choice and participation in society. Essential to this form of action is the demand for anti-discrimination legislation (Shakespeare, 1993; Barnes & Oliver, 1995; Barnes, 1996).

Issues of equality and citizenship are central concerns in the process of emancipation because as Rioux (1994), a disabled analyst, notes:

> Disability is not measles. It is not a medical condition that needs to be eliminated from the population. It is a social status and the research agenda must take into account the political implications attached to that status (Rioux, 1994, pp. 6–7).

Disability is thus a social and political category in that it includes practices of regulation and struggles for empowerment and rights (Fulcher, 1989). Portrayals of disabled people as passive, incomplete and unfortunate inhibit the development of conceptions which view such people as actively seeking to change their circumstances. Alternatively, portraying disabled people as heroic/heroine figures minimizes the very real costs of oppression and underplays the importance of group effort and solidarity. Both these perspectives are offensive and counter-productive to the fundamental changes required for the removal of disabling barriers. Nor must it be assumed that 'disability' is a unitary category involving conceptions of sameness. This would be to minimize the degree to which, for example, class, race, gender and age factors cushion compound the experience of disability. Through this means some disabled people experience *simultaneous* forms of oppression (Stuart, 1992).

These qualifications reinforce the importance of how we define disability. This is vividly illustrated in Hahn's (1985) analysis of the medical approach. He supports a social model of disability and argues that:

A medical definition not only imposes a presumption of biological or physiological inferiority upon disabled persons, but it also inhibits a recognition of the social and structural sources of disability. From this perspective, the problems of disability arise from physical flaws within a person rather than from defects in an unadaptive environment or society, and the solutions to these difficulties must be sought primarily through individual rather than collective efforts (p. 89).

An individual's impairment must not be viewed as determining the degree of independence that person may exercise. This should not be taken to imply that disabled people do not experience pain or need medical support. Rather, the issue is the grounds on which that is provided and the forms of social relationships that are involved. Questions concerning power-relations, expertise and choice are central to this issue.

Engaging with disabled people on the basis of dignity requires the removal of low expectations, patronizing and over-protective practices, including viewing them as being permanently children (Brizenden, 1989). This constitutes a major agenda for all those professional groups (including educationists) who claim to work on behalf of disabled people.

CITIZENSHIP, HUMAN RIGHTS AND DISABILITY

The demands for citizenship need to be set against the stubborn realities of unequal social conditions and relations which disempower and disenfranchise disabled people (Finkelstein, 1993). Institutional discrimination is still a powerful force to be engaged with, as can be seen from the following factors:

Segregated provisions tend to encourage negative labels, suspicion, stereotypes and ignorance of a reciprocal nature (Morris, 1990; Barnes, 1991).

The ideology of 'caring' for someone which underpins practice in the social and health services, predominately means 'taking responsibility for them, taking charge of them (p. 38)'. This necessarily involves relations of dependence and contributes to a custodial notion of caring (Morris, 1993).

Little opportunity exists for disabled people to define the issues relating to Community Care which they think are important (Bewley and Glendinning, 1994).

Disabled people are more likely to be out of work than their non-disabled counterparts (Barnes, 1991).

Those who do work tend to find themselves in poorly-paid, low-skilled and low-status jobs (Helander, 1993).

Disabled people experience conditions of life inferior to those of the rest of the population. Thus there is a close association between disability and poverty (Coleridge, 1993).

The focus of criticism and concern therefore needs to move from an individualized, deficit approach to one in which institutional barriers can be challenged and the rights and value of disabled people as equal citizens can be achieved.

A commitment to human rights is based on the belief that the world is changeable and disability as a human rights issue reinforces the importance, as Starkey (1991) advocates:

. . . that differences, physical or cultural, should have no bearing on a person's entitlement to freedom, equality and dignity (p. 27).

In a discussion of disability issues in relation to the European context, Daunt (1991) supports this position and argues for the establishment of two complimentary principles:

1. The principle that all measures should be founded on the explicit recognition of the *rights* of disabled people.
2. The principle that all people are to be regarded as of *equal* value in the society and to the society (p. 184).

The importance of such principles and their implementation are related to the extent to which, on the one hand, we recognize the seriousness of the discrimination which disabled people experience and, on the other, acknowledge that the exercise of citizenship rights is independent of their economic contributions (Rioux, 1994).

CITIZENSHIP, DISABILITY AND DIFFERENCE

In attempting to understand some of the key issues involved in the question of democracy and citizenship it is important, for example, to distinguish between the content, style and function of political rhetoric and the lived reality of individuals or groups within specific socio-economic conditions and relations. This provides an added incentive for recognising, as Turner (1993) contends, that citizenship is necessarily and fundamentally concerned with issues of inequality and the distribution of resources in society. Thus, in the quest for citizenship and democratization, existing social and political inequalities and power differentials have to be challenged and changed.

From this perspective citizenship is to be viewed as a contested concept. Within a society characterized by gross inequalities disputes arise between and within groups over the criteria governing the use of citizenship, the kinds of rights involved, how membership is determined and the kind of obligations binding upon a citizen (Carr and Harnett, 1996). These and other factors constitute the focus of reflection and debate, through which the relationship between the citizen and state is redefined.

The quest for citizenship is also inextricably linked to the politics of difference. In an analysis of the political issues involved in the struggle for citizenship within a pluralist society, Phillips (1993) provides a feminist perspective based on a recognition of the limitations of socialist ideas, a critique of existing feminist ideas and an exposure of the myths of nation and country. She contends that:

> What distinguishes a radical perspective on democracy is not its expectation of future homogeneity and consensus, but its commitment to a politics of solidarity, and challenge, and change (p. 161).

From this approach the desires for an undifferentiated unity, the wishing away of group difference, forms of essentialism which define all individuals by a single criterion, are all severely criticized. A new politics of diversity and difference is advocated which necessitates a more active and participatory democracy.

Difference is now to be viewed as a challenge, a means of generating change and an encouragement for people to question unfounded generalization, hostility, prejudice and discrimination. This challenge needs to be viewed in terms of excluded groups themselves as well as a means of questioning and changing the perspectives of dominant groups. This fundamental task is to develop a vision of democracy through difference (Phillips, 1993).

In a discussion of feminism and democratic education, Arnot (1995) draws out some key insights from such research. These include the increasing awareness within the feminist movement of the existing social and economic inequalities *between* women, as well as the various ways in which women have been 'constructed' within official educational discourses and policies. Both of these are applicable to the question of disability.

A most significant development has been the emergence of a disability movement. This is being viewed as an example of a new social movement (Oliver, 1990; Shakespeare, 1993). One aspect of this has been the creation of Disabled People's Organizations. These are run by disabled people on behalf of disabled people. Part of the learning process has been recognizing and engaging with differences amongst their members – differences around issues of race, gender, sexuality and age (Priestley, 1995). In their collective struggle for civil rights, anti-discrimination legislation and the removal of all disabling barriers within society, a very difficult position has to be achieved with regard to the importance of *both* points of commonality and difference. This can have both local and national, even international dimensions.

However, we need to be cautious about an exaggerated claim and impression concerning the universal or global impact of such movements. The degree to which a disability movement actually exists differs across societies, as can be seen from Morgan's (1995) critical analysis of Northern Ireland in which he maintains:

> ... regretfully, ashamedly, it must be pointed out that the disability movement has made almost no headway among disabled people in Northern Ireland (p. 234).

One of the main reasons for this, he believes, is that disabled people in Northern Ireland primarily seek individual solutions to what are perceived as individual problems.

Part of the wider struggle is over how dominant groups define disability and seek to control the decisions affecting the lives of disabled people. Learning, for example, from the experiences of black people and their struggles over institutional racism, by refusing to enter into relationships of assimilation or accommodation with the State, disabled people's organizations face some difficult issues. Discussing the nature and function of the disability movement, Oliver (1995) high-lights some of these difficulties:

> The fine line between marginalization and incorporation remains one that the movement must address; it must be close enough to the political institutions of the state to be an effective change agent but must guard against being an establishment organization more concerned with OBEs for its leaders than representing the wishes of disabled people.

One of the essential features of the disability movement is its demand for the denial of the inclusion of disabled people into the political process to be removed and their social, political and civil rights of citizenship to be realized. It thus represents the continuing struggle for citizenship.

In the pursuit of social justice, participatory democracy and citizenship, the denial of difference needs to be resisted. Learning to live with one another necessarily involves learning to respect our differences. Part of this development also includes dealing with the issue of self-oppression. This process of empowerment enables people to have pride in themselves, in who they are. In a sensitive and personal self-analysis, Corbett (1994) provides some vivid insights into the difficulties and benefits of challenging stereotypes, discrimination and negative feelings of inferiority or personal inadequacy. Whilst the ultimate goal is the realization of a valued and dignified identity, she maintains that the pressures to conform or be 'normal' are extremely powerful. These have to be challenged in that:

> Fear can create monsters of us all. Fear of appearing different and difficult can make some disabled people deny their experience and feign normality, rejecting those who seem to be causing trouble and discontent. Super-heroes, overcoming adversity with supreme effort, may dissociate themselves from those who are weaker and unable to compete (p. 352).

Overcoming such oppressions requires, as Shakespeare (1993) so powerfully contends, the

> . . . subversion of stigma: taking a negative appellation and converting it into a badge of pride (p. 253).

Both the generation and use of proud and defiant self-labelling is an integral part of personal, group growth and political awareness.

INCLUSIVE EDUCATION

Inclusive education is part of a much wider vision relating to society itself. Issues of social justice, equity and choice are central concerns motivating policy, practice, and the demand for change. This agenda is about the wellbeing of *all* children and schools. Schools need to be welcoming institutions, irrespective of an individual's class, race or gender. The underlying principle is one of human rights and the recognition that the social and material worlds are changeable.

This approach is about fundamental values, priorities and the redistribution of adequate resources. It is more than mere questions of access that are at stake here. It is a quest for the removal of policies and practices of exclusion and the realization of effective participatory democracy involving the recognition and respect of difference.

Inclusive education is thus not about placing disabled children in mainstream schools. It is about how, where and why we educate *all* pupils. This clearly raises questions about the purpose and future of segregated special schooling. From the perspective we have adopted in this chapter such schools need to be closed and the human and material resources carefully transferred to supporting the development of inclusive policies and practices within mainstream schools. The grounds for such an approach are clearly articulated in the following statement by Dessent (1987):

> Special schools do not have a right to exist. They exist because of the limitations of ordinary schools in providing for the full range of abilities and disabilities amongst children. It is not primarily a question of the quality or adequacy of what is offered in a special school. Even a superbly well-organized special school offering the highest quality curriculum and educational input to its children has no right to exist if that same education can be provided in a mainstream school (p. 97).

It will be crucially important to utilize the experience and skills of staff from these schools to *support* the development of inclusive practices within mainstream schools. Part of the function of such a change will also be to contribute to the staff development of *all* staff within the school. This will be a challenging and educative process of change which will require sensitive and carefully planned courses of action.

Inclusive education is not about 'dumping' pupils into existing conditions and relations with the intention that schools will have to cope with these additional responsibilities. Schools will need to change. This process may comprise changes to the physical structure of the building in terms of access and appropriate facilities. But it is much more than this. It will also affect the curriculum, ethos and teaching practices. Importantly, it will also require carefully planned, adequately resourced and monitored staff development policies and practices. Teachers are key to this change process and must therefore be adequately supported and encouraged. -

'Education for all' as expressed in what Kemmis (1994) calls 'the socially just school' involves a serious commitment to the task of identifying, challenging and contributing to the removal of injustices. Part of this task includes a self-critical analysis of the role schools play in the production and reproduction of injustices such as disabling barriers of various forms. Coupled with this is the wider concern of clarifying the role of schools in combating institutional discrimination in relation to the position of disabled people in society. This entails identifying the sources of injustice in the social processes, practices, structures and institutions of society (Young, 1990).

We do need to dream, to have a vision of a better future society, one which inspires and motivates, but one which arises from an informed understanding of the injustices of the society we currently live in. Thus, given the stubborn realities of existing inequalities, discriminations and socially divisive policies and practices, the task will at times seem impossible, insurmountable and unrealistic.

Everything seems to be against such an outcome, including the increasing 'marketization' of educational planning and provision, the intensification of competitiveness, the publishing of league tables of examination results, the tendency to more selection both in terms of access and experience within schools, the introduction of grant-maintained schools and a set of values which celebrate individualism, thereby making the possibilities of co-operation and collaboration, at an institutional and individual level, less desirable or possible.

This *is* the context in which this struggle is taking place and it is because of the offensiveness of existing injustices and disabling barriers that we must not, on the one hand, underestimate the degree of the struggle involved if such a vision is to be realized, and, on the other, recognize the importance of establishing effective working relationships with all those involved in overcoming oppression and discrimination. This is itself a difficult but empowering experience.

Principles are being established as can be seen from the policy statement issued in Spain at the World Conference on Special Needs Education (1994). They include the belief that

Every child has a fundamental right to education and must be given the opportunity to achieve and maintain an acceptable level of learning.

Every child has unique characteristics, interests, abilities and learning needs.

Education systems should be designed and educational pro- grammes implemented to take into account the wide diversity of these characteristics and needs.

Regular schools with this inclusive orientation are the most effec- tive means of combating discriminatory attitudes, creating wel- coming communities, building an inclusive society and achieving education for all.

The struggle for their effective realization is part of the commit- ment to the wider pursuit of an inclusive society.

CONCLUSION

In this chapter I have briefly raised some of the key issues concerning the question of disability and citizenship. I have adopted a social model of disability which is critical of individualized, homogenized, deficit views of disabled people. The struggle for citizenship entails engaging with issues of difference, discrimination, power and the pol- itics of identity. I maintain that this needs to be part of an equal opportunities approach in which the demands for civil rights, choice and participation are essential components. Such a process of empowerment and critique necessarily involves the development of political awareness and action.

I have argued that historically disabled people have been funda- mentally excluded from concerns over citizenship for several reasons. They have been viewed as a sub-human species and therefore unworthy or unable to experience the entitlements and responsibil- ities associated with citizenship. They have been viewed as a menace or threat and therefore have forfeited any possible rights or entitle- ments. Finally, as a result of the extent of institutional discrimination in their lives, they have been so dependent and socially disadvantaged that they have been unable to experience the exercising of true citizenship.

The history of disabled people, has been one of discrimination, exclusion and dependency on the decisions of powerful professional groups over key issues affecting their lives. This has entailed their disempowerment and disenfranchise ment. The issues here are not merely about resources or access, but rather about fundamental values and ideologies influencing the way in which disability and disabled people are perceived and engaged with.

The role schools and teachers play in the pursuit of a barrier-free society is an important one. The extent to which the impact of marketization on educational planning and provision will militate against the introduction and effective implementation of 'education for all' values and practices, is an issue of very serious concern (Ball, 1993). Segregated special school provision has historically served to encourage stereotypes, ignorance and suspicion of a reciprocal nature between disabled and non-disabled people (Morris, 1990; Rieser & Mason, 1990; Barnes, 1991). Dealing with this particular barrier of exclusion will be an important task. Nor is the issue merely at the level of schools. Changes are required within post-school education, including higher education (Corbett & Barton, 1992; Hurst, 1996). Involving disabled people in discussions and decisions over these issues will be vitally important and a further means of their participation over factors affecting their lives.

Listening to the voices of disabled people is absolutely essential as they increasingly express their criticisms, needs and demands. The celebration of difference with dignity is being expressed through their songs, poetry, writings and other art forms. Yet there is no room for complacency. Part of the frustration that disabled people and their organizations experience is the result of the failure of the so-called democratic system to listen, or take their views seriously. Part of the response to this situation has been groups of disabled people taking to the streets to protest and undertake various acts of civil disobedience. Some of the most powerful examples of these actions have been the protests during the raising of monies for Telethon and recent attempts to gain anti-discrimination Legislation through Parliament. Such demonstrations were inspired by their refusal to be viewed as objects of charity and by their demands for real citizenship and participatory democracy.

A fundamental aspect of a democracy is the opportunity and encouragement to exercise freedom of speech, debate and dialogue. Part of the task, as Phillips (1993) notes, is to develop a form of political discourse that will enable *all* citizens to participate in this process. Any discussions concerning the sort of society this will entail and the forms of social change that it will require must include disabled people. Only through this means will we begin to recognize their rights and value them as equal citizens.

12 Knowledge of Most Worth to Citizens

Harold Entwistle

More than a century ago Herbert Spencer posed the question, 'What knowledge is of most worth to citizens?' His response was not to emphasize those subject areas which are most commonly associated with citizenship – history, geography, political theory, economics and civics, for example – but an affirmation of the primary place of science, 'without which the citizen cannot rightly regulate his conduct' (Spencer, 1861). History he dismissed as a 'mere tissue of names and dates and dead unmeaning events, (having) not the remotest bearing on any of our actions'. Science, however, as well as providing accounts of biological and physical phenomena of value to citizens, also embraces sociology, the science of society. Spencer eventually reinstated history as worthwhile knowledge for citizens, provided the emphasis was shifted from dynastic, imperial and military events towards those more intimately concerned with the everyday lives of ordinary people in their vocational, economic, political and cultural dimensions. For Spencer, history had practical value only as a 'descriptive sociology', recalling also John Dewey's similar characterization of history as 'an indirect sociology'.

Although this paper will argue that familiarity with the various disciplinary components of a liberal education is necessary to effective citizenship, the aim is not to dispute Spencer's claims for the importance of science, itself a crucial component of a liberal curriculum. But to argue for a wide general knowledge as a basis for effective citizenship is to point to a distinction which is not always explicit in discussions of education for citizenship. During most of this century, this has usually been predicated upon the belief that citizenship is primarily a political matter and that the educational correlate of this is that the curriculum should focus upon the machinery of government, its institutions and processes, and the relationship of citizens to these in their role as voters. Thus, citizenship education has been assumed to require political education concerned with the cultivation of political literacy. But in focusing upon science, Spencer had in mind the substantive issues which confront citizens – much as did his

near-contemporary, John Stuart Mill, who also saw the development, dissemination and application of scientific knowledge as crucial to ridding humanity of the terrible scourges of poverty, disease,
hunger, indigence and ignorance. It appears, then, that there are
two different questions to ask about the knowledge most worthwhile
to citizens: first, 'What knowledge is most appropriate to an understanding of the political process itself?' and second, 'What ought citizens to know in order to understand those substantive issues which
are concerned with the amelioration of impediments to human hap-
piness and the creation of those values and life-styles which are constitutive of the good life?'

Not withstanding that citizenship education has usually been
focused upon the former, I want to argue that it is the latter
knowledge which is of more importance to citizens. For the stuff of
political debate, whether in legislatures or in the pubs, bars, and
manifold voluntary associations where ordinary citizens congregate,
is not usually about the way government is structured, or how it
works (except, nowadays, that we have too much of it), but debate
about the substantive issues that concern citizens in the business of
everyday life: the environment, race relations, war and peace, the
education of their children, healthcare, taxation, the cost of living,
the fear of unemployment and the state of public transport. For
example, with reference to the sometimes obsessive preoccupation
with the environment, there are difficult questions about what
phenomena actually do threaten the planet, how serious the threats
are, and the methods and opportunity costs involved in dealing
with environmental pollution. But the question of what political
avenues and machinery exist to secure appropriate legislative and
executive action to achieve a healthy environment are quite distinct
from the substantive environmental questions. The political knowledge that is appropriate to political activity when dealing with any
matter of concern to citizens is different from the knowledge that
informs citizens about substantive issues of the kind we have just cata-
logued. No doubt it is arguable that both categories of knowledge,
the particular political and the general cultural, are of value to citizens in pursuit of the good life, but I wish to argue that it is general
cultural literacy of the kind advocated by Hirsch (1988) and others
that is of most value to citizens, while the knowledge of political institutions and processes that has generally been advocated as the stuff
of political education, is of little interest and importance to most
citizens.

If citizens are to be well informed about substantive political issues, such that they are able to discuss these with discrimination and understanding, armed against the clichéd, simplistic polemics of politicians, media pundits, and special-interest groups, the kind of knowledge most valuable is the historical, geographical, scientific, mathematical, literary, ethical, aesthetic, sociological, and economic knowledge – as well as the linguistic skills – that are the fruits of a liberal education. Ignorance or incompetence with respect to this kind of knowledge and skill does seriously impair the citizen's ability to act with understanding and discrimination when confronted with the substantive issues of politics.

However, there is perception of widespread and growing ignorance among the young that particularly disturbs many who are concerned about the quality and future of democratic citizenship. The 'well informed citizen' seems threatened with extinction. It seems that hardly a week passes when American television does not carry interviews with intelligent high school and college students who are ignorant of things like the place of the United States on a map of the world and the locations of major American cities; the timing of the American Civil War (not to mention similar ignorance of World Wars I and II) and the names of the generals of the contending armies; the whereabouts of Nicaragua; the meaning of the Holocaust. This last is widely believed to have occurred in the United States and to be connected with the Jewish New Year. Even with respect to people they do know, things of significance elude these young citizens. For example, few know of other connotations of the word 'madonna', thus missing both the irony and the audacity of the use of that name by the rock star, Madonna. In his controversial bestseller, *Cultural Literacy: What Every American Needs to Know*, cataloguing the demise of cultural literacy, Hirsch produces his own list of cultural *faux pas* committed by young Americans and concludes that there exist sufficient substantiated data to confirm the view that perceptions of youthful ignorance can no longer be considered merely impressionistic or a function of media hype. But this is not a phenomenon confined to the United States. Similar examples of cultural illiteracy are frequently cited from Britain. There also, large numbers of young people cannot identify their country on a map of the world. A recent survey pertaining to scientific knowledge reported widespread ignorance: for example, a third of all age groups have a pre-Copernican conception of the universe, believing that the sun daily circles the earth. Eighty-four percent of respondents to yet another recent inquiry confessed themselves to be Christian, but only one-third of these were able to explain the significance of Good Friday or Easter Sunday.

Often, these examples of cultural ignorance are dismissed as of no consequence to ordinary people in the business of everyday life, including, by implication, their daily lives as citizens. The general cultural knowledge that Hirsch and others would have people learn tends to be characterized, pejoratively, as 'high culture' or 'high status knowledge'; and Hirsch and people of like mind are dismissed as elitist. Yet, as a major reason for his insistence on the need to recover cultural literacy, Hirsch cites the demands that citizenship places upon people's cognitive repertoires. For him, as indeed for other educationalists who have made similar prescriptions for the health of American democracy, the knowledge which is one of the fruits of liberal education is not the prerogative of a cultural elite, but the birthright of every American. Hirsch's is perhaps the best known polemic on behalf of cultural literacy defined by reference to the kind of general knowledge which is the outcome of a subject-based liberal curriculum. And although his concern is with what every American should know (especially as a necessary basis of democratic citizenship), his identification of growing widespread ignorance amongst citizens is, as we have noted, far from being exclusive to America. Nor would the knowledge which Hirsch takes to be essential to every American citizen be unfamiliar to educated citizens elsewhere. In important respects the cultural capital of an educated American does not differ greatly from that of an educated Briton, Canadian, Australian, Dane, German or French citizen, for example. Hirsch's list of essential knowledge contains a few items of American esoterica which might not be familiar to non-Americans, but it also draws extensively on items from Greek, Roman, Judaic, French, German, Italian, Russian and other Western cultures, such that it is reasonable to suppose that a great variety of non-Americans also know what Hirsch believes that every American should know. With reference to large geographical conceptions that transcend national borders (the so-called Western world, for example) cultural literacy has always been more than an exclusively national phenomenon, for those who are liberally educated. And, no doubt, in the age of the global village, cultural literacy has a universal dimension.

If there is widespread ignorance of the geographical, historical, scientific, religious, economic and other aspects of general knowledge noted above, this clearly has deleterious implications for citizenship. For example, in the United States at the time of the Nicaraguan Civil War, one argument advanced in favour of supporting the Contras derived from the fact that Nicaragua is closer to Texas than Texas is to California. Again, since much Middle Eastern and, especially, Israeli politics (including the way Americans divide on this issue) derives from attitudes engendered by the Holocaust, and since problems of race in America are rooted in slavery and its consequences, the widespread geographical and historical ignorance pertinent to these matters that surfaces in surveys (see above) is hardly a promising basis for citizenship in a modern democracy. Similarly, informed judgments about the deterioration of the environment and various remedies to save the planet require familiarity with the appropriate scientific knowledge as well as the economic imperatives involved. Environmental problems are complex and their understanding and resolution require detailed reference to a variety of data from diverse sources. For example, anyone concerned at the deleterious impact of carbon fuels might be expected to welcome investment in an alternative renewable energy source like hydro-electric power. But environmental lobbies have effectively killed further hydro-electric development in James Bay, Quebec, by calling upon what they regard as a quite different environmental threat – the perceived threat to the traditional ways of life of native peoples and the migration patterns of wildlife in the Canadian North. Clearly, environmental arguments do not all point in the same practical directions, and resolution of these contradictions requires reference to a complex of scientific, economic, anthropological and zoological knowledge. And much the same is true of most substantive issues confronting modern citizens. Hirsch believes that the cultural literacy he advocates is essential precisely because it is necessary in order to read with discrimination the newspapers and magazines that address the current substantive political issues. But it is not only the so-called 'quality' media, appealing largely to cultural elites, that make demands on the reader by couching current affairs in the context of historical, geographical, literary, scientific, and other cultural allusions. The popular media make similar demands upon cultural literacy, as any evening devoted to watching television will indicate. The news, especially, is often presented with only oblique references to actual events, personalities or countries, employing instead geographical or historical allusion, such as when Washington joins Moscow in warning Baghdad, while London, Paris and Bonn lend support and Tehran feigns neutrality. A good deal of the news from any of the media would elude one without the appropriate cultural background.

There is a further reason why a broad cultural literacy is of greater value for citizens than specialized knowledge of the political system. Citizenship is not a purely political conception. It has a much wider cultural reference than to the political life of citizens. Historically, citizenship has intimated a more inclusive conception of human activity than is involved in the mere performance of political roles as voters, elected members of government and other public institutions, trade union officials, and the like. In particular, the classical conception of citizenship has an aesthetic dimension. The 'city' (as domicile of the citizen and the arena for the practice of citizenship) is, or ought to be, a thing of beauty.[1] One recalls Plato's claim that the young should be surrounded only with beautiful artifacts. When citizens speak with pride of their city (or state, province or nation), it is more likely to be with reference to its cultural amenities than to its political institutions. Among the decisions into which a modern democratic citizen may have an input are those affecting support of sculpture in public places, museums, orchestras, theatres, art galleries, libraries, parks, athletic stadia, and other public amenities. There is no doubt that, in the last analysis, public provision of this kind of cultural amenity is a political matter: public debate must focus on different social and economic priorities confronting citizens as an indication of what kind of place they want their city and country to be; what kinds of things they really value and what conception of social justice is implicit in decisions to provide cultural amenities at the expense of meeting 'bread and butter' needs like low-cost municipal housing, for example. But though their expressions of what they value are thus, in part, political decisions, when it comes to the provision of public amenities of one kind or another, unless citizens appreciate the value of cultural artifacts and institutions in their city and accept them as an enrichment of civic life (even if they do not enjoy or use them personally), political discussion will degenerate into mere consideration of the cost-benefit of such amenities, and the likelihood that they will add to the already onerous burden of taxation. Thus, even in their political capacity, citizens have to make judgments on the value of cultural objects – music, drama, literature, the plastic arts, athletic and sporting activities. Often such judgments also involve historical knowledge: citizen pride is apt to focus on what their city or nation has been as well as what it now is or might become. And it is because citizenship has these wider cultural dimensions that liberal education has often been considered the only educational option available to the free citizen. Clearly, the education of citizens should be as much an aesthetic education as it is a moral and political education.

As we have already noted, one of the criticisms made of Hirsch's advocacy of cultural literacy is that it is elitist. But it is odd that this charge of elitism should be directed at a proposal that seems essentially democratic; that is, at the requirement that all Americans (and, implicitly, all citizens of any democratic state) should have access to the cultural capital that has, historically, been the preserve of a ruling class. The paradox entailed in affirming the rights of everyone to citizenship, while doubting the capacity or inclination of a majority to acquire a liberal education, was underlined half a century ago by Robert Hutchins:

> (The) foundation of democracy is universal suffrage. It makes every man a ruler. If every man is a ruler, every man needs the education that rulers ought to have. . . . The kind of education we accept now when everybody is destined to rule is fundamentally an extension of the kind that in Jefferson's time was thought suitable for those destined to labor not to rule. When we talk of our political goals, we admit the right of every man to be a ruler. When we talk of our educational program, we see no inconsistency in saying that only a few have the capacity to get the education that rulers ought to have. Yet the choice before us would seem to be clear: either we should abandon the democratic ideal or we should help every citizen to acquire the education that is appropriate to free men. (Hutchins, 1953)

To put Hutchins's point bluntly, if people have neither the capacity nor the appetite for a liberal education, they ought not to be allowed to vote.

This democratic dilemma articulated by Hutchins remains as acute today, so long as there are educationists who assert that a liberal education is irrelevant to a majority of citizens, being merely a repository of high-culture or high-status knowledge of interest and relevance only to an elite. For, to the contrary, what is really elitist is the belief that only a few 'blue chip' or 'blue riband' citizens have any interest in or need for the kind of cultural literacy that is the fruit of a liberal education.[2] Until relatively recently, political radicals have usually taken the view that the fundamental problem of democratic education was not to define an alternative, 'relevant' curriculum for the masses, but to provide universal access to the humanistic liberal curriculum formerly denied to the subaltern classes; thus ensuring that every future citizen has the opportunity to acquire the best of knowledge and skill that historically has been available only to a privileged few.

If Hirsch's proposals are democratic in being predicated on the need for the benefits of a liberal education to be universally available to all citizens, in what sense, if any, can they also be characterized as elitist? 'Elitist' is an adjective which is almost always used pejoratively to denote those values, activities, and institutions that justify, promote, and legitimate an elite, especially those educational arrangements that appear designed to set selected individuals apart from the population at large in order to recruit and train them for social, professional, or political eminence. It is clear that Hirsch's proposals are not elitist in this sense. His concern is with *every* American: 'The educational goal advocated is that of mature literacy for all our citizens.' There is no elite minority group designated as the beneficiary of cultural literacy and consequent political empowerment, though Hirsch does claim that, inevitably, it is the disadvantaged who will benefit most from its universalization. In his view, cultural literacy is also an instrument of 'social justice and more effective democracy'.

Clearly, the epithet 'elitist' can only be attributed to Hirsch's proposal in quite a different sense, the sense that refers to individuals like himself who, allegedly presuming their own culture to be superior, wish to impose it upon other people's children. In this sense, the elite are not the beneficiaries of privileged educational arrangements, but a group of educationists, bureaucrats, pundits, and politicians who define what everybody else ought to know, irrespective of the culture they already have. But this latter charge of elitism applies to any individual or group (political revolutionaries, religious evangelists, dieticians, societies for the prevention of all kinds of alleged oppressions and evils) that advocates any alternative set of values, practices, or norms. Especially, it would apply to generations of Marxists who have believed that the working class should not be fobbed off with a curriculum of something called proletarian or working class culture. When answering fellow revolutionaries who wanted the curriculum of the post-revolutionary Soviet school to transmit proletarian culture, Lenin argued that this was something which did not yet exist: 'proletarian culture must be the result of the natural development of the stores of knowledge which mankind has accumulated under the yoke of capitalist society, landlord society and bureaucratic society'. He believed that this had also been the position of Marx himself, who 'took his stand on the firm foundation of human knowledge which had been gained under capitalism' (Lenin, 1920). In similar vein, Gramsci believed that 'the entire thought of the past' is the appropriate cognitive capital for political revolutionaries. And as I have observed elsewhere (Entwistle, 1979), working-class students in the various traditions of adult education have usually demanded a 'liberal' curriculum, not a hand-to-mouth 'relevant' curriculum, parochially rooted only in the here and now (also see Entwistle, 1989).

Similar to the contention that Hirsch and other advocates of cultural literacy are elitist is the claim that liberal education as historically manifest in the school curriculum represents the cultural imperialism of white males. The claim, voiced by some minority groups and left-wing radicals and feminists, is that the liberal curriculum is merely a celebration of Western culture that neglects not only the contributions to human knowledge of non-Westerners but also of women. Given that modern citizens are now members of multicultural nations, it is argued that cultural literacy should be conceived in terms of contributions from a wide variety of cultures.

However, it has already been noted that Western culture is itself a multiculture. One of the ironies of the multicultural education debate (in, for example, multicultural Canada) is that a quarter-century ago it was immigrant communities of Greeks and Italians who were deemed excluded from the mainstream curriculum. This was an odd claim, since the cultures of Greece, Rome/Italy, France and Germany, for example, have always figured prominently in the curricula of schools in the English-speaking world. Half a century ago, you could not have gone to school in England without being taught Greek, Roman and Norse mythology; the ancient histories of Greece and Rome; the Old Testament and the history of the Holy Land and Mesopotamia; the French revolution; the unification of Germany and Italy; as well as the contributions to philosophy, art, music and literature of non-English European people. Many students, especially in continental Europe, also learned one or more foreign languages. And, it should be noted, this teaching of other contributions to human culture was rarely xenophobic; to the contrary, it was almost always laudatory and appreciative, in the spirit of Matthew Arnold's claim that this international cultural tradition represents 'the best that has been thought and said in the world'. So today, as then, the charge of cultural exclusion has to refer to the alleged neglect of non-Western cultures, especially in the curricula of those schools having significant minorities of students from Africa, Asia and the Middle East. The question is, as contenders for inclusion in the curricula of English-speaking schools, what contribution have non-Western cultures made to 'the best that has been thought and said'? Two responses to this question are necessary.

First, it is a commonplace that non-Western cultures have contributed, seminally, to our knowledge of the human condition and the natural universe. Mathematics, for example, is far from being an exclusively 'western' invention: that we owe our system of arithmetical notation to the Arabs is legendary. Nor does Hirsch's list neglect Eastern cultures: Confucius, Buddha, Mohammed and Ghandi figure alongside Christ.

Secondly, however, it is interesting that school curricula in many non-Western societies frequently include the same curriculum content as Western schools, especially with reference to the sciences. Western science is axiomatically the basis for most technological development throughout the world: Air Japan, Malaysian Airlines and other non-Western airlines would be foolish if they tried to build and fly aircraft on scientific principles other than those bequeathed us by Western science. But this Asian reference to Western culture is not confined to the sciences. I am reliably informed that if, tonight, there is an orchestral concert in Tokyo, the Tokyo Symphony Orchestra will be playing the works of the great European dead white males – Haydn, Mozart, Beethoven, Brahms, Tchaikovski, Dvorak and the rest – and only occasionally works or concerts by Japanese composers. Any day in Europe will also reveal droves of Japanese gazing admiringly at the works of the great dead white European painters, sculptors and architects. Intellectuals who have no appreciation or respect for the great Western European traditions of literature, art, music philosophy and science may deplore the fact that Asians are so easily seduced by Western culture, but it is important to consider why this fascination exists. And, arguably, it is because they recognize these cultural creations of dead white European males to be amongst the best that has been thought and said (and, one might add, done) in the world. Perhaps intense scholarly activity in the future will discover non- Western scientific, literary, philosophical and artistic artifacts which are demonstrably superior to anything we currently know. A similar claim is often made for allegedly lost or suppressed literature, art and music created by women in the past. And, indeed, it might make for a considerable amelioration of the human condition if the whole world, and the Western world especially, took cognizance of non-Western science, religion, philosophy, literature, and so on in the school curriculum, as well as of the contribution of women to the arts and sciences. But that prospect remains unrealized in default of the research that would uncover such hidden, suppressed, or neglected female or non-Western contributions to human culture.

As Hirsch is quick to emphasize, the cultural capital, which is the school's stock in trade, is not a static museum piece. The best of human thought and action that the liberal, humanistic curriculum represents is subject to constant re-evaluation and renewal, open to new forms of knowledge from whatever cultural source, whilst rejecting that which becomes obsolete. The pedagogical correlate of this curricular dynamic is that abstract knowledge, which is the stuff of the academic disciplines, needs to be appropriately concretized in order to speak to a variety of student interests, talents, aspirations, and needs.

Earlier, the distinction was drawn between different kinds of knowledge appropriate to the different aspects of citizenship: particular knowledge of the political culture related to the machinery and processes of government, as means toward ends; and the general cultural knowledge necessary for understanding and intelligent activity in relation to substantive political issues. It was argued that the latter is the knowledge of most worth to citizens. However, it is not possible to envisage cultural literacy that does not also embrace political literacy. The political culture is an integral part of general culture. Among the best that has been thought and said in the world is the great tradition of political theory contained in the works of Plato, Aristotle, Machiavelli, Hobbes, Locke, Rousseau, Montesquieu, Hegel, Marx and Engels, Paine, Madison, de Tocqueville, the Utilitarians, and Dewey. Clearly, any comprehensive catalogue of cultural literacy must include these names as, indeed, Hirsch's list does with few exceptions. However, as distinctively political knowledge, political theory of this kind has rarely figured in the curriculum as knowledge relevant to all future citizens. The political content of the curriculum has largely been confined to a mainly descriptive civics concerned with the facts of the constitution and political institutions. I have argued that this is of little interest and relevance to the average citizen. But political theory, focusing upon seminal figures such as those listed above, is potentially a more fruitful educational experience in itself, and more relevant to the political development of citizens.

It may seem unrealistically demanding to suggest that these seminal ideas of the great political philosophers should be part of the curriculum of all future citizens. But this tradition of political thought is not mere esoterica. The point has often been made, notably by Jerome Bruner, that the key ideas that lie at the heart of the sciences and humanities are as few as they are simple, such that they can be taught to any student at any age in some intellectually honest form. To take just one example, it should not be beyond the ability of primary schoolchildren to grasp the Hobbesian thesis that without an agreement to curb individual appetites and aggressions through the creation of political institutions concerned with law and order, life will be 'poor, nasty, brutish and short,' even and especially in school. Indeed, the social relationships and values manifest in the organization of any school are sufficient to illustrate the principles immanent in the great tradition of political theory. For these are the principles that are fundamental to all discussions of the questions that concern all citizens, albeit at the level of concrete experience if not abstract theory, in the daily business of life: concern with rights and freedoms, duties and obligations, law and order, as well as the machiavellianism of governments in dealing not only with foreign powers, but also with their own citizens.

Finally, no doubt there are those who will object that what really matters if citizens are to act responsibly and humanely is not so much that they have detailed information about substantive political issues but that they develop 'correct' feelings and attitudes about the issues confronting modern societies; arguably, intellectual elites will tell them what are the politically correct responses to any issue, irrespective of the facts of the matter. As some of the classical accounts of the nature of citizenship remind us, without virtue and passion citizenship is barren. It is often argued that schools have neglected the emotions in favour of an exclusively cognitive approach to learning. But nothing could be further from the truth. All national educational systems cultivate a passionate xenophobia in young citizens, usually masquerading as patriotism but often nakedly, uncompromisingly and aggressively nationalist. Evidently passion and emotion without the constraint of intellect is as dangerous as knowledge without passion. A former colleague recently reminded me that when we both taught in a northern English university in the 1960s, our students informed us one afternoon that they would not be attending classes next day since they would be on a protest march downtown. When asked what they were protesting about we were told that they would be putting pressure on Prime Minister Harold Wilson to bring British troops out of Vietnam. It might be argued that to have told them that there were no British troops in Vietnam would have been insensitive and irrelevant, since theirs was really a sincere protest against a war which was widely regarded as obscene. But even righteous anger is, politically, vain unless grounded in relevant accurate knowledge about what is the case. No doubt appropriate citizen activity does depend upon prompting by a humane affective sensibility. But the sincere ignoramus is as much a threat to the future of mankind as is the clever machiavellian. The education of citizens needs to cultivate virtue and passion, themselves immanent in a curriculum which includes literature, history and the arts, but that citizens should also be well informed is inescapable if they are to contribute autonomously and creatively to the intelligent and humane development of modern democratic societies.

NOTES

1. Here the word 'city' in quotation marks acknowledges the origin of citizenship in the city states of the ancient world, whilst standing also as a shorthand for the different levels at which modern citizenship is exercised – the local community, the state or province in federal jurisdictions, the nation-state and even in supra-national communities like the European community; as well as globally, as in expressions like 'citizen of the world'.
2. The terms 'blue chip' and 'blue riband' have recently been used in North America to denote groups of citizens (often former politicians, businessmen, academics and other pundits) who believe themselves to have superior wisdom to that of 'ordinary' citizens. No doubt experts have a useful function to perform in illuminating the complex issues which confront all citizens in the modern world. But expertise of one kind or another lies in the experience of most citizens in all walks of life (including, especially, the 'expertise' that comes from being poor, handicapped, unemployed or

otherwise disadvantaged) and the possession of expertise does not privilege the knowledge of any expert when matters of political or moral judgment are at issue.

Bibliography

Abberley, P. (1987) The Concept of Oppression and the Development of a Social Theory of Disability, in *Disability, Handicap and Society*, 2: 1.

Acton, H. B. (ed.) (1951) *Utilitarianism, Liberty and Representative Government*. London: Dent and Sons.

Amin, K. with Oppenheim, C. (1992) *Poverty in Black and White*. London: CPAG and the Runnymede Trust.

Anderson, M., Bechhofer, F. and Gershuny, J (eds) (1994) *The Social and Political Economy of the Household*. Oxford: Oxford University Press.

Anderson, P. and Blackburn, R. (eds.) (1965) *Towards Socialism*. London: Fontana.

Aristotle *Politics*. Harmondsworth: Penguin (1981 edn).

Arnot, M. (1995) Feminism and Democratic Education, in Santomé, J. (ed.) *Volver a pensar la educación*. Madrid: Morata Press.

Association for Education in Citizenship (1935) *Education for Citizenship in Secondary Schools*. Oxford: Oxford University Press.

Atkinson, J. and Papworth, R. (1991) *Literacy and Less skilled Jobs*. IMS Report No. 211. University of Sussex: Institute of Manpower Studies.

Atkinson, J. and Spilsbury, M. (1993) *Basic Skills and Jobs*. London: Adult Literacy and Basic Skills Unit.

Atkinson, J., Spilsbury, M. and Williams, M. (1993) *The Basic Skills Needed at Work : a Directory*. London: Adult Literacy and Basic Skills Unit.

Australian Education Council (1990) *A National Literacy Strategy*. Darwin: Australian Education Council.

Avineri, S. and de-Shalit, A. (eds) (1992) *Communitarianism and Individualism*. Oxford: Oxford University Press.

Bahmueller, C. (1991) *Civitas: A framework for civic education*. Calabasas, California: Center for Civic Education.

Baldaur, R. and Luke, A. (eds) *Language Planning and Education in Australia and the South Pacific*. Sydney: Multilingual Matters.

Ball, S. J. (1990) *Politics and Policy Making in Education*. London: Routledge.

Ball, S. J. (1993) Education markets, choice and social class: the market as a class strategy in the UK and US, in *British Journal of Sociology of Education*, 14: 1.

Ball, S., Kenny, A. and Gardiner, D. (1990) Literacy, Politics and the Teaching of English, in Goodson, I. and Medway, P. (eds).

Barbalet, J. M. (1988) *Citizenship*. Milton Keynes: Open University Press.

Barnes, C. (1991) *Disabled People in Britain and Discrimination: A Case for Anti-Discrimination Legislations*. London: Hurst and Company.

Barnes, C. and Oliver, M. (1995) Disability Rights: rhetoric and reality in the UK, in *Disability and Society*, 10: 1.

Barnes, C. (1996) Theories of Disability and the Origins of the Oppression of Disabled People in Western Society, in Barton, L. (ed.).

Barth, F. (1969) *Ethnic Groups and Boundaries*, London, Allen and Unwin.

Bartolini, S. (1983a) The European Left since World War I: Size, Composition and Patterns of Electoral Development, in Daalder and Mair (eds).

Bartolini, S. (1983b) The Membership of Mass Parties: The Social Democratic Experience 1889–1978, in Daalder and Mair (eds).

Barton, D. (1994) *Literacy: An Introduction to the Ecology of Written Language.* Oxford: Blackwell.

Barton, L. (ed.) (1996) *Disability and Society: Emerging Issues and Insights.* London: Longman.

Bassett, K. (1984) Labour, Socialism, and Local Democracy, in Boddy, M. and Fudge, C. (eds).

Batho, G. (1990) The history of the teaching of civics and citizenship in English schools, *The Curriculum Journal,* 1: 1.

Bauman, Z. (1990) *Thinking Sociologically.* Oxford: Blackwell.

Beck, U. (1992) *Risk Society: Towards a new modernity,* London: Sage.

Bellamy, R. (1993) Citizenship and Rights, in Bellamy, R. (ed).

Bellamy, R. (ed.) (1993) *Theories and Concepts of Politics.* Manchester: Manchester University Press.

Bellamy, R. et al. (eds) (1995) *Democracy and Constitutional Politics in the Union of Europe.* London: Lothian Foundation Press.

Bellamy, R. (ed.) (1996) *Constitutionalism, Democracy and Sovereignty: American and European Perspectives.* Aldershot: Avebury Books.

Benhabib, S. and Cornell, D. (eds) (1987) *Feminism and Critique.* Cambridge: Polity Press.

Berenstain, S. and Berenstain, J. (1975) *He Bear She Bear.* London: Collins.

Bewley, C. and Glendinning, C. (1994) Representing the Views of Disabled People in Community Care Planning, in *Disability and Society,* 9: 3.

Bines, H., Baroness Perry, and Demaine, J. (1992) Freedom, Inequality and the Market in Further and Higher Education, in *British Journal of Sociology of Education,* 13: 1.

Birnbaum, N. (ed.) (1977) *Beyond the Crisis.* New York: Oxford University Press.

Blunkett, D. (1987) Facing up to the new realities, *Times Educational Supplement,* 25 September.

Bock, G. and James, S. (eds) (1992) *Beyond Equality and Difference.* London: Routledge.

Boddy, M. and Fudge, C. (eds) (1984) *Local Socialism? Labour Councils and New Left Alternatives.* London: Macmillan.

Bottery, M. (1992) Education for citizenship in the 21st century, *Curriculum,* 13: 3.

Bowe, R., Ball, S. J. and Gold, A. (1992) *Reforming Education and Changing Schools.* London: Routledge.

Bowles, S. and Gintis, H. (1976) *Schooling in Capitalist America.* London: Routledge and Kegan Paul.

Bowles, S. and Gintis, H. (1986) *Democracy and Capitalism.* London: Routledge.

Briceno, S. and Pitt, D. (eds) (1988) *New Ideas in Environmental Education.* London: Croom Helm.

Bridgeman, J. and Millns, S. (eds) (1995) *Law and Body Politics.* Aldershot: Dartmouth.

Brisenden, S. (1989) Young, Gifted and Disabled: entering the employment market, in *Disability, Handicap and Society,* 4:3.

Bromage, A.W. (1930) Literacy and the electorate, *American Political Science Review,* 24: 4.

Brunt, R. (1989) The politics of identity, in Hall, S. and Jacques, M. (eds)

Butler, J. and Scott, J. W. (eds) (1992) *Feminists Theorise the Political.* London: Routledge.

Buttershaw Community (1992) *The GBH Report: An Integrated Comprehensive Regeneration Strategy for Buttershaw.* Bradford: Buttershaw Advice and Social Centre et al.

Cameron, D. and Bourne, J. (1989) *Grammar, Nation and Citizenship: Kingman in Linguistic and Historical Perspective.* Occasional Paper No. 1, Department of English and Media Studies, Institute of Education, University of London.

Carr, W. (1991) Education for Citizenship, *British Journal of Educational Studies,* 39:4.

Carr, W. and Hartnett, A. (1996) *Education and the Struggle for Democracy.* Buckingham: Open University Press.

Carr, W. and Hartnett, A. (1996) Civic Education, Democracy and the English Political Tradition: Chapter 4 in this collection.

Carroll, L. (1947) *Alice through the Looking Glass.* London: Pan Books.

Carter, R. (ed.) (1982) *Linguistics and the Teacher.* London: Routledge and Kegan Paul.

Center for Civic Education (1994) *National Standards for Civics and Government.* Calabasas, California: Center for Civic Education.

Children's Society (1991) *Education for Citizenship.* London: Children's Society.

Christodoulidis, E. (1995) 'A New Constitutional Reality for Civil Society'? Some Cautionary Remarks on Republican Citizenship, in Bellamy, R. et al. (eds).

Citizenship Foundation (1995) *Young Citizen's Passport.* London: The Citizenship Foundation.

Civics Expert Group (1994) *Whereas the People... Civics and Citizenship Education.* Canberra: Australian Government Publishing Service.

Cohen, P. (1990) *Really Useful Knowledge: Photography and cultural studies in the transition from school.* Chester: Trentham Books.

Coleman, J. (1957) *Community Conflict* New York: The Free Press of Gencoe.

Coleridge, F. (1993) *Disability, Liberation and Development.* Oxford: Oxford Publications.

Commission on Citizenship (1990) *Encouraging Citizenship.* London: HMSO.

Commission on Social Justice (1993) *Social Justice in a Changing World.* London: IPPR.

Commission on Social Justice (1994) *Social Justice: Strategies for National Renewal.* London: Vintage.

Connell, W. F. (1950) *The Educational Thought and Influence of Matthew Arnold.* London: Routledge & Kegan Paul.

Connell, R. (1989) Working class curriculum, in McCrae, D. (ed.)

Cook, D. (1993) Defrauding the state: who benefits?, in Sinfield, A. (ed.).

Coote, A. (1992) *The Welfare of Citizens.* London: IPPR and Rivers Oram Press.

Corbett, J. and Barton, L. (1992) *A Struggle for Choice: Students with Special Needs in Transition to Adulthood.* London: Routledge.

Corbett, J. (1994) A Proud Label: exploring the relationship between disability politics and gay pride, *Disability and Society,* 9: 3.

Corcoran, P. (1994) Environmental education in the former Soviet Union: problems, practice, collaboration, *International Research in Geographical and Environmental Education,* 3: 2.

Cox, B. (1991 or 3) *Cox on Cox: An English Curriculum for the 1990s.* London: Hodder and Stoughton.

Croft, S. and Beresford, P. (1989) User-involvement, Citizenship and Social Policy, *Critical Social Policy,* 26.

Croft, S. and Beresford, P. (1990) *From Paternalism to Participation*. London: Open Services Project.

Crowley, Tony (1989) *The Politics of Discourse: the standard language question in British cultural debates*. London: Macmillan.

Curriculum Development Group (1989) *Welfare Rights in Social Work Education*. London: CCETSW.

Crook, S., Pakulski, J, and Waters, M. (1992) *Postmodernization: Change in Advanced Society*. London: Sage.

Crossman, R. (1976) *Diaries of a Cabinet Minister*. London: Hamish Hamilton.

Daalder, H. (1983) The Comparative Study of European Party Systems, in Daalder, H. and Mair, P. (eds.).

Daalder, H. and Mair, P. (eds.) (1983) *Western European Party Systems*. London: Sage.

Dahl, R. A. (1985) *A Preface to Economic Democracy*. Cambridge: Polity Press.

Dahrendorf, R. (1987) The erosion of citizenship and its consequences for us all, *New Statesmen and Society*, 12 June.

Dalton, R. J. and Kuechler, M. (eds) (1991) *Challenging The Political Order: New Social Movements in Western Democracies*. Cambridge: Polity Press.

Darke, P. (1995) *Screening Lies? Portrayals and Betrayals: Disability in the Cinema*. Bristol: Watershed Media Centre.

Daunt, P. (1991) *Meeting Disability. A European Response*. London: Cassell.

Dearing, R. (1994) *The National Curriculum and its Assessment*. London: School Curriculum and Assessment Authority.

Delaney, C. F. (ed.) (1994) *The Liberalism- Communitarianism Debate*. Maryland: Rowman and Littlefield.

Demaine, J. (1981) *Contemporary Theories in the Sociology of Education*. London: Macmillan.

Demaine, J. (1988) Teachers' Work, Curriculum and the New Right, *British Journal of Sociology of Education*, 9: 3.

Demaine, J. (1990) The Reform of Secondary Education, in Hindess, B. (ed.) (1990).

Demaine, J. (1992) The Labour Party and Education Policy, *British Journal of Educational Studies*, 40: 3.

Demaine, J. (1993) The New Right and the Self-Managing School, in Smyth, J. (ed.) (1993).

Demaine, J. (1996) The Politics of Identity and the Identity of Sociology. A paper to the International Sociology of Education Conference in Sheffield, England; January 3–5.

Department of Education and Science (1975) *A Language for Life* (The Bullock Report). London: HMSO.

Department of Education and Science (1977) *Education in Schools: A Consultative Document*. London: HMSO.

Department of Education and Science (1985) *Education for All* (The Swann Report). London: HMSO.

Department of Education and Science (1988a) *Report of the Committee of Inquiry into the Teaching of English Language* (The Kingman Report). London: HMSO.

Department of Education and Science (1988b) *National Curriculum: Task Group on Assessment and Testing*. London: HMSO.

Department of Education and Science (1988c) *Mathematics for 5–16. Proposals of the Secretary of State for Education*. London: HMSO.

Department of Education and Science (1988d) *English for ages 5 to 11.* London: HMSO.

Department of Education and Science (1989) *English for ages 5 to 16.* London: HMSO.

Department of Education and Science (1991) *The Parent's Charter.* London: DES.

Despouy, L. (1991) *Human Rights and Disability.* New York: United Nations Economic and Social Council.

Dessent, T. (1987) *Making The Ordinary School Special.* London, The Falmer Press.

Dietz, M. (1992) Context is All: Feminism and Theories of Citizenship, in Mouffe, C. (ed.).

Donnison, D. (1994) *Act Local: Social Justice from the Bottom Up.* London: IPPR.

Drucker, H. (1979) *Doctrine and Ethos in The Labour Party.* London: Allen and Unwin.

Duverger, M. (1954) *Political Parties.* London: Methuen.

Edwards, J. and Fogelman, K. (1991) Active citizenship and young people, in Fogelman (ed.).

Edwards, J. and Fogelman, K. (1993) *Developing Citizenship in the Curriculum.* London: David Fulton.

Edwards, J. and Pathan, L. (eds.) (1993) *Cross-Curricular Resources and INSET Pack.* London: Pearson Publishing.

Edwards, L., Munn, P. and Fogelman, K. (eds) (1994) *Education for Democratic Citizenship in Europe – New Challenges for Secondary Education.* London: Swets and Zeitlinger.

Enticott, J., Graham, P. and Lamb, B. (eds) (1992) *Polls Apart.* London: Spastics Society.

Entwistle, H. (1979) *Antonio Gramsci: Conservative Schooling for Radical Politics.* London: Routledge & Kegan Paul.

Entwistle, H. (1989) The Citizenship Tradition in Adult Education, O'Sullivan (ed.).

Etzioni, A. (1961) *A Comparative Analysis of Complex Organizations.* New Jersey: Prentice-Hall.

Etzioni, A. (1964) *Modern Organizations.* New Jersey: Prentice-Hall.

Etzioni, A. (1968) *The Active Society.* New York: The Free Press.

Etzioni, A. (1993) *The Spirit of Community: The Reinvention of American Society.* New York: Simon and Schuster.

Eurobarometer No. 38 (1992) Luxembourg: Office for Official Publications of the European Communities.

Faith in the City (1985) London: Church House.

Field, F. (1989) *Losing Out.* Oxford: Blackwell.

Field, J. H. (1982) *Towards a Programme of Imperial Life: The British Empire at the turn of the century.* Oxford: Oxford University Press.

Feinberg, W. (1983) *Understanding Education.* Cambridge: Cambridge University Press.

Fien, J. (n.d.) *Education for the Australian Environment.* Canberra: Curriculum Development Centre.

Fien, J. (1993) *Education for the Environment: Critical curriculum theorising and environmental education.* Geelong: Deakin University Press.

Finkelstein, V. (1993) *Being Disabled.* Milton Keynes: Open University Press.

Flude, M. and Hammer, M. (eds) (1990) *The Education Reform Act 1988: Its Origins and Implications.* London: The Falmer Press.

Fogelman, K. (1990) Citizenship in Secondary Schools: a National Survey, Appendix E in Commission on Citizenship.

Fogelman, K. (1991a) Citizenship in Secondary Schools: The National Picture, in Fogelman, K. (ed.).

Fogelman, K. (ed.) (1991b) *Citizenship in Schools*. London David Fulton.

Forrester, T. (1976) *The Labour Party and The Working Class*. London: Heinemann.

Fountaine, P (1994) *A Citizen's Europe*. Luxembourg: Office for Official Publications of the European Communities.

Frazer, E. and Lacey, N. (1993) *The Politics of Community: A Feminist critique of the Liberal–Communitarian Debate*. Hemel Hempstead: Harvester Wheatsheaf.

Friedman, M. (1992) Feminism and Modern Friendship: Dislocating the Community, in Avineri, S. and de-Shalit, A. (eds.)

Fulcher, G. (1989) *Disabling Policies? A comparative approach to education policy and disability.* London, The Falmer Press.

Gaine, C. (1988) *No Problem Here*. London: Hutchinson.

Galbraith, J. K. (1994) *The Good Society considered: the economic dimension*. Cardiff Law School.

Gallie, W. R. (1956) *Essentially Contested Concepts. Proceedings of the Aristotelian Society, (1955–56).*

Gershuny, J. (1989) *Time Budgets as General Social Indicators*. Mimeo: School of Social Sciences, University of Bath.

Giddens, A. (1993) *The Transformation of Intimacy.* Cambridge: Polity Press.

Gilbert, R. (1992) Citizenship, education and postmodernity, *British Journal of Sociology of Education*, 13: 1.

Gilroy, P. (1987) *There Ain't no Black in the Union Jack*. London: Hutchinson.

Glendon, M. A. (1991) *Rights Talk: the Impoverishment of Political Discourse*. New York: The Free Press.

Goodson, I. and Medway, P. (eds.) (1990) *Bringing English to Order*. London: The Falmer Press.

Gough, N. (1989) From epistemology to ecopolitics: Renewing a paradigm for curriculum, *Journal of Curriculum Studies*, 21: 3.

Goulbourne, H. (1989) *The Communal Option: Nationalism and Ethnicity in Post-Imperial Britain.* Warwick: Centre for Research in Ethnic Relations.

Graham, D. (with Tytler, D.) (1993) *A Lesson For Us All: The Making of the National Curriculum*. London: Routledge.

Green, A. (1991) The peculiarities of English education, in *Education Limited: Schooling, Training and the New Right in England since 1979*. London: Unwin Hyman.

Greenall Gough, A. (1990) Red and green: Two case studies in learning through ecopolitical action, *Curriculum Perspectives*, 10: 2.

Greenall Gough, A. and Robottom, I. (1993) Towards a socially critical environmental education: Water quality studies in a coastal school, *Journal of Curriculum Studies*, 25: 4.

Guardian The (1995) Incentives call to aid parents. 28 September.

Gutmann, A. (1987) *Democratic Education*. Princeton: Princeton University Press.

Hahn, H. (1985) Towards a Politics of Disability: Definitions, Disciplines, and Policies, in *The Social Science Journal*, 22: 4

Hall, S. (1988) Invited Lecture to Department of Sociology. Lancaster: University of Lancaster.

Hall, S. and Jacques, M. (eds.) (1989) *New Times: The changing face of politics in 1990s.* London: Lawrence and Wishart.

Halsey, A. H., Floud, J. and Anderson, C. A. (eds.) (1961) *Education, Economy and Society.* New York: The Free Press.

Hamilton, M. A. (1939) *The Labour Party Today.* London: Labour Book Service.

Hampton, W. (1970) *Democracy and Community.* Oxford: Oxford University Press.

Hastie, C. (1986) History, Race and Propaganda, in Palmer, F. (ed.).

Hayek, F. A. (1976) *The Road to Serfdom.* London: Routledge and Kegan Paul.

Heater, D. (1990) *Citizenship: The Civic Ideal in World History, Politics and Education.* London: Longman.

Hebdige, R. (1990) Fax to the future, *Marxism Today*, January.

Hechter, M. (1975) *Internal Colonialism*, London, Routledge.

Helander, E. (1993) *Prejudice and Dignity: An Introduction to Community-Based Rehabilitation.* New York: United Nations Development Programme.

Held, D. (1987) *Models of Democracy.* Cambridge: Polity Press.

Held, D. (1989) *Political Theory and the Modern State.* Cambridge: Polity Press.

Hillgate Group (1987) *The Reform of British Education.* London: The Claridge Press.

Hindess, B. (ed.) (1990) *Reactions to the Right.* London: Routledge.

Hindess. B. (1993) Citizenship in the Modern West, in Turner, B. S. (ed.) (1993).

Hirsch, E. D. (1988) *Cultural Literacy: What Every American Needs to Know.* New York: Vintage Books.

Hirst, P. Q. (1990) Democracy: Socialism's Best Reply to the Right, in Hindess, B. (ed.) (1990).

Holmwood, J. (1993) Welfare and Citizenship, in Bellamy, R. (ed.).

Honey, J. (1983) *The Language Trap: race class and the 'standard English' issue in British schools.* Kay Shuttleworth Papers on Education, No 3. Middlesex: National Council for Educational Standards.

Honeyford, R. (1988) *Integration or Disintegration: Towards a Non-racist Society.* London: The Claridge Press.

Horrel, S., Rubery, J., and Burchell, B. (1994) Working Time Patterns, Constraints and Preferences, in M. Anderson et al. (eds).

Hosking, G. (1995) Mother Russia's prophet returns, *The Independent*, 21 September.

Hubback, E. M. (1934) *Education for Citizenship.* Morley College of Working Men and Women.

Huckle, J. (1987a) Environment and development issues in the classroom: the experience of one curriculum project, in Lacey, C. and Williams, R. (eds.).

Huckle, J. (1987b) *What We Consume.* London: Richmond and World Wildlife Fund.

Hurst, A. (1996) Reflecting on Researching Disability and Higher Education in Barton, L. (ed.).

Hutchins, R. M. (1953) *The Conflict in Education in a Democratic Society.* New York: Harper Brothers.

Hyatt, S. (1991) Accidental Activists: women and politics on a council estate. Paper presented to the American Anthropological Association Annual Meeting, Chicago, Illinois, November.

Inglehart, R. (1990) Values, Ideology and Cognitive Mobilisation in New Social Movements, in Dalton, R. and Kuechler, M. (eds.).

Institute for Citizenship Studies (1994a) *Encouraging Citizenship.* London: Institute for Citizenship Studies.

Institute for Citizenship Studies (1994b) *The Hallmarks of Citizenship*. London: Institute for Citizenship Studies.

Janowitz, M. (1983) *The Reconstruction of Patriotism: Education for civic consciousness*. Chicago: University of Chicago Press.

Jenkins, R. (1994) 'Rethinking Ethnicity: identity, categories and power', *Ethnic and Racial Studies*, Vol. 17, No. 2, pp 197–223.

Johnson, R. W. (1985) *The Politics of Recession*. London: Macmillan.

Johnston Conover, P., Crewe, I. and Searing, D. (1990) The nature of citizenship in the United States and Great Britain: Empirical comments on theoretical themes, *Journal of Politics*, 52: 4.

Jones, K. (ed.) (1992) *English and the National Curriculum*. London: Kogan Page and the Institute of Education.

Jones, T. (1993) *Britain's Ethnic Minorities*. London: Policy Studies Institute.

Kauffman, L. (1990) Democracy in a postmodern world? *Social Policy*, 21: 2.

Kemmis, S. (1994) *School Reform in the 90s: Reclaiming Social Justice*. Institute for the Study of Teaching, The Flinders University of South Australia.

Kerr, J. (1968) *The Tiger Who Came to Tea*. London: Collins.

Kimber, J. and Cooper, L. (1991) *Victim Support Racial Harassment Project*. London: Polytechnic of North London.

King, A. S. and Reiss, M. J. (eds.) (1993) *The Multicultural Dimension of the National Curriculum*. London: The Falmer Press.

Kingdom, E. (1994) Review of M. C. Regan, *Political Theory Newsletter*, 6: 2.

Kingdom, E. (1995) Body Politics and Rights, in Bridgeman, J. and Millns, S. (eds).

Kingdom, E. (1996) Rights Discourse, New Social Movements, and New Political Subjects, in Bellamy, R. (ed.).

Knight, C. (1990) *The Making of Tory Education Policy in Post-War Britain 1950–1986*. London: The Falmer Press.

Labour Party (1995) *Diversity and Excellence: A New Partneship for Schools*. London: The Labour Party.

Lacey, C. and Williams, R. (eds) *Education, Ecology and Environment: The case for an education network*. London: World Wildlife Fund and Kogan Page.

Laclau, E. and Mouffe, C. (1985) *Hegemony and Socialist Strategy: Towards a radical democratic politics*. London: Verso.

Lane, D. (1987) The Commission for Racial Equality: The First Five Years. New Community, 14: 1 and 2.

Lash, S. and Urry, J. (1994) *Economies of Signs and Space*. London: Sage.

Lawton, D. (1975) *Class, Culture and the Curriculum*. London: Routledge and Keegan Paul.

Leca, J. (1992) Questions on citizenship, in Mouffe, C. (ed.)

Lee, T. and Piachaud, D. (1992) The Time Consequences of Social Services, *Time and Society*, 1: 1.

Lenin, V. I. (1920) *The Tasks of the Youth Leagues: Speech Delivered at the Third All-Russian Congress of the Russian Youth Communist League* (2 October 1920), reprinted in *Collected Works*, Vol. 31. Moscow: FLPH.

Levine, K. (1986) *The Social Context of Literacy*. London: Routledge.

Lewis, R. (1988) *Anti-Racism: A Mania Exposed*. London: Quartet Books.

Lieven, A. (1992) Far-right violence and fascist rallies erupt in Europe, *The Times*, 23 November.

Lister, R. (1990) *The Exclusive Society: Citizenship and the Poor*. London: Child Poverty Action Group.

Lister, R. (1991) Citizenship engendered, *Critical Social Policy*, 32.

Lister, R. (1992) *Women's Economic Dependency and Social Security*. Manchester: Equal Opportunities Commission.

Lister, R. (1993a) Tracing the contours of women's citizenship, *Policy and Politics*, 21: 1.

Lister, R. (1993b) Welfare rights and the constitution, in Barnett, A., Ellis, C. and Hirst, P. (eds.) *Debating the Constitution*. Cambridge: Polity Press.

Lister, R. (1995) Dilemmas in Engendering Citizenship, *Economy and Society*, 24:1.

Lloyd, J. *et al.* (1993) *Democracy Then and Now.* London: Heinemann.

Lloyd, T. O. (1984) *The British Empire 1558–1983.* Oxford: Oxford University Press.

Lo Bianco, J. (1990) Making language policy: Australia's experience, in Baldaur, R. and Luke, A. (eds.).

MacKenzie, J. M. (1984) *Propaganda and Empire*. Manchester: Manchester University Press.

MacPherson, C. B. (1973) *Democratic Theory: Essays in Retrieval*. Oxford: Clarendon Press.

MacPherson, C. B. (1977) *The Life and Times of Liberal Democracy*. Oxford: Oxford University Press.

Marenbon, J. (1987) *English Our English*. London: Centre for Policy Studies.

Marshall, T. H. (1950) *Citizenship and Social Class*. Cambridge: Cambridge University Press.

Marshall, T. H. (1964) *Class, Citizenship and Social Development*. Chicago: Chicago University Press.

Marshall, T. H. (1981) *The Right to Welfare and Other Essays*. London: Heinemann.

Marx, K. (1871) *The Civil War in France*. London. Reprinted in *Marx & Engels Selected Works*. London: Lawrence and Wishart (1968).

Massey, R. (1994) Parents to fight RE mish-mash, *Daily Mail*, 6 July.

McCrae, D. (ed.) *Imagining the Australian curriculum*. Canberra: Curriculum Development Centre.

Michels, R. (1962) *Political Parties*. Glencoe, Illinois: The Free Press.

Middleton, S., Ashworth, K. and Walker, R. (1994) *Family Fortunes*. London: Child Poverty Action Group.

Miliband, D. (ed.) (1994) *Reinventing the Left*. Cambridge: Polity Press.

Mill, J. S. (1951) Considerations on Representative Government, in Acton, H. B. (ed.).

Morgan, M. (1995) The Disability Movement in Northern Ireland, in *Disability and Society*, 10: 2.

Morris, J. (1990) Progress with Humanity: The experience of a Disabled Lecturer, in Reiser, R. and Mason, M. (eds.).

Morris, J. (1993) *Community Care or Independent Living?* York: Joseph Rowntree Foundation.

Morrison, K. (1994) *Implementing Cross-Curricular Themes*. London: David Fulton.

Mort, F. (1989) The politics of consumption, in Hall, S. and Jacques, M. (eds.).

Mouffe, C. (1988) The civics lesson, *New Statesman & Society*, 7 October.

Mouffe, C. (1988) Hegemony and New Political Subjects: Toward a New Concept of Democracy, in Nelson, C. and Grossberg, L. (eds.).

Mouffe, C.(1992) Feminism, Citizenship and Radical Democratic Politics, in Butler, J. and Scott, J. W. (eds.).

Mouffe, C. (ed.) (1992) *Dimensions of Radical Democracy: Pluralism, Citizenship, Community.* London: Verso.

Murray, C. (1989) Underclass, *Sunday Times Magazine,* 26 November.

Murray, C. (1994) *Underclass: The Crisis Deepens.* IEA / Sunday Times.

Murray, C. and Herrnstein, R. J. (1994) *The Bell Curve: Intelligence and Class Structure in American Life.* New York: Simon and Schuster.

Murray, R. (1989) Benetton Britain, in Hall, S. and Jacques, M. (eds.).

Murray, S. (1905) *The Peace of the Anglo-Saxons.* London: Watts and Co.

NACAB (1991) *Barriers to Benefit.* London: National Association of Citizens' Advice Bureaux.

Nairn, T. (1965) The Nature of the Labour Party, in Anderson, P. and Blackburn, R. (eds.).

National Commission on Education (1993) *Learning to Succeed.* London: Heinemann.

National Curriculum Council (1989) *The National Curriculum and Whole Curriculum Planning: Preliminary Guidance* (Circular Number 6). York: National Curriculum Council.

National Curriculum Council (1990a) *The Whole Curriculum* (Curriculum Guidance Series: Number 3). York: National Curriculum Council.

National Curriculum Council (1990b) *Education For Citizenship* (Curriculum Guidance Series: Number 8). York: National Curriculum Council.

Nelson, C. and Grossberg, L. (eds) (1988) *Marxism and the Interpretation of Culture.* Urbana and Chicago: University of Illinois Press.

Newbolt, H. (1921) *The Teaching of English in England* (The Newbolt Report). London: HMSO.

No Turning Back Group (1986) *Save Our Schools.* London: Conservative Political Centre.

Norfolk and Norwich Race Equality Council (1994) *Not in Norfolk: Tackling the Invisibility of Racism.* Norwich: Norfolk and Norwich Race Equality Council.

Noyes, J. H. (1961) *History of American Socialism.* New York: Hilary House.

OFSTED (1994) *Spiritual, Moral, Social and Cultural Development* (An OFSTED discussion paper). London: Office for Standards in Education.

Oldfield, A. (1990) *Citizenship and community: Civic republicanism and the modern world.* London: Routledge.

Oliver, M. (1990) *The Politics of Disablement.* London: Macmillan.

Oliver, M. (1993) *Disability, Citizenship and Empowerment.* Milton Keynes: Open University.

Oliver, M. (1995) *Understanding Disability: From Theory To Practice.* London: Kingsley Press.

O'Sullivan, D. (ed.) (1989) *Social Commitment and Adult Education.* Cork: Cork University Press.

Pahl, R. (1995) Friendly society, *New Statesman & Society,* 10 March.

Palmer, F. (ed.) (1986) *Anti-Racism: An Assault on Education and Values.* Wiltshire: The Sherwood Press.

Parry, G., Moyser, G., and Day, N. (1992) *Political Participation and Democracy in Britain.* Cambridge: Cambridge University Press.

Parsons, T. (1935) The Place of Ultimate Values in Sociological Theory, *International Journal of Ethics,* 45.

Parsons, T. (1938) The Role of Ideas in Social Action, *American Sociological Review*, 3.

Parsons, T. (1949) *Essays in Sociological Theory Pure and Applied*. Illinois: The Free Press.

Parsons, T. (1951) *The Social System*. Illinois, The Free Press.

Parsons, T. (1952) The Superego and the Theory of Social Systems, *Psychiatry*, 15.

Parsons, T. (1959) The School Class as a Social System: Some of Its Functions in American Society, *Harvard Educational Review*, 29: 4.

Parsons, T. and Shils, E. A. (1962) *Towards a General Theory of Action*. New York: Harper and Row.

Parsons, T. (1964) *Social Structure and Personality*. New York: The Free Press.

Parsons, T. (1966) *Societies: Evolutionary and Comparative Perspectives*. New Jersey: Prentice-Hall.

Pateman, C. (1980) *Participation and Democratic Theory*. Cambridge: Cambridge University Press.

Pateman, C. (1992) Equality, Difference Subordination, in Bock, G. and James, S. (eds).

Phillips, A. (1993) *Democracy and Difference*. Cambridge: Polity Press.

Phillips, D. L. (1993) *Looking Backward: a Critical Appraisal of Communitarian Thought*. New Jersey: Princeton University Press.

Pizzorno, A. (1970) An Introduction to the Theory of Political Participation, *Social Science Information*, 9.

Plant, R. and Barry, B. (1990) *Citizenship and Rights in Thatcher's Britain: Two Views*. London: IEA Health and Welfare Unit.

Plaskow, M. (ed.) (1985) *The Life and Death of the Schools Council*. London: The Falmer Press.

Policy Studies Institute (1995) *Changes in Lone Parenthood 1989–1993*. London: HMSO.

Pollak, A. (ed.) (1993) *A Citizens' Enquiry: The Opsahl Report on Northern Ireland*. Dublin: Lilliput Press.

Porter, A. (1983) *Principle of Political Literacy* (Working papers of the programme for political education). London: University of London Institute of Education.

Preecy, R. and Marsh, J. (1989) *Community Links with GCSE*. London: Community Service Volunteers.

Priestley, M. (1995) Commonalty and Difference in the Movement: An Association of Blind Asians in Leeds, in *Disability and Society*, 10: 2.

Prosser, W. R. (1991) The underclass: Assessing what we have learned, *Focus*, 13: 2.

Putnam, R. D. (1993) The Prosperous Community: Social Capital and Public Life, *The American Prospect*, Spring.

Radice, G. and Pollard, S. (1993) *More Southern Discomfort*. London: The Fabian Society.

Rae, J. (1982) The decline and fall of English grammar, *Observer*, 7 February.

Ranson, S. (1990) From 1944 to 1988: Education, Citizenship and Democracy, in Flude, M. & Hammer, M. (eds).

Regan, M. C., Jr. (1993) *Family Law and the Pursuit of Intimacy*. New York and London: New York University Press.

Reiser, R. and Mason, M. (eds) (1990) *Disability Equality in the Classroom: A Human Rights Issue*. London: Inner London Education Authority.

Rex, J. and Tomlinson, S. (1979) *Colonial Immigrants in a British City: A Class Analysis*. London: Routledge.

Rex, J. (1986) *Race and Ethnicity*, Milton Keynes, Open University Press.

Rich, P. (1986) *Race and Empire in British Politics*. Cambridge: Cambridge University Press.

Rioux, M. (1994) New Research Directives and Paradigms: Disability is not Measles, in Rioux, M. and Bach, M. (eds).

Rioux, M. and Bach, M. (eds) (1994) *Disability is not Measles: New Research Paradigms in Disability*. Ontario: Roeher Institute.

Robottom, I. and Hart, P. (1993) *Research in Environmental Education: Engaging the Debate*. Geelong: Deakin University Press.

Roche, M. (1992) *Rethinking Citizenship*. Cambridge: Polity Press.

Rootes, C. (1992) The New Politics and The New Social Movements – Accounting for British Exceptionalism, *European Journal of Political Research*, 22.

Rosenblum, N. (1994) Romantic Communitarianism: Blithedale Romance Versus the Custom House, in Delaney, C. F. (ed.).

Rousseau, J.-J. *The Social Contract*. Harmondsworth: Penguin (1968 edn).

Rowe, D. and Thorpe, T. (1993) *Living with the Law*. London: Hodder and Stoughton.

Ryan, J. and Thomas, F. (1980) *The Politics of Mental Handicap*. Harmondsworth: Penguin.

Sandel, M. (1982) *Liberalism and the Limits of Justice*. Cambridge: Cambridge University Press.

Savage, S. P. (1980) *The Theories of Talcott Parsons*. London: Macmillan.

Schumpeter, J. (1976) *Capitalism, Socialism and Democracy*. London: Allen and Unwin.

Scott, J. W. (1987) History and Difference, *Daedalus*, 116:4.

Scull, A. (1982) *Museums of Madness. The Social Organisation of Insanity in Nineteenth-Century England*. Harmondsworth: Penguin.

Senate Standing Committee on Employment, Education and Training (1989) *Education for Active Citizenship in Australian Schools and Youth Organisations*. Canberra: Australian Government Publishing Service.

Senate Standing Committee on Employment, Education and Training (1991) *Active Citizenship Revisited*. Canberra: Australian Government Publishing Service.

Sennett, M. (1977) Destructive Gemeinschaft, in Birnbaum, N. (ed.).

Sexton, S. (1987) *Our Schools: A Radical Policy*. London: Institute of Economic Affairs.

Seyd, P. and Whiteley, P. (1992) *Labour's Grass Roots*. Oxford: Oxford University Press.

Shakespeare, T. (1993) Disabled People's Self-Organisation: a new social movement? in *Disability, Handicap and Society*, 8: 3.

Sherry, S. (1995) Responsible Republicanism: Educating for Citizenship, *University of Chicago Law Review*, 62: 1.

Sinfield, A. (ed.) (1993) *Poverty, Inequality and Injustice*. Edinburgh: Edinburgh University Press.

Skolimowski, H. (1981) *Eco-philosophy: Designing new tactics for living*. Boston: Marion Boyars.

Slocombe, D. (1987) Environmentalism and the evolving information society, *Environmentalist*, 7:4.

Smith, A. D. (1986) *The Ethnic Origins of Nations*. Oxford: Blackwell.

Smyth, J. (ed.) (1993) *A Socially Critical View of the Self-Managing School*. London: The Falmer Press.

Solzhenitsyn. A. (1995) *The Russian Question at the End of the Twentieth Century*. London: Harvill Press.

Spencer, H. (1861) *Education: Intellectual, Moral and Physical*. London: Manwaring. Reprinted by Watts & Co., London 1929.

Spretnak, C. and Capra, F. (1985) *Green Politics: The Global Promise*. London: Paladin.

Starkey, H. (ed.) (1991) *Socialisation of School Children and their Education for Democratic Values and Human Rights*. London: Swets and Zeitlinger.

Stewart, J. (1993) The Challenge of Urban Transformation, *Inner City Focus*, London: Hackney Council.

Stone, L. (1969) Literacy and education in England: 1640–1900, *Past and Present*, 42.

Stradling, R. (1975) *The Political Awareness of the School Leaver*. London: Hansard Society / Politics Association.

Stradling, R. (1987) *Education for Democratic Citizenship*. Luxembourg: Office for Official Publications of the European Communities.

Street, B. (1984) *Literacy in Theory and Practice*. Cambridge: Cambridge University Press.

Stuart, O. (1992) Race and Disability: Just a double oppression? in *Disability, Handicap and Society*, 7: 2.

Stubbs, M. (1980a) *Language and Literacy: The Sociolinguistics of Reading and Writing*. London: Routledge and Kegan Paul.

Stubbs, M. (1980b) What is English? in Carter, R. (ed.)

Stubbs, M. (1986) What is Standard English? in Stubbs, M. (ed.) *Educational Linguistics*. Oxford, Blackwell.

Sweeney, J. (1994) Curse of the Tabloid haunts Mr. Lucky's wildest dreams, *The Observer*, 18 December.

Tarrant, J. M. (1989) *Democracy and Education*. London: Gower Press.

Thatcher, M. (1982) Speech to Conservative Rally, Cheltenham, Gloucestershire.

Thatcher, M. (1987) Speech to Conservative Party Conference, Blackpool.

Thatcher, M. (1993) *The Downing Street Years*. London: Harper Collins.

The Times (1990) Tebbitt defends comments on Asians, 21 April.

The Times Educational Supplement (1990) Editorial: Section A, 8 June.

The Times Educational Supplement (1994) Language funding crisis hits poorest, 26 August.

Thomas, H. (1990) From Local Financial Management to Local Management of Schools, in Flude, M. and Hammer, M. (eds).

Thompson, E. P. (1968) *The Making of the English Working Class*. Harmondsworth: Penguin.

Thornton, M. (1990) *The Liberal Primise: Anti-Discrimination Legislation in Australia*. Oxford: Oxford University Press.

Titmuss, R. M. (1958) *Essays on the Welfare State*. London: Allen and Unwin.

Titmuss, R. M. (1970) *The Gift Relationship*. London: Allen and Unwin.

Tomlinson, S. (1982) *A Sociology of Special Education*. London: Routledge and Kegan Paul.

Tomlinson, S. (1983) *Ethnic Minorities in British Schools: A Review of the Literature*. London: Heinemann.

Tomlinson, S. (1990) *Multicultural Education in White Schools*. London: Batsford.

Tomlinson, S. (1993) The Multicultural Task Group: The group that never was, in King, A. S. and Reiss, M. (eds).

Tomlinson, S. (1994) National Identity and a National Curriculum, Conference Paper to the International Sociological Association, Bielefeld, Germany, July.

Treaty on European Union. (1992) Luxembourg: Office for Official Publications of the European Communities.

Turner B. (ed.) (1990) *Theories of Modernity and Postmodernity*. London, Sage.

Turner, B. S. (1990) Outline of a Theory of Citizenship, *Sociology*, 24: 2.

Turner, B. S. (ed.) (1993) *Citizenship and Social Theory*. London: Sage.

Turner, B. S. (1993) Contemporary Problems in the Theory of Citizenship, in Turner, B. S. (ed.) (1993).

Turner, B. S. (1994) Postmodern Culture: Modern Citizens, in van Steenbergen, B. (ed.).

Turner, R. H. (1961) Modes of social ascent through education: sponsored and contest mobility, in Halsey, A. H., Floud, J. and Anderson, C. A. (eds).

Twine, F. (1994) *Citizenship and Social Rights: The Interdependence of Self and Society*. London: Sage.

UNICEF–Save the Children (1990) *The Rights of the Child*. London: UNICEF-UK.

van Steenbergen, B. (ed.) (1994) *The Condition of Citizenship*. London: Sage.

Vogel, U. (1991) Is Citizenship Gender-Specific? in Vogel, U. and Moran, M. (eds).

Vogel, U. and Moran, M. (eds) (1991) *The Frontiers of Citizenship*. London: Macmillan.

Walby, S. (1994) Is Citizenship Gendered?, *Sociology*, 28: 2.

Walzer, M. (1983) *Spheres of Justice*. Oxford: Blackwell.

Wardle, D. (1976) *English Popular Education 1780–1975*. Cambridge: Cambridge University Press.

Ware, A. (1985) *The Breakdown of Democratic Party Organization, 1940–1980*. Oxford: Clarendon Press.

Webster, P. and Charter, D. (1995) Tory plan to take over all schools, *The Times*, 23 October.

Wexler, P. (1990) Citizenship in the semiotic society, in Turner B. (ed.) (1990).

White, M. (1994) Big oration for tilt against the 'rot from Brussels': Fresh push to the right by Portillo, *The Guardian*, 13 October.

Whitty, G. *et al*. (1994) Subjects and themes in the secondary school curriculum, *Research Papers in Education*, 9: 2.

Williams, R. (1965) *The Long Revolution*. Harmondsworth: Penguin.

Willis, P. (1990) *Common Culture*. Milton Keynes: Open University Press.

Wolfensberger, W. (1993) A Reflection on Alfred Hoche, the Ideological Godfather of the German Euthanasia Program, in *Disability, Handicap and Society*, 8: 3.

Wong, F. (1994) The political dimensions of environmental education in Hong Kong, *International Research in Geographical and Environmental Education*, 3: 1.

World Commission on Environment and Development (1987) *Our Common Future*. Oxford: Oxford University Press.

World Conference on Special Needs Education (1994) Framework For Action on Special Needs Education, in *International Review of Education*, 40: 6.

Worsthorne, P. (1982) Editorial, *The Sunday Telegraph*, 23 May.

Yeatman, A. (1994) *Postmodern Revisionings of the Political*. London: Routledge.

Young, H. (1988) 'Citizen' The catch-all rallying cry, *The Guardian*, 1 September.

Young, I. M. (1987) Impartiality and the Civic Public: Some Implications of Feminist Critiques of Moral and Political Theory, in Benhabib, S. and Cornell, D. (eds).

Young, I. (1990) *Justice and the Politics of Difference*. Princeton: Princeton University Press.

Index

liberal individualism, 43–46; *see also* individualism
Lieven, A., 119
Lister, Ruth, ix, 4, 19, 29 n, 35, 163–178
literacy, 2, 92–113 *passim*, 144, 196–201, 203
literary tradition, 97, 102–3
Lloyd, J. 88
Lloyd, T. O., 119
Lo Bianco, J., 112
local community, 16, 24, 91, 163–178 *passim*
local government, 143, 163–178 *passim*
lone parents, 10–11; *see also* families

Maastricht Treaty, 131, 139; *see also* Social Chapter
machiavellian, 204, 205
MacIntyre, Alasdair, 8, 32
MacKenzie, J. M., 121
MacPherson, C. B., 67, 69
Major, John, 25, 29 n
Marenbon, J., 106–8
market model of democracy, 71–72, 73–74, 76
marketisation of education, 189; *see also* consumerism
Marsh, J., 84
Marshall, T.H., 19–20, 35–6, 52, 62, 68, 86, 117–19, 165–7
Marx, Karl, 7, 201
Marxists, 200
Mason, M., 191
Massey, R., 128
McDonaldization of youth culture, 14–16
media, 195, 197–98; *see also* teledemocrary
meritocracy, 77
Michels, R., 143
Middle East, 202
Miliband, D., 29 n
Mill, J. S. 194
moral education, 12, 199
moral model of democracy, 69–70, 72
Morgan, M., 186
Morris, J., 183, 191

Morrison, K., 87
Mort, F., 53
Mouffe. C., 6, 37–9, 62
Moyser, G., 154
multicultural education, 201
multiculturalism, 126–8
multiracial schools, 122–4
municipal socialism, 143
Munn, P., 83
Murray, C., 119, 175
Murray, S., 119
mystification thesis, 20

Nairn, T. 146
National Commission on Education (Britain), 89–90
National Council for One Parent Families, 11; *see also* lone parents
National Curriculum, 3, 24, 38, 64, 83–113 *passim*, 124–130
National Curriculum Council, (Britain) 21–23, 42, 84–9, 126–30
national identity 114–122; *see also* identity
national service, 13–15
nationalism, 115
New Left, 65
New Republicanism, 2, 6, 30
New Right, 22–24, 64–5, 79–82
New Social Movements, 154–5, 160
Newbolt Committee 92
Nicaragua, 197
No Turning Back Group, 24
Noyes, J. H., 7
Nozick, Robert, 8

OFSTED (Office for Standards in Education) in Britain, 90
Oldfield, A., 43, 47–8
Oliver, M., 170, 179, 182, 186
Ombudsman, 131, 134
Oppenheim, C., 172
Opsahl Commission, 169

Pahl, Ray, 10, 16–18, 24
Palmer, F., 123
Papworth, R., 96, 113 n
Parry, G. 154
Parsons, Talcott, 13, 20, 29 n